MYTHS AND SYMBOLS OF

VEDIC ASTROLOGY

Lotus Press
Vedic Astrology Titles
by Bepin Behari

FUNDAMENTALS OF VEDIC ASTROLOGY
Vedic Astrologer's Handbook
Volume I

PLANETS IN THE SIGNS & HOUSES
Vedic Astrologer's Handbook
Volume II

MYTHS & SYMBOLS OF VEDIC ASTROLOGY

Myths
&
Symbols
of Vedic
Astrology

Bepin Behari

Edited by David Frawley

LOTUS
PRESS
Twin Lakes, WI

All requests should be directed to:
Lotus Press, P.O. Box 325, Twin Lakes, Wisconsin 53181
Web: www.lotuspress.com   Email: lotuspress@lotuspress.com
(800) 824-6396

2nd U.S. edition 2003

ISBN: 0-940985-51-9

Library of Congress Control Number: 2002108741

Printed in the United States of America

CONTENTS

Abbreviations

BPHS	*Brihat Parasara Hora Sastra,* Trans. by R. Santhanam.
C	*The Chakras* by C. W. Leadbeater.
CJW	*Crest Jewel of Wisdom* by Sri Sankaracarya.
EW	*Esoteric Writings of T. Subba Row.*
HWHB	*Hidden Wisdom in the Holy Bible* by G. Hodson.
IU	*Isis Unveiled* by H. P. Blavatsky.
SAO	*A Study in Astrological Occultism* by Bepin Behari.
SD	*The Secret Doctrine* by H. P. Blavatsky.

EDITOR'S FOREWORD
By
David Frawley

Astrology had a certain universality in the ancient world, appearing as a global science in ancient times. While details vary, there is much in common between all ancient astrological systems. We note that all ancient cultures including Egypt, India, China and Mexico relate the seven days of the week to the same seven planets, from Sunday, the day of the Sun, to Saturday, the day of Saturn. Is this only a coincidence? There was either a diffusion of information or a commonality of knowledge between these cultures. Similarly today, with the blending of East and West in the world, astrology is again emerging in a global context.

Eastern or Vedic astrology is again becoming important along with the systems of Yoga and meditation and the greater wisdom of the orient. Astrology has always been given a more significant place in Eastern than in Western culture. It remains in use and is respected by the majority of people in India today. It was never consigned to the domain of superstition, nor was attention ever removed from it by the great minds of the land, many of whom, even today, also study and practice astrology. While astrology has been criticized, ridiculed and even suppressed in the Western world, it has flourished in India since ancient times. If there is any threat to its prestige in India today, it is only through those who are adopting Western culture.

Most ancient myths relate to the heavens. It would not be exaggerated to say that all mythology is astrological, at least in one major line of interpretation. Hence, a modern reexamination of myth must also take us back to astrology. Without understanding astrology, our understanding of mythology must be partial. Even if we do not recognize the validity of astrology as a science, we cannot ignore its role in shaping and expressing the myths and legends of the world.

Solar, lunar and planetary symbolism is common in many myths, as among the ancient Greeks and Hindus. The constellations play a very prominent place in them as well, like the Greek myths of Perseus and

Orion. It is likely that most myths were first devised while contemplating the sky, or while telling stories at night under the stars. The sky is a good field of projection for the creative imagination. Contemplating the stars also connects us with the cosmic intelligence or universal mind and thereby its energies, laws and symbols come to us to reveal its workings. Mythology is in this way part of a language of cosmic consciousness, with the symbol being a more profound and universal statement of truth than logic or abstract thought. If there is any wisdom in mythology, it must also have an astrological meaning and significance.

Ancient Hindu mythology, like the Greek, has a very strong astrological orientation. While its stories and symbols often appear different than the Greek, if we look deeper we find much in common. The messages they give about man and the universe are very similar. The basic nature of the planets is the same in all systems of astrology, as for example, the aggressive and war-like nature of the planet Mars. Yet in many instances, the Hindu interpretations of the planets are of a more spiritual implication than Greek myths, as the Hindus were of a more spiritual bent of mind than the more scientific Greeks. Hence, the Hindu Mars is also the son of the great God Shiva. He destroys the demons of ignorance who oppress mankind, and is not just a crude God of war. As such, Vedic astrological symbols may give us a better key to the spiritual meaning of the stars and planets. This will be important for any students of the deeper aspects of astrology.

The relationship of the stars and planets with the practice of Yoga, with the different chakras or force-centers of the subtle body, and so on, can be found in Vedic and Hindu myths and stories. All the great scriptures and legends of India from the Vedas to the *Puranas*, the *Mahabharata* and *Ramayana* are filled with astronomical and astrological symbols, so much so that there is an entire tradition of astrological interpretation for them. Most ancient teachings including the *Bible* and Homer have such a significance if we look beneath the surface. As man and the cosmos are linked, even if we do not intend it, our deeper thoughts and intuitive visions must link us up with the cosmic energies that come through the planets.

According to modern ideas of history, we consider that astrology was developed first in Babylonia and then refined by the Greeks, and that the Hindus got their astrology from these two sources. While a few Greek terms do occur in medieval Hindu astrological books, this is scarcely enough grounds to derive the Eastern system from the West. Hindu influences can also be traced in much of Greek thought as well, particularly among the Greek mystics and mystery religions, like Pythagoras, which groups were also famous for their astrological knowledge. We also observe that Hindu astrology is more complex and often very different than the Greek. Nor does the Vedic tradition concur with a Western origin for its knowledge. Vedic astrologers relate their knowledge to their own tradition which speaks of equinoctial positions of great antiquity to support their claim. Vedic astrology, unlike Western astrology, figures the precession of the zodiac into its calculations, which in itself suggests a great antiquity for the system. As we move towards the Age of Aquarius today, we may appreciate that different Vedic texts speak of the ages of Taurus, Gemini and Cancer (by relating the equinox to the asterisms that mark the beginning of these signs), taking astrological knowledge back at least to 6000 B.C. In this regard the Vedic may be the oldest astrological system in the world, and the source of all ancient systems of astrology.

As the scholarly world may be now beginning to afford a greater antiquity to Vedic culture, with new evidence that the Indus Valley civilization in ancient India of the third millennium B.C. was Indo-Aryan, this claim may yet be substantiated. The Hindu mythology of the planets does not derive from outside sources, as the reader can observe in this book. As Hindu mythology is the largest mass of mythological literature in the world, its mythology of astrology, is also the largest and most complex, the richest remnant of ancient astrological knowledge.

Ancient Europeans — the Greeks, Romans, Kelts and Slavs — spoke languages closely related to Vedic Sanskrit. They practiced a similar religion of fire worship and had Gods akin to the Vedic. Ancient European God and planet names are traceable to the Vedic. Jupiter is Sanskrit Dyaus Pitar, Mars is Sanskrit Marut, Venus is Vedic Vena, the Sun (Greek Helios and Roman Sol) is Sanskrit Surya. Hence, ancient European and Vedic mythology are akin. Indo-European people of the ancient Middle East, like the Persians, Hittites, Kassites and Mittani, also worshipped Vedic Gods and had strong astrological traditions. The Kassites, who ruled Babylonia in the second millenium B.C., may have been a point of transmission of Vedic astrology to Babylonia and Greece. In this way Vedic mythology has a relevance far beyond the boundaries of India.

Vedic astrology does differ somewhat from Western or Tropical astrology. It employs the sidereal zodiac or the zodiac of the fixed stars. This causes its sign positions to shift backwards about 23 degrees from tropical positions. The main factors of astrology are otherwise the same — the use of the planets, signs, houses and aspects — though aspects are figured rather differently. This will cause students of Tropical astrology to have to shift their orientation in approaching the Vedic system. They will have to think of the signs more in terms of the visible constellations than in the seasonal division of the zodiac.

In addition, Vedic astrology puts much emphasis on a twenty-seven-fold division of the zodiac, the Nakshatras or lunar asterisms. This system and the mythology about it is special to the Hindus, yet it also follows from the basic meaning of the planets. Similar systems have been used by the Chinese, since their earliest era, and by the Arabs, since medieval times.

*

Bepin Behari, the author of this volume, is one of the more well-known and widely published astrologers in India. He is most recognized for his spiritual and esoteric view of astrology, in which he uses both Vedic and Theosophical approaches. He employs this methodology here as well. Students of Theosophy will find this particularly helpful in giving them a bridge to Vedic astrology. Behari is one of the few modern astrologers in India who concentrates on the spiritual meaning in chart interpretation rather than the more mundane and predictive side. As such he preserves much of the deeper and older wisdom tradition.

Behari not only uses Hindu myths, he also examines in great depth the Western symbols for the planets and signs and shows their greater meaning. He adds aspects of Western and Middle Eastern thought through his Theosophical background. Very importantly he introduces the Nakshatras or asterisms and helps us to understand them according to the same astrological symbols as the planets and signs. Another important factor of Vedic astrology is the importance it gives to the nodes of the Moon. Behari explains the Vedic view of the nodes (which is rather different than what is ascribed them in western astrology) and shows their profound affect on the human psyche and its transformations.

Vedic astrology may appear strange and difficult to understand for the Western mind. This is because much of the background of the system is not known to us. *Myths and Symbols of Vedic Astrology* gives this background information of how the planets are viewed, so that the student approaching this system can make sense of it. The book is also useful for students of Western astrology who are interested in the broader world-wide symbolism and mythology of the planets. In addition, anyone interested in astrological mythology will find it an important book.

*

I began examining this book to see how helpful it could be for introducing Vedic astrology to a Western audience. I soon discovered a depth of thought in it that understood the system of Yoga and the profound science of the relationship between Spirit and Matter called Sankhya in India. The book explains the whole process of human and cosmic evolution and relates human life to the highest goal of spiritual knowledge and liberation from the cycle of rebirth. It shows the depth of astrology as a cosmic science. As such, this is indeed an important book and fundamental text for anyone wishing to approach Vedic or Hindu astrology, particularly with concern for its deeper aspects. Yet it does not require that one is an astrologer. It gives much of myth and philosophy that will stimulate any sincere reader toward a deeper examination of the meaning of life.

David Frawley
Santa Fe, NM
September 1990

PREFACE

The relevance of Vedic knowledge has greatly increased with the rapid growth of modern science and technology. Knowledge of the expanding universe, the development of international communication, and the spread of a materialistic way of life are modern developments that have stimulated insecurity and caused people to lose faith in life. The individual human being has become indistinct, having lost his uniqueness. Man faces a dilemma in that traditional values no longer satisfy modern emotional and intellectual needs while the human mind has developed to the point where it cannot blindly accept just any philosophy. The Vedic concept of life — the identity between the individual and the universe, the possibility of unlimited growth and expansion of human faculties — couched as it is in a difficult symbolism or abstract philosophy, transcends the understanding of most people. Unless such inner knowledge can be convincingly demonstrated to the inquiring mind, it will not be accepted. Yet, with an objective study of the principles of Vedic astrology, it is possible to demonstrate that an individual's personal life, in spite of innumerable frustrations and immense complications, is looked after and guided by natural forces and cosmic intelligence.

The present study, therefore, does not require any belief in such things on the part of the reader. Vedic knowledge is not a body of doctrines to be spread through organized religion. Rather, it attempts to pierce the veil of the external images that permeate us, to reveal their inner reality. An understanding of such reality does not create divisive beliefs. Every individual and atom in the universe is unique and has its individual special destiny to fulfill. Certain patterns describe the course of this spiritual pilgrimage. The sevenfold principle in life — represented by the seven planets, the seven ancient seers and the seven sheaths of the human soul — offers such a pattern. It indicates that there are seven main categories of souls evolving along their different paths. Each of them will have a radically different approach to the problems of life. The ancient seers, therefore, did not lay down any dogmatic injunctions to be followed. They pointed the way by which each human being could discover his or her own light. The approaches may vary but the investigative method and general principles are useful to all.

Vedic mantras emphasize the identity and connection between the human being and the universe. This Vedic understanding was not based on speculation that could be disproved by later discoveries. It is an immutable truth that man and the universe are subject to the same laws and are one and the same — an integral unity. Through scientific knowledge, man can measure the limits of the external world and discover the finer laws of nature, something he cannot do with his crude sense organs alone. He needs a new apparatus, a new means of acquiring further knowledge. Modern man can confidently assert that behind the reality perceived by his sense organs are many layers of concealed laws and mysteries. He is now recognizing the vast depths of his own consciousness and the mysteries surrounding the brain and mind. The synthesis between the knowledge of the human mind and the understanding of the laws of the expanding universe has not yet been seriously attempted. But such a synthesis can be found hidden in the ancient teachings. Because each individual is unique, the real integration of the knowledge of man and the universe must be done by each individual himself. Only when this is accomplished can there be harmony in human relationships and actions. Understanding Vedic astrology in its deeper implications can be very helpful in this regard.

The present study hopes to assist the individual searching for the truths concerning himself and the universe. Its aim is to enable the individual to directly experience the inner and deeper forces working within his psyche. *Myths and Symbols of Vedic Astrology* shows that the various impulses which induce cosmic evolution are applicable to the conscious growth of the individual as well. The planets, signs and asterisms do not deal in mystifying hocus-pocus designed to confuse the credulous. They attempt to place the individual in the wider perspective of the cosmic evolutionary growth pattern. The descriptions given in Vedic mantras, which are elaborated in Puranic mythologies and Vedantic philosophy, relate to both macrocosmic and microcosmic evolution. The individual can apply them to himself and perceive the non-physical impulses working through his everyday life and mental activity. In order to pursue this course of self-examination and introspection, it is advisable to grasp a few of the basic concepts of Vedic philosophy in a practical way.

In this study, references are frequently made to the allegory of the churning of the ocean by the gods and demons in their war with each other in Heaven. This churning process produced various precious items, including an immortality-giving nectar and a death-inflicting poison.

Such an apparently strange allegory represents a universal phenomenon occurring at each stage of manifestation. This struggle takes place every day when the individual is torn between conflicting loyalties or upset by emotional stress. In it, one receives both the nectar as well as the poison. One cannot choose one and discard the other. This churning operation takes place because the gods and demons, the opposites, fight with each other. It represents the duality or opposition in everyday life which is necessary for the unfoldment of one's inner faculties, for the emergence of real unity. It is only the constant churning of pleasure and pain, joy and sorrow, gain and loss, success and failure, that causes us to look beyond this transient world to an enduring and non-dualistic reality.

A creation hymn in the Vedas states, "In the beginning the non-existent was not, nor was the existent; the earth was not, nor the firmament nor that which is beyond. There was neither death nor immortality; there was no sign of night, nor of day. That One breathed without breath by His own nature. Other than Him there was nothing beyond." On this everlasting void, the cosmic Spirit, Purusha, was conceived "alone as this all, that which was and that which will be."

This process of manifestation essentially requires a triplication of forces from the original unity. The universal creative potency is externalized from the void, and upon polarization becomes Purusha and Prakriti, spirit and matter, positive and negative energy. When the polarized energies interact with the universal matrix, the world soul (anima mundi) or the Golden Egg (Hiranyagarbha), the cosmic fire emerges in seven flames and creation begins. The Vedas reveal this sevenfold cosmic being, "Who has seven rays, who is strong like a bull, who is mighty, who lets the waters of the fast running rivers flow on, who armed with the thunderbolt spreads at the rising clouds." Such cataclysms symbolized by the "war in Heaven" are necessary to the process of uncovering the hidden potentials in the evolving being, cosmic as well as mundane. The planetary influences which disturb human life are not Divine curses signifying individual misfortune. Pain or sorrow is a necessary ingredient of life, a part of evolution indispensable to the process of manifestation.

At each stage of cosmic and human unfoldment, the current established state must be disturbed to allow for further growth. Great turmoil must ensue before a new equilibrium is attained at a higher state. In human life also, new relationships are established when new faculties are developed. It is an inevitable process. Therefore, planetary impulses do not precipitate any result on their own; they merely reveal a portion of the Divine plan for the individual.

The ancient seers saw that adequate preparation was necessary to understand such inner knowledge. For this purpose, they prescribed the

six Vedangas, the supporting studies for understanding the proper meaning and significance of Vedic mantras. One of these is Jyotish or astrology
which deals with the nature of planetary influences and the relationship
between astronomical forces and cosmic and human evolution. They did
not consider the planets and the signs to be unconscious material forces;
they saw them as highly sensitive, powerfully charged entities, almost
divine in their existence. In discussing the significance of these celestial
bodies, the Vedic seers were mainly concerned about the deities working
through them. In dealing with their impact, the seers demonstrated how
they connect the human individual and the universe around him with the
Supreme being. This relationship is not theoretical. It is possible to
perceive it even today on the basis of astrological prognostications. Such
predictions and the principles assumed in Vedic astrology do not pertain
to one period of history. They are timeless, though they require a constant
adaptation of their outer form. Their basic principles cannot, therefore, be
appropriately explained in terms of the concepts and values of only one
specific epoch or country. Vedic astrology reveals the essential core of
astrological impulses. This knowledge can either be imparted by a teacher
directly, or described in terms of symbols, allegories and mythologies so
that generations to come can comprehend. In the latter case, the deep
understanding of the basic astrological principles is only possible by
correctly understanding these indirect teachings. *Myths and Symbols of
Vedic Astrology* attempts to unravel some of the mysteries and profound
insights of Vedic astrology.

A special feature of this study which has not been available elsewhere
is a delineation of the impact of the Nakshatras or lunar asterisms on
human affairs. Vedic astrology lays great emphasis on them — they have
tremendous importance in predictive astrology and the determination of
planetary periods is done according to them — yet there is very little
information about them. Based on mythologies and philosophies not
directly related to astrology, an attempt is made here to give a systematic
account of them. This information opens many new predictive possibilities. For the general reader, it reveals many interesting features of the
cosmic evolutionary process.

I would like to record my appreciation for the unflinching assistance
and encouragement accorded for the preparation of this book by Robben
Hixson. His erudition in general, and profundity in Vedic and astrological
literature in particular, greatly influenced this work. But for his help, it
could not have been presented in the present form. I also owe a great deal
to David Frawley. He is a great scholar, gifted healer, experienced
astrologer and very discerning editor. His impact on the revival of Vedic
and yogic science has much affected the present study. In spite of the

assistance received from many quarters, I alone am responsible for any possible shortcoming in the study. I look forward to any suggestions and comments, and hope that this kind of study is useful to a wide audience and encourages a deeper examination of these topics by its readers.

May we together experience the Truth.

Bepin Behari
C-505 Yojana Vihar
New Delhi-110 092
INDIA

PART I

ASTROLOGICAL MYTHOLOGY

THE MEANING
OF ASTROLOGICAL SYMBOLS

There is no simple method to decipher astrological symbolism. The logic of the outer mind cannot uncover the subtle relationship that exists between the stars and events on earth. Yet it is clear that astrological symbols were originally chosen with great care. They were selected to conceal as well as to reveal our relationship with the universe. The ancient seers perceived that the cosmos is not a mere material formation but an expression of the spirit which is its very life and soul. All created things draw their strength, vitality and direction from the indwelling consciousness. In fact, the spirit is the real power in all things. Eastern philosophy and mythology aims at describing the deeply complex relationship between the outer world and the inner spirit. The knowledge of the indwelling spirit is difficult to express, as well as difficult to comprehend.

We are told that human beings can receive the keys to this secret knowledge either through divine inspiration or from a qualified teacher. No one can succeed in obtaining it without divine grace. The flow of grace is known as initiation in occult and spiritual literature and is symbolized in various ways. An inner preparation is required to receive the higher knowledge and this involves great discretion. Confidentiality is essential because the knowledge thus imparted reveals the subtle powers of nature. These can be used for the good of humanity or to cause harm. The symbols revealed to spiritual aspirants have thereby a dual purpose, both to teach and protect the knowledge. When the student reaches a certain level of awareness, he is entrusted with the keys to unravel the meanings of these symbols. Thus the same symbols reveal different levels of meanings to different grades of aspirants. They are capable of unveiling nature's secret forces and at the same time they obscure this knowledge if the right preparation has not been made.

The ancient seers gave us philosophy, religion, mythology and such spiritual practices as yoga, mantra and tantra. Astrology was part of this grand revelation. The seers uncovered the cosmic framework according to which we can understand the Divine plan for humanity. They gave us astrology so that we can understand our role in the cosmic order. Usually, the majority of people are neither interested in such subtle knowledge, nor is it relevant for their pursuits in life. The imparting of this knowledge is useful only to those conscious individuals ready to receive it and apply it in their daily lives. For such students, the whole system of knowledge is necessary, not merely one branch of it.

The medium of expression for imparting spiritual knowledge follows a certain pattern. Religious scriptures, mythology, philosophical discourses and yoga expositions are expressed in a similar language. Terms and concepts used in one area are applicable to the others. Astrological symbols form an important part of this unified system.

These teachings have to describe spiritual principles in an everyday language. This creates enormous problems. Deeper realities, which can only be comprehended with intuition, insight and awareness, elude superficial students. To the great spiritual teachers, written language and the spoken word are merely suggestive. The effective exploration has to be undertaken by students themselves within their own minds. In spiritual literature, the medium of expression has the difficult task to lead students in the right direction and provide them a useful way to explore the depth and expanse of the subject. The language of the spirit is not like a sculpture, a concrete object, but like a poem which arouses the sensitivity and imagination of the reader. Myths, allegories and parables, in their flexibility and multidimensionality allow a wide range of interpretation, a suitable base for such knowledge.

The finer forces of nature are ever active and involved in creative relationships. They are not restricted by time and space. They act on subjective realms of experience as well as on objective phenomena. Nature is never inert or static. A language that describes the dynamic impulses of nature has to recognize this. Concepts used to explain the profound and ever changing creative impetus must have an affinity with it. They must reveal the nature and characteristics of the underlying realities if approached correctly. They are, however, merely indicators, and not the realities themselves. Depending on the intensity and depth of contemplation, they reveal the inner truth.

The ancient seers gave us knowledge of the Divine plan of evolution. Many who are ready to receive it come from different geographical, social and personal backgrounds. To teach them requires a consistency of terms and concepts. In the absence of a common medium of expression, there can be more confusion than illumination. A symbolic language was used for this purpose as it reflects the truth in terms which are universal, but to reach its universal core requires a certain insight. A proper study of astrological symbols requires adequate knowledge of related teachings and the spiritual implications of allegories employed but, above all, rests on true intuition.

A modern student has to realize his potential limitations. He may not possess the necessary inner preparation and spiritual training. His geographical, social, religious and educational background, and general approach to life differ significantly from that of the ancients who received their lessons in close proximity to their spiritual guides. Such widely varied students are confronted with allegorical teachings which not only originated in a radically different society but are superficially very confusing. When they pierce the veil of superficiality and with patience begin to appreciate this method of communication, they will glimpse the realities behind these at first seemingly meaningless fantasies. When confronted with such strange symbols, if they ponder over their essential features and go to the root of their universal implications, they will come to understand their true message. These symbols and mythologies may appear colored in an Eastern way of thinking and philosophy, but underneath their cultural forms they represent certain universal processes of psycho-physical transformation that transcend all cultural boundaries.

For comprehending the hidden meanings of different symbols, the intellect, especially in the absence of spiritual insight, requires an extensive study of related teachings and an ability to see the inner truth of Nature's workings. Spiritual study is basically practical. Unless the student is moved by the spirit of cooperation with nature, his studies remain barren, superficial and misleading. In ancient times the knowledge was only revealed to students who had the intention to harness nature's secret powers for the good of all. The studies were undertaken as part of an integral approach to the problems of everyday life. There was no scope for personal aggrandizement or the acquisition of knowledge for intellectual curiosity. Such study was a lifelong mission done by dedicated investigators of truth. It was inspired by a deep-rooted aspiration to become a conscious collaborator with Nature and the Divine.

Different Kinds of Astrological Symbols

Astrological symbols are of many kinds. Some are clothed in the historical, religious and social traditions, and the beliefs of the region where they originated. Most myths, allegories and stories are examples of this category of expression. There are other symbols which are universal in their application. Geometrical figures and diagrams, natural objects like animals, precious stones and flowers all belong to this group. Sometimes one finds both natural and man-made figures in stories woven around astrological forces. Whatever the reason for selecting a symbol, the basic consideration is their suitability to reveal the essential character of the astrological factor indicated.

Whether the symbol is a natural object like a lotus or a pearl, an animal like a bull, horse, or lion, a plant like the Ashwatha tree*, or a man-made object like a scale or potter's wheel, the external appearance of the symbol is like the husk which must be discarded in order to comprehend the inner and universal meaning behind it. One has to approach these symbols in their wider ramifications, their cosmic implications, to understand what they are pointing out.

Sometimes symbols are merely a veil. The obvious is not what they signify. In such cases one must look for related factors to arrive at the real meaning, or even examine the values of the different letters used in their names, such as the Kabbalistic number. Once a particular key is found for deciphering the meaning, its correctness can be tested by application in similar cases and contexts. Knowledge of the process of cosmic creation, the evolutionary course of the human soul, the various subtle sheaths of man, and the workings of the Kundalini are helpful in this study.

The depth of meanings revealed by symbols depends upon the keys employed. The student should realize that there is no end to the secrets of nature. In this exploration, veil after veil will be lifted, but there will remain veil upon veil behind. The eye of the student will pierce the veil of the mystery depending upon the truth he has put into practice and the universality of consciousness he has gained. Each symbol is thereby a channel for further discovery. The same symbol may assume a deeper significance when the student further expands his consciousness. The study of spiritual symbols in this sense is a voyage into the great unknown. The essential preparation for it does not lie so much in the study of books as in the right spiritual orientation in one's personal life. This is as much true in astrological studies as in alchemy, mantra and yoga.

The ancient wisdom preserved in symbol and mythology often appears as fantasy or superstition. The forms of the gods and goddesses transcend common sense. Hindu mythology abounds in such examples. Lord Shiva appears with the Moon among his forelocks and the river Ganges flowing through his hair. Ganesh, his son, has an elephant head, rides on a mouse and likes to eat a round shaped sweet called laddoes. Hanuman, the monkey god, has vermilion smeared all over his body and he floats in the air rather than walks on earth. These descriptions are full of spiritual implications. Such revelations enable the student to control

---

*   Ashwatha tree is a mythical tree which is supposed to have its roots in the sky while its branches, leaves and fruits grow downwards toward the earth.

and harness subtle natural forces and give him greater power over his own destiny.

Among the geometrical figures used in astrology, the cross, circle and arrow are most important. They are the basis for the symbols of the planets and signs of the zodiac. Almost every planet has some portion of the circle attached to it. The cross appears prominently in regard to Venus, Mercury, Jupiter, and Saturn. The arrow is associated with Mars. In the case of the zodiac the arrow appears relative to Scorpio and Sagittarius, and among the asterisms it symbolizes Ardra and Purvashadha. The significance of these astrological entities becomes clear if the implications of their geometrical designs are understood.

The Symbol of the Cross

Geometrical symbols represent different aspects of cosmic evolution. They indicate the dynamic movement in nature's creative impulse. Beginning at the point where soul breaks off and ending where it unites again with the Original Flame, the total movement is represented by a circle, the most primary geometrical design. The circle has several components. The formation of the cross is also based upon it.

The point is the basic constituent of the all-pervading circle that represents the cosmic life. Every point receives vertical as well as horizontal thrusts to give it circularity in shape and direction. These two directional movements are inherent in every point. The point in movement becomes an arc. From one view, a portion of the grand circular movement can be perceived as a vertical arc, almost like a straight vertical line. Another arc similarly perceived, if the length is considered infinitely small, becomes a straight horizontal line. A cross is composed of two such lines intersecting in the middle. As each point is a center of horizontal and vertical impulses, while every point flows from an earlier point and further merges into a later one, the whole sequence of the grand cosmic design can be conceived as the movement of a very rapidly whirling cross usually represented as a Swastika.

When the beginning of manifestation appears as a geometrical point it is already in motion producing a line. Every point is attracted to the central subjective source from which it has arisen. This provides the onward impulse, a central direction expressed as circularity of movement. At this cosmic beginning, however, the splintering of the Original Fire produces not just one spark or scintilla. Innumerable such fragmented points of energy arise. Each contains within itself the nature of holding together or passivity, as well as that of externalization or activity. These two polarized aspects of the Divine Spark become the two arms of the Swastika which represents the creative principle in nature. It has the original status in the cosmic evolutionary process, all subsequent stages of manifestation being produced by the interplay of its dual forces. This stage appears allegorically as the churning of the ocean under which the dual cosmic principles represented as the gods and demons, or the centripetal and centrifugal impulses, confront one another and precipitate storms and stresses that produce various emanations and set in motion the ever changing universe. These polarized forces in their perpetual interaction are symbolized by the cross.

The circle and the cross are very ancient symbols. They reveal the basic impulses in nature ever present at all levels of manifestation. The cross did not originate with Christianity. It was used thousands of years before Christ. The cross formed an important component in symbols and rituals used in ancient Egypt, Greece, Babylonia, India, China, Mexico and Peru. It was a cosmic as well as a psychological symbol. As the Tau, it was used as a magic talisman. Essentially the cross is a symbol of eternal life, the four points representing birth, life, death and immortality. As a symbol of the dual generative power, it was placed upon the breast of the Initiate after his "new birth." It was used as a mystic sign that the student was spiritually reborn — signifying the union between his astral soul and divine spirit — and that he was ready to ascend in spirit to the blessed land of light and glory. It was a symbol of the revealed mysteries of life and death.

H.P. Blavatsky indicates that the Brahmatma, the chief of the Hindu priests, carried on his headgear two keys arranged like a cross (*IU Vol II pp. 253–56*). In some Buddhist regions like Mongolia, the entrance of a chamber, generally containing a staircase leading to inner shrines, was ornamented with a cross formed with two fishes. In the dome monuments of Chaldea, Persia and India there are inscriptions of a double or an eight-pointed cross. There is a Masonic tradition which says that Solomon's temple was built on three foundations, forming the temple Tau or three crosses. A.F. Orchard states that the symbol of the cross was engraved on rocks in Egypt and Central Asia, while the ancient cave temples of Ellora, Elephanta, Varanasi and Mathura in India are also cross shaped. Such an extensively used symbol was not an isolated phenomena or confined to one group or region. It is a simple expression of deeply significant and universally relevant knowledge of nature's secret creative process.

The cross is used in astrology to indicate the polarized cosmic impulse working both within the human psyche and on a vast cosmic level. For this reason it is employed in many planetary designs. An understanding of the relationship between the cross and the planets reveals many deeper

The Divisions of the Circle

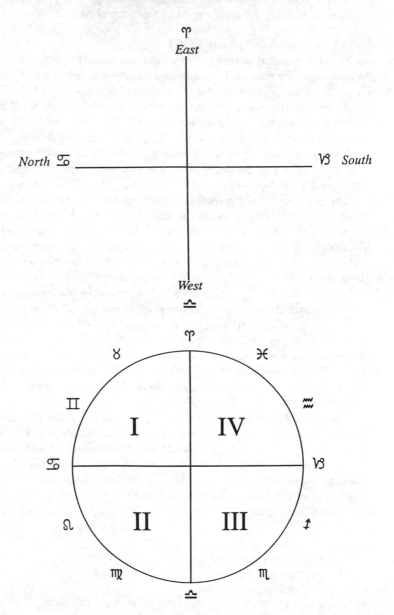

aspects of world religions. According to it the predictive principles described in astrological texts can be better comprehended.

The Essential Nature of the Cross

The cross consists of two lines, one horizontal and the other vertical, intersecting in the middle. It symbolizes the union of Spirit and Matter. The Life-Eternal in Spirit is represented by the ascending line, while Life-Eternal in Matter is represented by the horizontal. The vertical line represents the spiritual male principle, while the horizontal line is the materially creative female principle. Yogic philosophy (Sankhya) describes these as Prakriti, the female principle of cosmic creative energy, and Purusha, the male principle of cosmic awareness. The cross thereby represents the fundamental law of the cosmos.

The horizontal line represents Hiranyagarbha, the Golden Egg of Hindu mythology, which is also reflected as Mother Nature and the psyche in man. It contains within itself all the components of the cosmic manifestation; the five prime sensory qualities (Tanmatras*), five sense organs (Indriyas**), five elements (Bhutas+) and three prime qualities (Trigunas++). The various levels of manifestation are produced as a result of their combination and permutation. They enable the consciousness or spirit to undergo the materialization process. This occurs when its original pure nature is veiled by Illusion, Maya. They also enable it to undergo its spiritualization process which leads to Liberation, Moksha or Nirvana. The horizontal line consists of atoms (points), each with its individual destiny, like an ovum awaiting impregnation. Each atom is destined to achieve the blossoming of its inherent potential, but working alone it does not have the power to do so.

The vertical line represents the Purusha or positive creative potential. It is of the nature of freedom but being in manifestation it is under self-imposed limitation. This does not mean isolation or captivity but shows its self-constraint in order to assist the cosmic mission. In the process of manifestation, the Absolute first differentiates itself as Mula-Prakriti, primordial matter, and Daivi-Prakriti, primordial spirit or consciousness. Then it begins immersing itself in varying densities of matter

---

*   smell, taste, sight, touch and hearing.
**   nose, tongue, eyes skin and ears.
\+   earth, water, light, air and ether.
\+\+   Trigunas — Three attributes, viz., *Sattwa* (harmony), *Rajas* or activity, and *Tamas* considered as inertia or lassitude.

thus limiting its capabilities and thereby departing from its original state of pure freedom.

In spite of this immersion, the Cosmic Male represented by the vertical line, remains positive, creative, and ever ready for action. Without his impress, matter remains inert and unable to fructify. Yet this positive creative potential can only become actual in union with matter. The passive material potential is represented by the horizontal line.

The cross represents the manifestation process in which both active and passive impulses function together. It shows how the Unmanifest involves itself in the process of manifestation resulting in creation. The assumption of motion by the Absolute, which is expressed as evolution, is represented by the cross. In this sense, the cross symbolizes life in all aspects. The same relationship is represented as the Tree of Life, the Hammer of Creation and the outbreathing and inbreathing of the Great Breath. It is a symbol for both man and God. The cross stands for sacrifice. It is a symbol of generation and regeneration, life and death, rebirth and immortality, union, separation and reunion. It shows past, present and future, night and morning, sleep and awaking and thereby eternity in time. The cross expresses the rhythmic movement of life. It stands for all the pairs of opposites like male and female, light and dark, happiness and sorrow, and indicates thereby the androgynous dualism at the very core of nature. It is a symbol of the descent of spirit into matter and the fall of mankind into generation.

The cross also symbolizes the Sun, Moon and planets through which the energy of time is projected. It is a a spiritual, physical, cosmic, anthropological and magical symbol, with seven keys to its meanings. The cross is the alpha and the omega of creation, the force of involution and evolution linking pure spirit and gross matter. It applies to geometry, mathematics, astronomy, biology and many other sciences.

These metaphysical implications of the cross may be confusing to the student examining the symbol in the context of predictive astrology. In this regard the cross stands for a stage in evolution where important changes occur in the life of the individual. Under the impact of a planet associated with the cross, the individual changes and radical transformation takes place according to the interplay of spiritual and material forces. In Mercury the cross is at the base, and the circle with a portion of the arc is above it. In Saturn the cross is at the top with the arc below it. The position of the cross on these planetary symbols indicates the nature and significance of the turmoil confronting the individual. Under the Saturnian impulse, the conflict between spiritual forces and the material tendencies rules supreme and other forces are subordinated to the conflict. In the astrological context, the cross always signifies some kind of conflict, trial, tension and subjective activity directed towards changing the nature of man and the direction of his course of life.

Significance of the Circle

The circle expresses the central evolutionary impetus and shows the original principle of cosmic manifestation. It indicates harmonious movement in nature. No movement in nature is linear. The flight of birds, the growth of trees, the flow of rivers, the movement of the Sun, Moon and planets, the shape of clouds, the distant horizon skirting the landscape and touching the sky, are all curvilinear. Such movements reveal harmony. They show attraction towards a central nucleus, a point from which all creation, all curving movements have arisen. The vision of such a central referral point is perhaps the main reason for the strong theistic belief of primitive man.

The circle consists of a central point and a circumference, which together form a unity. The circumference can be used mathematically to determine the position of the central point. Therefore, whenever the ring of the circle is described, it assumes the existence of a central point or referral source. This nucleus sustains the essence of the peripheral line, the circumference. The dropping of the central point from the symbol signifies that it more specifically refers to the outer manifestation. It is not concerned with the unity between the center and circumference, or the creator and creation. The circle with a central point represents the Divine unity from which all proceeds and to which all returns.

The circle with its central point very appropriately represents the Sun, which in its splendor is the Supreme as far as the human world is concerned. The circle without the central point represents the delimitation of the area marked for manifestation. The circle with its central point is the first differentiation of the Absolute as the Prime Source of visible existence. The symbol of the Sun is not so much a physical representation of the visible planet; rather, it describes the original evolutionary impulse that leads to manifestation. The point in the center of the symbol emphasizes this origin of creation.

The development of the Absolute from its unmanifest to manifest stage is a very subtle affair. This incomprehensible dynamic process is well expressed by a circle with a central point. Through it the subjective potential is objectified. Mother Nature swells to give birth to numerous forms at different planes of existence. This process extends from the complete negation of everything, the void, to all that has been, is and will be.

From the first objectification of Divine consciousness expressed as a central point, there is a polarization which is quite mysterious. The

Absolute contains within itself the power to expand in all directions. It thereby produces the pair of opposites. Operating simultaneously in two directions, there is expansion as well as contraction. Polarization is an expression of this inherent dual nature of manifestation. The movement of the point leads to the Unmanifest being manifest, the subject becoming object, the sexless becoming masculine and feminine. Polarization gives rise to attraction and repulsion simultaneously.

Whatever takes place in manifestation has its germ or potential in the point. Yet by itself the central point has no direction. It is the starting point for all directions. The point in motion operates in every direction. It is the urge to creativity. The horizontal and vertical movements of the point are not restricted to merely two directions, rather they represent an ever increasing expansion on different planes. All planes of existence are both horizontal and vertical to some other plane of existence. This establishes the simultaneous existence of masculine and feminine aspects in every form of manifestation. The concept of Ardha-Narishwara* in Hindu mythology, Shiva and Shakti in one body, one side male and the other female, refers to this essential fact of cosmic polarity.

Each particle of energy in the universe is charged with centripetal and centrifugal forces which generate attraction and repulsion. This gives rise to magnetism and electricity and arouses motion and activity. The interaction between the polarized force-centers also leads to the ever existing war between the gods and demons, which brings about the churning of the cosmic ocean. It leads to differentiation, materialization and the production of all the multi-colored forms of existence. The process of differentiation and expansion which begins with the objectification of the central point continues along the evolutionary cycle on all planes of existence. The evolutionary force moves not only in three but in multiple dimensions making it not only an ever expanding sphere, but an unfolding whose depth cannot be measured by the human mind.

This expanding movement is stopped when the Divine consciousness restricts the parameter of growth. At this stage the innermost point of the expanding blades of energy-particles is restricted from further growth. Then the energy-particles begin to revolve around the center and sustain a certain limit to the manifestation. The circle with a central point, which establishes the connection between the creator and the creation, also refers

---

* Literally means Half-woman-god. The concept refers to the Supreme God consisting of a half male and a half female body but together forming a harmonious unity.

to this delineation of the power of the Absolute. The Sun, represented by the circle with a central point, makes our solar system the visible representative of the Absolute. It shows in its limitation the power of the unlimited.

Both the central point and circumference of the circle have their special implications. The point has two main qualities. First, it is a swelling of the inner outwards. It is the impulse to grow. By this action, that which is within and unmanifest comes out on the periphery and becomes manifest and expressed. The central point itself becomes the circumference. The center and the circumference form a unity. The seed and the fruit exist together. In life the point represents germination. It enables the Divine Potential in man to flower which implies expansion in all directions. The point as an impulse to grow leads the soul to the unknown, to growth and splendor beyond limit.

Second, the point is the beginning of all linear movement — horizontal, vertical and in other directions. The seed or original impulse in man enables him to engage in all forms of activities, positive and negative. Together with the circumference, the point stands for the expansion of the spirit and its energies within the delineated field of its activity. They show the field of observation or arena of activity. As a symbol of the Sun, the circle does not merely represent the solar globe but includes the entire solar system up to the furthest point where the Sun's gravitational pull operates. As a symbol it represents intense activity, both physical and mental, in which the circumference is always a limitation to the basic urge of the central point to grow and expand.

Key expressions for the circle in an astrological context are spontaneity, movement, growth and expansion outwards of that which is within, the subject becoming object. There is expansiveness, perfection, simultaneous attraction and repulsion, and ultimate frustration if the urge for growth is thwarted.

The circumference has yet other characteristics. In its wholeness it represents duration, the matrix of the innumerable dimensions of manifestation. It shows the entire creation from beginning to end. It is thereby represented as a serpent swallowing its tail. It indicates rhythmic movement, periodicity, cyclic rise and fall from the highest dimension of activity to the lowest depth. It is, in short, the universal life.

The different portions of the circumference represent different phases of the evolutionary process. These are important when they are associated with different planets. Which portion of the circumference is related to a specific planet determines the characteristic of the planet. For this purpose the circumference can be viewed in certain segments. First, the top of the circle represents the zenith of growth and expansion as well as future destiny. It refers to the ultimate possibility of actualization of latent faculties. The lower portion of the circumference also links the latent with the actualization process, but it emphasizes the depth of materialization that the soul can experience before extricating itself to return to its true nature. In the first instance, actualization takes place through inspiration while in the latter, the soul traverses through the vale of sorrow and suffers severe trials that force it to go beyond.

The circle corresponds to different directions. The uppermost point is generally regarded as the East, the lowest point the West, the leftmost point the North and the right the South. These points correspond to the astrological chart. East is the Ascendant, First house or first sign Aries, while West is the Descendant, Seventh house or seventh sign Libra, North is the Nadir, Fourth house or fourth sign Cancer, while South is the Zenith, Tenth house or tenth sign Capricorn. However, please note that this is a little different than the usual orientation of the astrological birth chart where the Ascendant is to the left and the Tenth house at the top. We must put the Ascendant at the top of the chart to view it in this way.

This circle is divided into four divisions based on the intersection of the horizontal and vertical axes. Divided by the vertical line, the circle becomes two semi-circles, one representing the involutionary course and the other the evolutionary course of the soul. The left semi-circle beginning at the top and ending at the bottom represents the course of materialization of the Divine Impulse. The right semi-circle rising from the bottom and ending at the top represents the evolutionary path during which the veil of matter is gradually removed and the divinity of man realized.

When a horizontal line intersects the vertical line four quadrants are created. The upper left quadrant represents the urge towards materialization. At this stage the involutionary movement of the Spirit causes it to become increasingly embedded in matter. The lower left quadrant represents intensification and concretization of this material urge. The third or lower right quadrant indicates the Spirit-ward urge as the soul seeks to ascend back to its origin. During this stage the impact of materialization decreases and the individual is gradually prepared for spiritual transformation. The last or upper right quadrant stands for the gaining of Liberation and reabsorption in the Ultimate, the Absolute. The arc curving up on the right represents the return movement or homeward journey of the soul, while that turning down on the right shows the prior descent of Spirit into matter.

The Arrow As Dynamic Movement

The arrow is a symbol used sparingly in astrology. It stands for dynamic movement in a special direction. Actually all astrological impulses represented by different planets, signs and asterisms give rise to movement in certain directions. The use of the arrow may therefore seem redundant. However, this symbol is used to indicate acceleration of primary energies.

Ordinarily the arrow has two aspects. The first shows direction in movement, and the second the purpose for which it is employed. The arrow is used as an aid for combat with an opposing force. The skill in archery attained by hard work, arduous training and great austerity has made the symbol both dynamic and austere. Furthermore, an arrow can be shot only by the voluntary action of the archer. It implies self-will and determination.

The arrow is a symbol of spiritual pursuit, something which requires a special category of human being and a special mission. Such activities are not possible for everyone. That is why the arrow represents the spiritual urge in many ancient teachings. In the *Upanishads*, the arrow stands for one-pointed spiritual efforts. The disciple is urged to shoot his arrow pointedly, with attention and concentration, to his ultimate source and goal, the Divine Self or Atman. The arrow is an instrument for achieving noble aims as well as for defending oneself. Warriors expressed their reverence by shooting arrows at the feet of their teachers and elders. Allegorically, the arrow is used to indicate submission to the higher self and thereby the opening of oneself to the mighty flow of spiritual forces.

The arrow is an instrument to express one's prowess. It is a pointed instrument to hit an object, an aim to be achieved. The success in such efforts is attained by concentrated and controlled attention, adequate physical strength and necessary psycho-physical coordination. These are the qualities which are realized only when the soul has reached a certain stage of evolution. Only when the individual becomes fearless and is able to lay down even his own body for the task in hand can he acquire the skill for higher spiritual attainments. One can appreciate the appropriateness of this symbol in relation to Mars, as we will see. During the course of our examination we will discover that whenever the arrow is used in astrological description it indicates the spiritual quest.

PART II

THE
PLANETS

1
THE SUN
SURYA

Hindus give great importance to the solar deity. Even today various ancient forms of Sun worship are performed, which are very powerful in their effects. Such practices give spiritual healing, as curative energy itself derives from the solar radiation. During the course of history, Hindu adoration for impersonal solar light became personalized. In Puranic mythology the solar deity became couched in strange fantasies. This served to deflect the attention from the inner to the outer expressions of this energy. Nonetheless, these mythological accounts contain the most sacred wisdom. It is possible to discover the essential features of the Sun by studying these stories on the basis of certain esoteric keys. The myths, allegories and symbols assigned to the Sun are capable of revealing the meaning of all cosmic energy.

The Sun is the most important planet of the solar system. The harmony between the planets depends upon its gravitational pull. The Sun provides the vital forces which energize all forms of existence, and when withdrawn, bring about their dissolution. Geometrically the Sun is represented by a circle with a central point ⊙. The central point refers to the fountainhead of primeval energy from which every form of manifestation arises, whereas the outer ring describes the realm of manifestation. In the visible Sun the indentification of the center is impossible, while in the symbolic representation it is conspicuous. A center without a circumference is non-existent: if a central point is located, there must always be a circumference. It is possible to increase the dimension of the circumference if the length of the radius is altered, but all such circles remain concentric with the identical central point. Moreover, as long a circumference is not assumed, the central point becomes meaningless; it loses its very referal existence. When the outer circle and the central point are both specified, the relationship between the manifest universe and the primeval cause is already postulated. Given the circumference, the central point can always be located. Thus this symbol suggests the all pervasive nature of the Sun. Whatever exists in manifestation is the result of solar radiation, and the Sun includes within itself every aspect of manifestation and nourishes it.

Second, the symbol emphasizes the fact that the circumference is necessarily an outcome of the central point. Without the central point there cannot be any circumference. In fact, the expansion of the central point itself becomes the outer circle. The central point demonstrates another important inner law — all objective forms are merely externalizations of the subjective essence. The point itself is non-existent in the true geometrical sense. A real geometrical point has no dimension at all and in this sense cannot be perceived. But the point shown in the Sun-symbol informs us that the Sun externalizes subjective into objective form. Evolution is a process by which what lies hidden within is made evident without, what is at the core expands and blossoms to the periphery.

Third, there is always a direction to the solar impact. In all movement, whether from the central point to the circumference, or along the outer ring itself, there is a direction that can be accurately traced. There is nothing random. The central direction may be the externalization of an inner potential, or an evolutionary impetus within the externalized life form. The circularity of the outer ring represents, during its downward movement from the top, the immersion of the soul in materiality, which having reached the densest physical sheath moves back upwards to its primeval state of purity and spirituality (see pp. 27-33).

Fourth, there is rhythmic movement in the symbol. The relationship between the center and circumference, and between the different points on the curvature of the circumference, show perfect symmetry and coordinated movement. They form a beautiful pattern of dynamic change. In all solar action, whether diurnal, annual or seasonal, or connected with the pattern of growth in living beings, there is perfect order. This orderliness enables scientists to discover the hidden laws of nature. The orderliness of the solar influence is characteristic of the Sun and a guiding principle under which it operates. It ensures predictability and effective action in the world.

Lastly the symbol, though expressed in a two dimensional figure, is capable of limitless extension and representation. It can be visualized as a sphere on a three dimensional plane. It can also be comprehended on other dimensions according to one's capacity to visualize them. In spite of the externalization of the inner potential from the center, the essential features and relationships between the central point and the outer ring are not compromized. The Sun always behaves according to its own law. The Sun is the supreme deity of the universe and its expression and movement are governed by itself.

These characteristics of the Sun are described in detail and great depth by the various allusions and allegories scattered in Hindu mythology and sacred books of the East. Even in the earliest Vedic civilization Indian sages delved deep into the planetary mysteries. The Vedic seers gave one of the profoundest glorifications to the radiant Sun. They called the Sun Loka Chakshu, "the Eye of the World." This appellation is very profound. The function of the eye is threefold: it is creative, preservative and destructive. Modern psychologists have begun to acknowledge the far-reaching consequences of "seeing." By looking at a situation or phenomenon, the viewer provides a form for the viewed object. All form perceived is a subjective reality. Whatever is believed to be seen by the viewer, the object perceived gradually assumes that form. The viewer perceives only that which is contained in his subjective consciousness and the object or situation is fitted into that pattern. In addition, thinking about a situation in a specific way impinges on it and gradually molds it into the desired pattern. The ancient seers were aware that tortoises hatch their eggs from a distance by sending their thought currents to them. Mothers protect their children, shape their character and even their physical characteristics through the thought currents generated by the images existing in their mind. By "seeing" their children to be of a particular nature, by seeing goodness in their every action, the children must become good. Seeing is watching, observing, and wishing things to approximate their desired archetype. It is possible, therefore, to effect the growth and development of seen or observed entities to a desired pattern.

The Sun watches the universe and nothing escapes its observation. The required quantum of nourishment flows from the Sun. The karma of the individual is recorded in the consciousness of the Sun. Like an able architect or efficient sculptor, the Sun observes all the imperfect or unwanted protrusions and chisels them into the proper shape. From the watchful eye of the Sun nothing can escape, so in the case of any disharmonious occurrences, the solar radiance is able to correct the aberrations. The Sun is the final directing force. Nothing happens in the universe without its wishes. Not a sparrow falls in the world without being registered in the Sun's consciousness.

The eyes also have much destructive power. By the light radiating from his third eye, Lord Shiva burnt to ashes Kamadeva, the Indian Cupid, when he tried to arouse passion within him. In ordinary life we see that anger radiates from the eyes. Such expression arouses fear in the persons thus looked upon. This capability gives the Sun the power of complete annihilation. As long as the Sun desires the universe to continue, it grows and evolves, but when the Sun withdraws its benefic rays, the entire universe merges back into it. The dissolution of the universe is also an aspect of the solar radiance. The triple manifestation of the Divinity which was later symbolized by the Hindu Trinity of Brahma, Vishnu, and Shiva was conceived by the Vedic seers as the triple nature of the Sun itself. Such tremendous power was attributed not so much to the visible Sun as to the solar deity who is the soul of the Sun.

Being the Eye of the World, the Sun is not only associated with the universe objectively, the consciousness of the universe is also the consciousness of the Sun. Whatever is experienced by the universe is registered in its awareness as a result of its unity with the Sun. The Sun the inner spirit dwelling in all things. It is often stated that the Sun is the heart of the world. The Sun is called the Atman or "Self of the universe." As the consciousness of the Sun and that of the manifestation are linked together, the Sun is ever present in all aspects of creation. The subjective being of the objective manifestation is the Sun. This relation is also expressed by considering the Sun, or the Deity presiding over it, as the Inner Ruler Immortal of all beings.

The Vedic phrase "Eye of the World" implies that there is no objective existence outside the Solar consciousness. All forms of life experience, all modes of action, every thought current, and aspirations at all levels are contained within the Sun as parts of its own being. The phrase describes the universality of the central planet of our solar system, its omnipresence on all levels of existence.

Hindu literature describes the solar mysteries in three ways. It gives mythological allegories about the origin of the Sun, it describes the lineage of the planet, and it couches its basic features in symbolic characteristics.

There are one hundred and eight names given to the Sun. Some are superficial in meaning while others are very abstruse. Important names of the Sun are: Ark, meaning a ray of light, fire, the Sun-plant, or the number twelve; Tamishrahan, destroyer of darkness, or dissolver of illusion; Divakar, maker of the day; Loka-Chakshu, Eye of the World; Savitar, the Father, a ray of light, or a Vedic chant to the Sun known as Gayatri; Vivaswat, the early morning, a name of the present Manu; Bhaskara, creator of brightness, reflection or desire; Dinakara, creator of day and night; Arhapati, worthy of adoration; Karma-sakshi, witness of the deeds of men; Graha Raja, king of the planets; Gabhastimat, one who posesses a beam of light, or one of the seven divisions of Patala, the nether world; Sahasra-kiran, having a thousand rays of light; Vijartana, a son who has usurped his father's kingdom; Martanda, son of a dead-egg; and Surya, the Sun, or the number twelve derived from the twelve forms of the sky.

Each name indicates a significant feature of the planet. A common feature of them is the association of the Sun with a ray of light. But light itself refers to the essential nature, the essence or soul of all that exists. In the absence of light, there is death. When the radiance of the Sun, its life giving energy is withdrawn, there is the dissolution of the universe.

One of his most interesting and mysterious names is Martanda or son of the dead egg. In some myths we are told the genesis of this name. The *Puranas* tell us that Aditi, the mother of the gods, bore eight Adityas, but she retained only seven and discarded the eighth believing it to be dead. As our Sun was born of this supposedly lifeless egg, he is called Martanda. The rest of the Adityas became his attendant deities.

Aditi, the mother of the gods, who bore the various Adityas, is a word which essentially means "the beginning and the end." As time arose through placing limitations on timelessness without any beginning or end, it is the offspring of eternal. The *Secret Doctrine* teaches that there is "the universal perpetual motion which never ceases, never slackens nor increases its speed not even during the interludes between the pralayas, or "nights of Brahma" but goes on like a mill set in motion, whether it has anything to grind or not." This is the eternal and uncreated Deity. Aditi corresponds to the timeless Deity whose nature and characteristics are beyond description. But from this transcendent state of perpetual motion cosmic evolution begins. The early deities who were requested to assume responsibility for creating the universe refused to do so, because it required their immersion in materiality which meant renouncing their everlasting freedom. The inability of the first seven sons of Aditi to create the world shows that they represent these higher forces which held back from the process of material creation.

The eighth effort from which the Sun was born appeared at first as "a dead egg." The word Mrityu or death refers to Yama, the god of death, Vishnu who preserves the universe, Maya which is creative illusion as well as ignorance, and to Kamadeva, the god of love. These references point to the mystic nature of the cosmic womb. Seen from the standpoint of the eternal and uncreated deity, Aditi, this manifestation with its expression of life's movement could not be considered to be dead. Since the wheel of creation can rotate only when both life and death equally participate in the process, the Universal Mother Aditi approached Martanda, the Sun, to undertake the function of cosmic ideation and in deference to the will of his mother he created day and night as symbols of life and death. It is believed that on dissolution, when the role of the visible Sun is over, all the immortal suns will once again shine in their radiance.

This allegory emphasizes the importance of death as an integral part of creation. The egg is a symbol of potential life. The Sun as the creator of life and death is necessarily the beginning and the end, the alpha and the omega. That the Sun came out of the egg also shows that it contains within itself all the potentials of growth and development. The world that we perceive around us is merely an externalization of the Sun's inner powers. The manifestation of the universe is like the swelling of the eternal womb, expanding from within to without, like the bud of the lotus which contains within itself the full potential of all the creative force from which it has arisen. The primary function of the Sun is to externalize what is contained in it.

The geometrical symbol of the Sun as the circle with a central point shows this idea of externalization with the central point swelling and expanding outward as the periphery of the circle. The central point gradually expands in the evolutionary process until the limit imposed by the circumference is reached which becomes the death of the evolving spirit. In this sense the central point represents origin and birth and the circumference is the end or death. The area circumscribed demarcates the realm of manifestation. Once the restrictive limit imposed by the circumference is reached the life-wave recedes, finally merging back into the central point. It indicates the rhythmic circularity of the evolving spirit. The Sun is therefore essentially one its own eternal nature, Sadaikarupa, the changeless and immutable Self, while in manifestation it is named as Ekaneka-rupa, the One that becomes many. The Sun is eternal as well as transient, both unity and multiplicity. He is the cause of the creation but also part of it and one with it.

In the process of his descent to the lower planes of manifestation the Sun is given different names which indicate the level of his expression. These are:

1.	THE MAHAPURUSHA OR PARAMATMAN	The Supreme Spirit.
2.	ATMAN OR PURVAJA	The living spirit of nature.
3.	INDRIYATMAN OR HRISHIKESHA	The intellectual soul.
4.	BHUTATMAN	The life soul.
5.	KSHETRAJNA	The embodied soul or spirit in matter.
6.	BHRANTIDARSHANATA	False perception, the material universe.

The solar deity is the Primordial Essence, the Atman of the universe. During the course of the evolutionary process it assumes different forms at different levels, but also pervades the universe with its radiant energy and remains in wholeness by itself. The visible Sun can be considered the heart of the solar system while its brain is the solar deity behind it. From it sensation is radiated into every nerve centre of the great body and waves of the life-essence flow into each artery and vein of the solar system. The planets are the limbs and pulsations of the Sun.

Describing the lineage of the Sun, Surya is said to be the son of Kashyapa and Aditi. Kashyapa is a designation used to refer to several degrees of creative energies. In the Vedas he figures in an important way. As a Prajapati or Creator he fathered gods, demons, men, beasts, birds and reptiles. According to the *Mahabharata* and other accounts, he married Aditi and twelve other daughters of Daksha. He begot the twelve Adityas through Aditi, and from Diti (which means splitting or division) he fathered the Daityas or demons. Surya, our Sun, was the eighth Aditya born to Aditi and Kashyapa. The Sun belongs to a large family with many brothers and sisters.

The Sun married the daughter of the celestial architect Vishwakarma, who was called Twashtri or Sanja, but his radiance was unbearable to her. Vishwakarma cut the solar effulgence into several parts from which he made Shiva's trident, Vishnu's disc, Kubera's mace, Yama's rod and Skanda's spear, all of which are invincible weapons. With a view to visiting her parents, Twashtri put her shadow called Chhaya in attendance on the Sun and left him. The Sun became infatuated with Chhaya and through her begot the planet Saturn. Later on, when Twashtri returned to her husband she was dismayed by his union with her shadow and left to wander in the form of a mare. On realizing his mistake the Sun followed her assuming the form of a horse and uniting with her produced the Ashwins, the two celestial doctors. Upon resuming their ordinary forms they had three children; Manu the progenitor of men, the Death god Yama, and the goddess Yami or the Yamuna river. The Sun also had several illegitimate children, of which the important ones were Sugriva, Karna and Savarni.

Manu was the father of Ikshwaku who began the solar dynasty of kings, to which the avatar Rama belonged, and in which Buddha was a prince. An important characteristic of the solar dynasty is adherence to the highest order of ethics, truthfulness, and the keeping of their promises regardless of the cost.

The lineage of the Sun shows his association with feminine counterparts or creative energies to further cosmic development. The Sun has to reduce his primeval effulgence to function at lower levels of creation. The Sun is closely linked with the ruling class, and wherever invincible power is displayed there dwells the radiance of the Sun. All creative beginnings, like the breaking of the dawn, are energized by the Sun. Similarly, the cessation of the working of life-energy takes place with the withdrawal of solar radiance: Yama, the God of death, is a son of the Sun. The end was created by the Sun himself. The river Yamuna is a companion of Vishnu, the preservative principle of the universe. In this way the lineage of the Sun shows that he is the life-giver, the preserver and the death inflictor. Wherever there is any glory, any victory, any success, there shines his effulgence. All positive creative energies come from the Sun who is always ready to fructify or stimulate all creative desires in human beings.

The third approach to understanding solar symbology is through the various pictorial representations of the Solar Deity. The Sun or Surya is pictured in a chariot having only one wheel but yoked to seven horses which include a mare. Often the horse is described as being only one but with seven heads. These seven horses are named after the seven colors: orange (Rochika), violet (Mochika), white (Shukl), yellow (Pita), red (Rakta), green (Nila), and blue (Indranila). They also represent the seven Vedic meters — Gayatri, Ushnik, Anushtup, Brihati, Pankti, Trishtup, and Jagati. The wheel is the visible form of the year. It has five spokes showing an apex of five points joined at the center which form a nave. There are three naves representing the triple nature of man bounded by one belly or the body. The triple nature is physical, psychic and spiritual, but it also indicates the three primary attributes of Nature as Rajas (activity), Tamas (inertia), and Sattwa (harmony). The wheel is eight-fold representing the eight Vasus or Gods of light who guide the evolution of the universe by assisting the visible Sun. The Great Naga or serpent draws the wheel.

On this chariot the Sun sits as a dwarf. His body glows like burnt copper and is yellow like honey in appearance. He has slightly red eyes, big arms and a neck like a tortoise shell. He wears bracelets and the earrings given to him by his mother Aditi, and is adorned with a diadem.

Surya, the most important name for the Sun, derives from the root words Sur, Swar, and Sura. Sur means the Sun, a god, a learned man, and numerically represents the number thirty-three. Swar represents the galaxy or the milky way; it stands for sound, the voice, a musical note, scale, tone or tune, and refers to the number seven. Sura is associated with courage, valour and might.

If we examine deeply the concepts associated with the Sun we realize their significance. The singleness of the chariot's wheel stands for perfect balance, non-dependence on any external support, and the tremendous speed with which the Sun moves. The Sun's chariot moves in Time which is always associated with space. It can have its existence only with the support of the three Gunas or primary attributes of objective manifestation. The objective existence also requires the energy and vitality provided by Prana or the vital force circulating in the three Nadis or nerves of the subtle body, the Ida, Pingala and Sushumna. These are twined around the human spinal cord. The three naves also stand for the threefold extension of time as past, present and future which enables the unfoldment of the inner potential in time. The desire for bodily existence or Trishna, the craving for sensual existence, also arises from three primary motivational impulses, those for wealth, honor and pleasure (Artha, Dharma and Kama). The three naves of the Sun's wheel express the triple nature of the manifesting energy.

The five spokes refer to the five bases on which the objective manifestation comes forth. For the macrocosm these are the five elements of earth, water, fire, air and ether. For the microcosm they are the five sheaths; Annamaya kosha (the physical body), Pranamaya kosha (the vesture of the vital airs), Manomaya kosha (the sensorial vesture), Vijanmaya Kosha (the cognitional vesture), and Anandamaya Kosha (the vesture of beatitude). The duration in which these live and move is described by five various parameters. These are Tithi (date), Var (day), Nakshatra (constellation), Yoga (combination of stars), and Karan (division of the day which are eleven in number). For astrological considerations these are very important.

The five vital airs energizing all forms of life are: Prana, the breath of life; Apana, the vital air which goes downward; Vyana, the life-wind diffused throughout the body; Udana, the life-wind which rises up the throat and enters into the head; and Samana, the vital air in the navel responsible for digestion. The functioning of the human being both for outward expression or for inward reception of impressions takes place with the five organs of action and the five sense organs. The organs of action are the mouth, hands, feet, anus and generative organ. The sense organs are eyes, ears, tongue, nose and skin. The various five-fold divisions, represented by the five spokes of the Sun's chariot wheel, are well integrated and act together with intelligence. The mind receives various impressions via sensations generated by smell, taste, sight, touch and hearing. These sensations arise from the activities of the sense organs. The impressions through these senses are produced from the five elements of earth, water, fire, air and ether. The wheel that runs the Sun's chariot moves on these spokes implying that the central core of the physical as well as psychic existence is the solar deity. Seated in his chariot he commands the movement of all the forces in the universe and guides the cosmic journey.

The eight Vasus who surround the wheel are personifications of the mighty natural forces directing the manifestation. The serpent god (Naga Deva) who leads the wheel is the embodiment of wisdom. He is the medium by which the "churning of the ocean" was carried out and who is the foundation of all creative deities and spiritual knowledge. The horses drawing the chariot represent the seven-fold principle according to which the Sun operates in the universe.

The ancient seers adored the Sun as the visible embodiment of the invisible, subjective Absolute. He is the Will of the Unmanifest. The creation and dissolution of the universe results from the outbreathing and in-breathing of the Solar Deity. The life-force energizing the manifestation is personified as Agni, the god of fire. Whether we considered the Sun or Agni as the basic source of energy, both are described as operating in rhythmic emanations. The Sun moves in a chariot drawn by seven horses while the Fire rises in seven flames. The *Mundaka Upanishad* names these seven flames as Kali (the black), Karali (the fierce), Manojava (the mind-swift), Sulohita (the deep red), Sudhumravarna (the smoke coloured), Sphulingini (the scintillating), and Visvaruchi (the bright all-shining). Emphasizing the importance of the septenary emanation, it further states that "from Him, too, the seven senses in the head are born, so are the seven flames or the powers of cognition, the seven fuels (objects), seven oblations (knowledge) which in their seven-fold channels operate in various realms of manifestation." Each of these seven channels has been classified and its distinct characteristics indicated. This enables the great yogis to practice their meditations and austerities in accordance with the vibrations of their specific Ray.

The first ray is called Sushumna. Its function is to light up the Moon. It is related to the central subtle channel (Sushumna) associated with arousing the Kundalini, emphasized by yogis. Similarly, other Rays have their specific functions. In their totality, the seven Rays are spread throughout the solar system. They constitute the foundation on which all other impulses are impressed such as light, heat, electricity, magnetism and other forces. Operating together in various ways they produce all actions on Earth. As the solar rays express the Will of the Unmanifest from the subtlest to the most material levels, all physical, psychic, spiritual and cosmic effects arise from them. These Rays are the horses which represent the solar energy in action in the process of cosmic ideation. Through them the power locked up in the Primordial Point, which radiates through the spokes of the wheel, is carried to different levels of manifestation.

The seven solar horses as different solar energies cover the different states of consciousness as well as the objective realms of manifestation. As creative energies they give rise to seven Prajapatis, the creative cosmic agents, while as far as the realms of creation are concerned, they form the seven worlds. The seven planets also arise from the solar out-breathing. The seven ancient Rishis, the progenitors of all life on earth, represent the seven flames of Agni and the seven horses of the Sun. These horses on the positive side created Bhu Loka, the earth of which we live; Bhuvar Loka, the world of air; Suvar Loka, the world of the planets; Maha Loka, the abode of the ever young ascetics, the Kumaras; Jana Loka, the heaven of deified mortals; Tapa Loka, the abode of Viraj-Devas; and Satya Loka, where Brahma resides. The seven worlds on the negative side thus created are Atala, the world of sensual women and vain men; Vitala, where Rudra resides with his ghosts and is seated in embrace with his consort Bhavani; Sutala, the abode of egoistic persons like Bali who was destroyed by the God Vamana for his pride in the sacrifice; Talatala, where the Asuras reside in their ignorance; Mahatala, the abode of the great serpents; Rasatala, the abode of the enemies of the Gods; and Patala, where resides Vasuki and other Lords of the Nagas whose lustre from the gems of their hood dispel darkness. Beyond all these floats Lord Vishnu on the bed of his thousand-headed serpent to carry the entire plan of manifestation. He is the Perserver who gives unity to the fourteen worlds emanating from the Primordial Fire, the Solar Energy.

The septenary principle operates in connection with terrestrial evolution which occurs in seven cycles. Each cycle has seven sub-cycles containing the impulses of all cycles within it. Thus the total is made up of 7X7 or 49 evolutionary impulses. These impulses flow through the planetary deities in their primary and secondary aspects; they are directed by Root and Seed Manus. The Primary Manu, as indicated earlier, arose from the Sun, as do the others who are seven in number. Each of them in turn produces seven other Manus, who guide the evolution of seven root-races, each with seven sub-races. There are thus 49 root-races during one full course of evolution. A number of cycles take place during the total evolutionary period between the beginning and the dissolution of the universe. The Manus who assist the evolutionary process of the universe derive their ultimate authority and power from the Solar Deity.

In order to arouse the subtlest potential inherent in Life, the seven ever youthful ascetics — Sanaka, Sanandana, Sanatana, Asuri, Kapila, Barhu and Panchashika — and the seven ancient Rishis — Gotama, Bharadwaja, Vishwamitra, Jamadagni, Vasishtha, Kashyapa and Atri — along with Prajapatis and Manus are ever engaged in creation. They work under the seven principles represented by the seven emanations of the Sun, taking their direction, authority and power from the Solar Deity himself.

Terrestrial evolution provides the necessary conditions under which the spiritual power in man can blossom to its fullness. At each stage of evolution, such solar representatives radiate their influence so that the cosmic and psychic principles gradually blossom and reach their perfection. After the course of evolution extending over several Manwantaras and Kalpas dissolution takes place. The twelve Adityas shine in their effulgence once more before everything merges in Aditi, the cosmic perpetual motion.

This explanation of the solar allegory represents but a fragment of the inner knowledge hidden in the exoteric literature on the Sun. But even a superficial study of such mythological references shows the supreme importance of the Sun. The Sun is the basis of the origin, maintenance and dissolution of the manifestation. He is the unity in the trinity. He is the most ancient, the primeval cause of manifestation, the deity who nourishes it and in whom it finally merges.

The Sun is meaningfully represented as a circle with a central point. Hindu mythology elaborates this basic idea and gives various descriptions of the mystic processes involved in manifestation. The rhythmic radiation of life-giving energy leading to birth, growth, and decay with seven positive and seven negative realms of existence arises from the Sun. The Sun governs the ruling dynasties of men as well as eminent human beings who show the divine spark within them. The Sun on the subjective plane stands for the Inner Immortal Ruler. In the working of the solar radiation the septenary principle is of supreme importance. As long as the solar benediction exists there is life; on its withdrawal life ceases. The solar influence always arouses the life-force on the inside, at the central core of the being, and from it the life and its various expressions expand to the periphery. It grows on its own energy, initiative and direction; everything else has to be subservient to its central motivational force.

In the individual horoscope the Sun indicates the total quantum of Divine energy flowing through the different levels of the individual and the quality of its manifestation. On the harmonious relationship between the Ascendant lord and the Sun depends the harmony between the life of the individual and the direction in which his inner urges lead him. The various impediments confronting him on his path can be apprehended according to the influences impinging on these two planetary forces. The Sun represents the central motivating force, the basic impulse in one's life, while the Ascendant and its lord signify the existing tendencies of the person. Unless the two are in harmony and well blended in everyday life, there will be struggle, dissatisfaction and imbalance.

The circle is the symbol of the Absolute and the Sun is the absolute in the manifest world. In human society this status is enjoyed by the monarch, the head of the state or the administrative head of the region. The relationship between the government and the individual can be examined by considering the disposition of the Sun with the house relating to the situation. Such a combination in relation to the Tenth house of profession enables the individual to receive promotions, titles, or high administrative status. In relation to the Sixth house, the Sun enables the individual to connect with the central fountainhead of energy and become free from disease. Also in relationship to the Sixth house, giving the favor of central powers, the Sun can lead the individual to victory in litigations or disputes with others. The basic principle is that the circumference indicating the objective existence or everyday life of the individual receives its sustenance from the central point representing the subjective or central seat of power. The circumference indicating the individual's outer life is represented by the Ascendant in the birth chart.

The circle with the central point includes everything manifest within its scope. But it does not lose its independent identity: the central point does not merge with others. Only when it merges with the Supreme is its objective existence annihilated, but then creation itself comes to an end. The effect of the Sun in actual life is observed by the fact that the central planet arouses in the individual a sense of oneness and independence. Identification with the masses of people will not take place on the level of equality. There will be a strong consciousness of aristocracy and a certain exclusiveness, though in the heart of the person there is usually no negative feeling or animosity toward others. Under adverse conditions, however, the impact of solar power is dictatorial, autocratic or despotic.

2
THE MOON
CHANDRAMA

𝄞

The Moon, the queen of the planetary hierarchy, is very mysterious and highly dangerous. The symbolic representation of the planet and allegorical references to it are generally elusive. Confusion persists even regarding its sex. It is worshipped as a male deity, but functionally, in its cosmic aspect, it represents the female generative principle. This androgynous depiction of the planet makes the examination of various allegories connected with the Moon complex. Moreover, the role of the planet at different stages of the cosmic creative process is so varied that a coherent picture of its workings is difficult.

Having glimpsed the basic solar impulse at the spiritual core of manifestation, we can consider the Moon as the Cosmic Mother, the Universal Womb, which the solar energy impregnates in order to concretize the spiritual fire into material forms. The main difficulty in interpreting lunar symbols and allegories arises from the fact that the planet is ever seated in the bosom of the Sun while it is continually involved in materializing the Divine Spark. Therefore, the Moon is a chalice for the downpour of the cosmic creative life-force. It is always withdrawing and in the process destroying life, thus becoming intimately linked with the death inflicting forces in nature. In fact, the Moon is Nature herself in the most universal sense, the custodian of all subtler forces. Sorcerers as well as sages worship her for the fulfillment of their wishes.

The geometrical figure for the Moon is easier to understand than the allegories about it. It is universally represented as two concave lines, 𝄞, joined at their extremities. This depicts the natural crescent appearance of the Moon, but a little thought indicates that the comparison is only partial. As the Moon changes its appearance every day, adherence to one form to represent it becomes misleading. In fact, this representation of the Moon suggests at least three possibilities. The first is the early phases of the waxing Moon and the last stages of its waning phase. Second is the condition of the Moon during the later phases of a lunar eclipse. Third, the figure can be seen as unconnected with the visible planet, being a symbolic indication of surging emotions like the waves of the sea. In all three approaches we see the Moon intimately linked with the psycho-physiological processes of human evolution.

All three interpretations make the Moon dependent upon the Sun. They recognize that the brightness of the Moon and its very energy is received from the Sun. The degree of reception, however, depends upon conditions. In showing this relationship, the figure indicates the inner or the psycho-mental state of the human individual. The brilliance of a man reflects his nearness to the central core of his being. As one endeavours toward this realization, one becomes qualified for greater enlightenment and better expression of one's latent divinity. In the event of being increasingly attracted towards materialism, one moves away from his central being, and becomes immersed more and more in ignorance and loses his grace.

Considered as a process of eclipses, the figure depicts this condition more explicitly. When the earth intervenes between the Sun and the Moon, the shadow of the earth (materialism) cast on the Moon (the human psyche) obstructs the (spiritual) light from the Sun and the Moon (psyche) becomes dark. This situation arises symbolically due to the demonic influence of Rahu swallowing the Moon. When adverse karmic forces represented by Rahu become powerful the human being is engulfed in immense darkness and ignorance. When these karmic forces are dispelled the individual becomes free to return to his original pure nature and the Moon begins to shine forth as before.

As surging waves of emotions and aspirations the lunar figure points out the goal of life. The curves do not merely show momentary upheavals, they indicate the long term direction of movement. The lower arc stands for a portion of the Sun-symbol. This becomes the periphery of the manifestation which is surging towards the center of the circle. The expansionary process can be indicated by the same symbol. Thus the Moon stands for outgoing as well as ingoing processes. Both of these are primarily functions of the solar radiation which in cyclic order swells from the center to the outside and having reached the assigned limit represented by the circumference recoils back. Thus as it periodically swells and withdraws with ever-increasing unfoldment of inner capabilities, the prime function of the Moon is to assist the Sun in the development of its light. It is said that the Sun bestows life to the whole planetary system, while the Moon gives life to our globe. This is the main difference between the two.

The nature of lunar radiance and its impact on terrestrial life are expressed in many ways. Blavatsky once stated that human beings in their spiritual sense have come from the Moon (*SD Vol I, p.274*). This expresses a triple mystery; astronomical, physiological and psychical at once. It shows the Moon functioning at different levels of human existence simultaneously. It is reflected in stories concerning the Moon's origin.

One legend makes Soma or the Moon the son of the Vedic sage Atri and his wife Anusuya. Atri is one of the seven Vedic seers on whom rests the balance of the universe, and Anusuya is the epitome of chastity and purity. Another legend makes the Moon a child of Dharma or righteousness. A third makes the Moon's father to be Prabhakar, which means the Sun, Fire, Ocean and Lord Shiva. From the Moon was born Budha, Pururavas, Ayus, Nahusha and the Kurus, the last who fought in the great battle of the *Mahabharata* which represents the complete destruction to the world. The Moon is the progenitor of the Lunar dynasty of kings, as the Sun is that of the solar dynasty. The difference between the two dynasties consists in the solar kings being righteous, wise, courageous, invincible and strictly adhering to their promises, while the lunar kings are courageous and learned but susceptible to worldly vices and suffer from internal conflicts.

The allegory of the churning of the ocean describes the battle between the gods and the demons. This yields several powerful important things including poison, Lakshmi or the goddess of fortune, the immortalizing nectar, and the Moon. As there was no place suitable for the Moon, it was placed by Lord Shiva on his forehead. Hence, the Moon is known as Shiva-Shekhar, meaning the crest of Shiva. From the Moon thus placed pours the celestial nectar which nourishes the universe and a few drops of which can give immortality.

The nature of the lunar influence is revealed by the names assigned to the Moon. Soma, nectar; Aushadpati, lord of herbs; Kumud-pati, lord of the lotus; Nakshatranath, husband of the asterisms; and Shwetajaji, drawn by white horses, are important names of the planet. Soma is a name given to the Vedic deity worshipped for "strengthening our life and conquering what opposes us." The *Rig Veda* regards him as the inspirer of all auspicious activities and the bestower of all desirable qualities, the progenitor of life on earth and the source of all wisdom. Because of the special power enjoyed by the Moon over the subtle forces of nature and his special status among the spiritual hierarchy, the *Sama Veda* lauds Soma as the great, wise hierophant who sustains the gods and gives birth to the different sense organs and powers of perception. He bestows on Indra, who represents the center of manifestation or the Universal Self, purity, strength and intellect. He gives light to the Sun who unfolds all siddhis or supernatural powers. The Moon is the deified soma-juice because it contains the celestial nectar that is the drink of the gods, which it pours down as its ambrosial rain through the sieve of heaven. This invigorating lunar influence on terrestrial life was well known to the sages.

According to the relationship between the phases of the Moon and the development of life on earth, plants, animals, birds and human beings in their procreative processes are deeply affected by the Moon (*SD Vol. I, p. 204, 211; Vol. II, pp. 102–119; Vol. III, p. 113*). The Moon has a special influence on the functioning of the female organism and on sexual impulses of both males and females. The psychological structure and emotional responses of human beings as well as their intellectual capacity are linked to the Moon. Yogis use the phases of the Moon to aid in their meditational practices. Blavatsky states that the influences of the Moon are wholly psycho-physical and the Moon is literally dead, sending out injurious emanations like a corpse. It vampirizes the earth and its inhabitants so that anyone sleeping under its rays suffers, losing some of his life-force. She stresses that plants which are benefic under the rays of the Sun are malefic under those of the Moon. Herbs containing poisons are most active when gathered under the Moon's rays at night. She considers the Moon as the friend of sorcerers and the enemy of the unwary. From ancient times of the witches of Thessaly down to some of the present Tantrics of Bengal, she continues, "her nature and properties have been known to every occultist but have remained a closed book to the physicists."

The influence of the Moon is largely felt on the physical, psychological and mental nourishment of the individual. Its name as Oushad-pati or Lord of herbs indicates the great influence of the Moon on herbs and its curative and healing potential. It refers to the connection between the lunar radiation and the inner sap energizing and vitalizing all living creatures on Earth — plant or animal. The Moon is inwardly linked with the power that animates all creatures.

The name Kumud-pati refers to the inspirational impact of lunar radiation. Kumad is a Sanskrit word for the white water-lily. Kumud-pati means the "Lord of Lotus" or more specifically the "Lord of the white water-lily." The lunar impulse controls and guides the growth and nourishment of the lily from its muddy (physical) bed, through watery (emotional) and airy (mental) states of existence (consciousness) which finally leads to its flowering of purity and freedom. This attraction of the water-lily to the Moon stands for the human response to "the celestial ambrosial rain through the sieve of heaven" which imparts the divine intoxication and draws the individual towards the purity and freedom of Divine wisdom.

Nakshatra-Nath or "Lord of the asterism" alludes to an important aspect of cosmogenesis (see p. 180). Daksha Prajapati, a great cosmic progenitor, gave twenty-seven of his sixty daughters to the Moon to further the creation. These twenty-seven became the various nakshatras or asterisms that the Moon regularly visits. During the course of his relationship with them, the Moon became extremely fond of Rohini, the fourth asterism which has great creative power and fertility. This special attention to Rohini aroused jealousy among the others. They complained of this discrimination to their father. Daksha became enraged and cursed the Moon to childlessness and to die of consumption. This harsh punishment was removed by the piety of his wives. They interceded with Daksha in the Moon's favor. As a curse once pronounced cannot be recalled, Daksha agreed to modify it. The Moon has to decay periodically but gradually it can regain its earlier strength.

This story about the Moon has a deep significance. Astrologically it is recognized that the power of the Moon's influence depends upon its association with various asterisms. The Moon and the asterism Rohini are both concerned with concretizing the creative potential in nature. They have much affinity between them, but such an intensification of the creative impulse is liable to make the individual emotionally unbalanced. The curse of childlessness cast on the Moon refers to the passivity of its creative potential. Being pure consciousness, the Moon must have the association of a masculine or active influence to make it objective. As the personification of the female generative principle, the Moon requires an active agent to make it fertile. For the actualization of the Moon's creative influence, it must be examined in its relationship with planets and the asterisms where it is placed.

The *Rig Veda* eulogizes Soma as the source of wisdom. This characteristic of the Moon is amplified in Puranic mythology as Taraka Rahasya or the Mystery of Tara's seduction. The Moon became fond of Tara, the wife of Brihaspati or Jupiter who was the priest of the Gods and engaged in the meticulous performance of religious rituals and the rules of ethical conduct. Tara had a craving for the direct perception of the realities of life or the higher wisdom. Jupiter was unable to satisfy her desire. This was represented by their inability to have children. The Moon wanted to seduce Tara; that is, he wanted to impart his inner understanding to her so as to enable both of them to be in unison. He induced Jupiter to proceed with his morning rituals. Meanwhile, he eloped with Tara, seduced her, and made her pregnant. He was not willing to part with Tara and return her to her husband, nor was she desirous of returning.

This led to a war in heaven. The Gods, along with Indra and Brahma were arrayed with Jupiter, and the Asuras, Danavas, Daityas, and other enemies of the Gods with the Moon. The sage Ushana or Venus, the priest of the Asuras, out of enmity to Jupiter sided with the Moon. A fierce battle ensued and "the earth was shaken at its center" (the axis of the earth began to wobble). Both sides were adamant. No one wanted to yield. Even Tara was not willing to return to Jupiter. Shiva with his trident cut Soma into two, but the contest continued as before. Realizing the imminent possibility of the world coming to an end as a result of this strife, Brahma interposed. He stopped the fight. He compelled Soma to return Tara to her husband. When Tara in time had a son, she would not reveal who its father was. At last, when she indicated Soma to be the true father, Jupiter did not want the child. But when the child turned out to be a charming creature, he became attracted to it and adopted him as his own. This child was named Budha, who became the planet Mercury and started the lunar dynasty of kings.

This allusion to Soma or Moon emphasizes that the lunar impact is necessary for producing inner wisdom which cannot be produced by mere outer religious rituals represented by Jupiter. The Moon has the quality of revealing the hidden secrets of nature. The Moon can be subdued by creative power (Brahma), while the mere exercise of force, even at the threat of reducing its power (Shiva's trident cutting Soma in two) cannot make the Moon swerve from its determination. Not only are the godly potentials (Tara) attracted towards the Moon, but even Ushana, the Daityas and Danavas who represent Asuric forces of nature and foes of the gods are ever willing to support the Moon in order to attain their own ends.

Blavatsky (*SD Vol. III, p.76*) once stated that "the Moon, masculine in its theogonic character, is, in its cosmic aspect only, the female generative principle, as the Sun is the male emblem thereof. Water is the progeny of the Moon, an androgyne deity with every nation." In the terrestrial evolution, the Moon has the primary role. The Sun is the giver of life to the whole planetary system, while the Moon specifically directs life to our globe. The relative status of the Sun and the Moon has often been described by associating the Sun with the Seventh Principle of our planetay system and the Moon with the Fourth, "shining in the borrowed robes of her master, saturated with and reflecting every passionate impulse and evil desire of her grossly material body, Earth." The Fourth Principle arouses thirst for sentient existence, Trishna as the Buddhists call it. It is the desire for experience rooted in the sense organs and sensory qualities which acting through the elements produces the mind. This interrelationship between the Sun and Moon has been described in many ways. Puranic mythology which refers to the Moon as seated in a chariot having three wheels and drawn by ten white horses, five on the right half of the yoke and five on the left, is one such allegory. The implications of this symbology are the same as those with the wheel of the chariot of the Sun and its three naves and five spokes.

The origin of consciousness, which the Moon represents and energizes, is a complex phenomenon. In it sensation and the sense organs both
act together. Whatever one understands is reflected in one's action.
Intelligence and the actual response to any stimulus — external or internal
— is conditioned by the basic attitude of the individual. This situation is
represented by the chariot symbology on which the Moon is drawn.

The similarity between the solar wheel and the lunar chariot emphasizes the special status of the Moon in carrying out the goals set forth by
the Sun. The special responsibility for its tasks on earth is taken over by
the Moon. But there is a radical difference between the two. The Sun leads
the universe towards the ultimate actualization of its potential in order to
attain its final destiny — liberation from the veil of matter. The Moon, on
the other hand, directs the individual to immerse himself in materiality
and become encased in the ignorance so that he may no longer be attracted
to it. This is why the Moon attracted Tara only after she was dissatisfied
with the fruitlessness of exoteric rituals and outer knowledge which could
not draw forth her creativity. The manner of operation of solar and lunar
forces are radically different from each other. There is an inherent
opposition between the two luminaries, one pulling us towards liberation
and the other pushing us towards materialization. Hence, much tension is
indicated in astrological predictions when a close association occurs
between the two.

The ten horses divided into two groups of five, and the three wheels
of the Moon's chariot reiterate the importance of the five sense organs
and five organs of action. They are all colorless and ready to draw Soma,
the Consciousness, wherever it wants to go. The three primeval attributes,
Sattwa, Rajas and Tamas induce the soul to engage itself in the manifestation at different stages of the evolutionary cycle. They follow the lead
given by the sensory and motor organs. As long as these organs are pulling
the chariot in different directions, there will be turbulence and disturbance
in the proper functioning of the human being. When these horses are well
coordinated and begin marching in unison, the movement of the chariot
will be swift and well directed. The Moon seated in the chariot is the
individual soul (Jiva), crystallized so as to involve itself in the evolutionary cycle wherein it assumes several incarnations before attaining final
freedom. Unless the mind has a clear perception of the goal, it cannot
effectively control and direct the horses.

This story emphasizes the helplessness of the mind in making any
progress unless the sensory and motor organs are disciplined and well
coordinated. The direction for this journey must come from a source
higher than the Moon. It has to come from the Sun or the Self, in whose
radiance the Moon or mind shines. The passivity of the Moon, therefore,

must be safeguarded, which implies that the nature of the person must be crystalline clear like the whiteness of the horses before he undertakes the pilgrimage destined for him. There should be no sediment born of material seeking in the consciousness. This passivity of Moon is best revealed both psychologically and astrologically when it reflects the radiance of the Sun without any impediment as seen on the day of the full Moon. The essence of all these teachings can be summarized in a statement from *The Secret Doctrine (Vol. III, p.121)* that the Divine Spirit is symbolized by the Sun or Fire, the Divine Soul by Water and the Moon, and that both stand for the Father and Mother of Pneuma, the Human Soul or Mind, symbolized by the Wind or Air. "The importance of the Sun and Moon is indeed very great, and it is stated in secret literature that between the Sun and the Moon almost every occult mystery is imparted. The whole cycle of Adeptship and Initiation and all its mysteries are connected with, and subservient to these two, the Sun and the Moon, along with the Seven Planets. Spiritual clairvoyance is derived from the Sun, while all psychic states, diseases and even lunacy proceed from the Moon. The birth of Adepts and Initiates who represent additions to the Inner Government of the World is the most effective creative assistance imparted by the Moon to Sun. The possibility of the Moon leading to nature's finer forces is so great that the occultists as well as the sorcerers greatly look forward to the favors of the Moon."

3
MERCURY
BUDHA

☿

Mercury, the prince of the planetary hierarchy, has a mysterious origin and deep meaning in alchemical literature. Diagrammatically, Mercury is represented by a circle placed on the top of a cross with a crescent as its crown ☿. This is the symbol of Venus with the crescent on top of it. Thus, the distinguishing feature between the symbols of Mercury and Venus is this arc at the top of Mercury's symbol.

Mercury contains within itself all the qualities of Venus; sensitivity, perception and the tendency towards materialization of the Divine potential. Under the Mercurian impulse, Venusian qualities are either pushed toward the deeper layers of materialization, or they are raised towards the realization of the soul's Divine origin and original purity. Such transformations depend upon the growth and development of intelligence. Mercury is related to Mind, which enables the individual to use his intellect. The arc that distinguishes Mercury from Venus at first sight appears to represent the Moon. Mercury is related to the Moon. The Sanskrit name for Mercury is Saumaya, meaning "son of Soma" or the Moon. The Moon is pure consciousness. It reflects the universal essence of life directed through the radiance of the Sun. The Moon projects this radiance onto lower levels of manifestation to energize and nourish life on earth. Pure consciousness, as it is the capacity of comprehension without any object, requires involvement in matter in order to get objectified and fructify the realm of manifestation. In this process, the intellect serves as a bridge between knowledge as an active potential and pure intelligence that enables the understanding of the essential being. This is the special feature of Mercury. The emblem for the planet as a cross which stands for manifestation, combined with a circle which represents evolutionary movement in its wholeness, and the Moon-like arc which relates it to pure consciousness indicates the totality of Mercurian function. The arc at the top represents the movement of various impulses after they have individualized and are struggling towards liberation. The semi-circularity of the arc links the last point of objectification of the subjective impulse with the beginning of the liberation of the soul. This wide field of Mercurian operation makes the planet a messenger between the gods and man.

The Mercurian arc reveals two additional aspects of the planet. First, the part of the arc touching the top of the Venusian circle signifies the immersion of the soul in matter. It shows the downward movement of the Divine Energy. Second, the movement of the arc away from the Venusian circle signifies escape from the material world. It therefore shows that the human intellect is capable of immersing the individual in the darkness of materialism as well as releasing him from it. Whether the individual is struggling toward the Spirit or to indulgence in the sensate experiences of the material world depends upon the disposition of Mercury. The proximity of Venus and Mercury relates to two adjacent sheaths of the human being, the Anandamaya Kosha or Bliss sheath (related to Venus) and the Vijnanamaya Kosha or Intelligence sheath (related to Mercury), which combine to greatly influence the nature of the man.

The alchemists gave much importance to Mercury*. They considered it to be a metal but under this symbol they discussed the nature and activities of consciousness. According to them, Mercury transforms base metal into gold. This represents the transformation of earthly and materialistic human beings into realized souls who have returned to their original pure nature. Due to its perceptivity and sensitivity, Mercury has the power to transform human experience into the realization of pure consciousness. Truth in every form of creation can be comprehended only with the freedom of intelligence from every material shackle and bias of thought. According to the view of Vedanta the ignorance that veils the true nature of creation can be rent asunder by the intellect provided that it is properly trained and directed.

The addition of the crescent to the Mercury symbol points to its ability to transmute all mundane experiences and involvements into Right Awareness. This aspect of consciousness is not tarnished by any experience; time does not make it old and no object impedes its movement. Pure consciousness can operate at the highest level of creation and attain the heights enjoyed by the gods. At its level of eternal duration and perpetual motion, there is no age, as there is no material content in it to alter its original perfection. In the state of pure awareness, there is no place for matter. Such a state has the quality of eternal youth. It is ever able to adapt itself to any situation. This ability to function at the highest level of

---

* See *Psychology and Alchemy*, C. G. Jung. Pantheon Books, 1952.

existence because intelligence has overcome all the shackles of ignorance enables Mercury to maintain the freshness of agelessness.

Mercury and Venus are nearer to the Sun than the other planets. Their symbols show a greater affinity to it also. The solar ideation is received on the level of consciousness by way of sensitivity and perception. In fact, conception and perception go together, but once the thought process has begun to operate, the intelligence functions in two ways, it can intensify materialization or help the individual gain release from its thraldom.

The arc at the top of the Mercury symbol stands for a chalice. It receives the Divine potential represented by the circle in the Sun symbol to channel its perception and creativity. This is then passed on to other planets for their articulation. Mercury contains within itself all potentials for further differentiation. The Vedantic concept of Mahat or Cosmic Intelligence, upon which further differentiation expresses itself as the manifest universe, is represented by this arc.

Mercury has the quality of agelessness; it is a chalice for the Divine downpour of its manifesting power, and it stands for Mahat, the cosmic thought principle. Furthermore, the arc, circle and cross are so arranged in its symbol that together they reveal the special role of Mercury in inducing the human being to ascend the spiritual heights. Beginning with gross matter, represented by a cross at the lower end of the symbol, one experiences the Divine potential as the underlying essence of all forms of manifestation represented by the circle. In its integrated wholeness, Mercury is more pleasing than Venus as far as diversity of interest, adaptability, intelligence and sociability are concerned. Mercury does not crave for personal gratification as Venus does. Being the Mahat principle, Mercury even transcends death. In everyday life one knows that the thought of a person survives his death. The circular arc moving from the Fourth to the Tenth house in the horoscope represents the individual uniqueness of the person covering his creativity (Fifth house), struggle against resistances experienced in earthly activities (Sixth house), interactive love and hate relationships in social life (Seventh house), problems of ill health, decay and death (Eighth house) and spiritual endeavors (Ninth house) (see p. 27). When all these experiences are transcended and assimilated in consciousness, the operation of Mercury ceases and thought no longer holds the soul under its servitude.

Allegorically, Mercury was born after Tara's abduction, seduction and her liaison with Soma (see p. 54). This simple story of adultery with the usual strains on both sides reveals the conflict in the human psyche at its deeper levels when the individual aspires for spiritual knowledge. The craving for higher wisdom possessed by Soma induced Tara to have a liason with him. This represents the blending of the consciousness of the two at higher levels where communication is inward. Tara was not satisfied with the husk of external rituals and was disenchanted with Jupiter who represented tradition, social order and exoteric religious practices. Prior to attaining enlightenment represented by the birth of Mercury, the soul has to pass through mundane religious rituals to experience their futility. Only on the perception of the superficiality of outer rituals does enlightenment dawn on the individual mind. Pure understanding is signified by the comprehension of the all-pervading life principle without any distortion. Mercury is the power of comprehension, the perceptiveness arising out of sensitized urge to understand Reality. In ordinary terms, it is intelligence as distinguished from mere collection of information.

Mercury is married to Ila or Ida and Pururavas was born to them, from whom starts the Lunar dynasty of kings. Ila is a daughter of Manu, who was a son of the Sun. Manu was saved from the Deluge with the assistance of Vishnu, the preserver of the universe. Later, Manu started the Solar dynasty of kings but he had no children. Wanting a son, he arranged for a sacrifice to Mitra (the Sun god) and Varuna (the Water god). The officiating priest mismanaged the performance and it resulted in the birth of a daughter Ila. The two deities, however, changed her sex and she became a man called Sudyumna. Under the malediction of Shiva, Sudyumna was again turned into a woman and she married Budha from whom she gave birth to Pururavas. Under the favor of Vishnu, she was once more changed to her male form of Sudyumna and in time became the father of three sons.

Another version of the legend refers to Ila as the eldest son of Manu. His sex was changed due to his trespassing on a grove sacred to Parvati, the consort of Shiva. Thus Ila was made into a female. Upon the supplication and prayer of Ila's friends, Shiva and Parvati conceded that he would be male one month and female the next.

In the *Sathapatha Brahmana*, Ila is represented as arising from a sacrifice which Manu performed with a view to beget an offspring. When Ila arose from the sacrifice, she was so charming that the Sun god, Mitra, and Water god, Varuna, both claimed her, but she remained faithful to the sacrificer who produced her. Manu lived with her for a long time praying and fasting to obtain an offspring. Finally, from her he succeeded in establishing a race of Manus.

Ila's marriage with Mercury is a psycho-spiritual phenomenon. Intelligence, which is pure subjectivity, requires a creative potential for its expression on the material planes of existence. The Manus or human progenitors are responsible for providing adequate facilities and opportunities for such activities. In this process, however, Ila's several changes of sex are significant. Ila, the offspring born as a joint benediction of the Sun (Mitra) and Water (Varuna) is the life giving energy which operates in active as well as passive aspects as the need arises. In marriage with Budha, the creative counterpart has to be passive in nature. Pure consciousness to be fruitful requires a placid environment. This is how thought produces pure awareness in its unending motion allegorized as the beginning of the Lunar dynasty of kings.

In the *Rig Veda*, Ila is described as food, refreshment or a libation of milk. She is the goddess of speech, the earth or a cow. In yogic literature, Ila or Ida is one of the three important channels (nadis) through which the vital air travels from the base of the spine to the crown chakra, on whose unimpeded flow depends the liberation of the mind. Vak (speech) is personfied through Ida, who Blavatsky *(SD Vol. II, p. 148)* calls the female Logos that Brahma created out of half of his body when he divided in two for furthering the creative manifestation. Ila is the subjective creative force, which emanating from the Creative Deity, becomes the manifest world of speech. She is often described as the celestial Saraswati, the voice that arises from the silent Brahman.

Ida as another name of Saraswati is the channel through which the creative impulse expresses itself in its concretization process. It is necessarily feminine in character as it is the receptacle for the downpour of the creative Ray represented by Mercury. To make speech effective in its generative mission, it requires the positive creative intelligence of Mercury. The creative intelligence by itself is not productive since in its primeval state it is pure subjectivity. It must blend itself with a channel which is creative and functions as a receptacle. This emphasizes the importance of androgynous Ila or Ida. Budha, the subjective intelligence requiring a channel for its creative mission, is married with Ida, the creative channel, to originate and perpetuate the Lunar dynasty of kings. The mystifying changes in Ida's sex take place because she has to act both as a creative agency, which is primarily a masculine function, while she is also a receptacle, an incubating agency which is a feminine.

Uniting with Ida, Mercury represents the positive, masculine, creative power described in the Tantras as Shiva tattwa, the truth of Shiva or pure being. However the intelligence principle in man, which Mercury represents, is passive in character. This is why Mercury is considered androgynous. Ida, which functions as the concretizing counterpart of Mercury must also have the characteristics of both forces: it must be androgynous acting in such a way that it plays the passive role when Mercury is active in operation, reassuming its active role when Mercury reverts to its natural state of passive awareness.

Ida or Ila as an offspring of Manu is basically masculine in character but was transformed in order to unite with Mercury. The marriage of the two results in the blending of their consciousness at a high level of the oneness of life. This was the seed essential for the propagation of the Lunar (representing the life-giving) dynasty of kings. Since Budha, representing Intelligence or Mind, is basically feminine, its harmonious unification can only be achieved with a partner who is basically masculine. The Buddha-nature, which is expressed as the urge for enlightenment, is inborn in every individual. Each mind has the quality of enlightenment, Bodhi, in potential form, but its activation cannot be induced by any external agency. To be effective, the energy which enables the mind to comprehend has to be sui generis, unique, not dependent upon any external factor or support. The aspiration aroused by external factors cannot wrest control over the secret energy that is the Kundalini or Serpent Fire.

The energy which illumines the mind is basically active, but it lies dormant until intelligence by its own power establishes control over it and rapport with it. The union between Ida, the channel by the side of the spinal cord for the movement of the vital air, and Budha, the pure consciousness giving energy to mind to arouse Intelligence, is a mystic ritual that occurs in the process of initiation. The marriage of Budha with Ida is a veiled and allegorised version of this ritual. It indicates the extraordinary role of Mercury in exploring the secrets of nature. Nature reveals her secret truths in marriage, opening the most secret part of the body to the searching mind which is not induced by any external attraction except the urge to know the truth. Such a mystic role for Mercury in acquiring the control over nature's secrets also explains the special status assigned to it by the Alchemists.

In the stories that refer to Ila turning into a female either as a malediction of Shiva or his consort Parvati, Vishnu is instrumental in Ila's return to his original nature. Shiva is the creative power functioning at the highest level while Vishnu is the preserver. The blending of the consciousnesses of Mercury and Ila was necessary for starting the Lunar dynasty of kings. Unless the subjective consciousness and its objective channels of expression are united together, no concretization of creative radiance is possible. Vishnu, the preserver, has the responsibility to maintain the channel, the womb or the Hiranyagarbha so that it can be utilized when required. This is the role of Vishnu in changing Ila back to an active male agent.

Such involved allusions point out the role of Mercury to blend itself with the cosmic creative energy that flows from the Sun and direct that energy to lower levels of manifestation. Mercury aims at concretizing the Divine Will. In every world religion, Intelligence personified as Mercury,

Hermes, or Nebo is considered the god of wisdom who represents the Word or Logos. Mercury is that principle in man which leads the blind and restores sight both mental and physical. He is the creative word of God, the creative speech scattered throughout the universe.

Blavatsky states that Mercury has to be ever near Isis as her minister for without Mercury neither Isis nor Osiris can accomplish anything. Isis is the goddess Virgin Mother who personifies Nature. She is the Egyptian equivalent of the Hindu goddess Saraswati, the goddess of music and sacred works. She possesses the esoteric knowledge and wisdom and is similar to Ila whom Mercury marries. Osiris is the First Cause, the Self-created god. For these two to be effective, there is the need of Cosmic Intelligence, Mahat. This raises the importance of Mercury and shows his place in the spiritualizing as well as materializing processes of the soul. At earlier stages of its operation Mercury accentuates egoism, the sense of I-am-I, but ultimately Mercury as pure consciousness is unaffected by the channel through which it functions. The nature of pure awareness in this sense is neither materialistic nor spiritual: it is unspoiled by either state.

To summarize, the geometrical figure for Mercury represents its channeling the solar radiance and reflecting it onto the entire field of manifestation. It can be interpreted either as a spiritualizing or material- izing force according to its direction of movement. Mercury transmutes matter into the universal energy represented by the wholeness of the circle and enables it to reflect the inner light pervading all forms of existence. The different stories show the details of the materializing and spiritualiz- ing processes by associating Mercury with the Sun and Moon. They show its inner wisdom by relating it with Soma and Jupiter. By relating Mercury with Saraswati, Ida and Parvati, it is represented as the subjective principle of Mahat or Cosmic Intelligence. Mercury is related to Manu to show its role in furthering the plan of manifestation. Mind represented by Mercury is a channel for serving Shiva or the supreme creative principle, and is preserved and assisted by the self-perpetuating intelligence represented by Vishnu. Mercury is a messenger who gives out the hidden secrets of inner teachings and the deeper meaning of outer rituals. Mercury functions as the messiah of the Sun by enabling the mind to understand the unifying principle in the universe. As a husband of Ida, Intelligence in man, Mercury, enables the individual to wrest the solar energy contained as the Serpent Fire and grant him enlightenment. Mercury makes the person a Buddha or enlightened one.

4
VENUS
SHUKRA
♀

Venus is the most occult, powerful and mysterious of the planets; the one whose influence upon the Earth is most prominent (*SD Vol. III, p. 42*). In Hindu mythology, Venus or Shukra is a male deity, the son of Bhrigu who was one of the Prajapatis and a Vedic sage. Shukra is the Daitya-Guru or the teacher of the demons or giants.

The symbols for Mercury and Venus are alike except for the crescent arc at the top of Mercury. The difference between the symbols of Venus and Earth lies in the latter being an inversion of the former. In the case of Venus, a cross hangs from a circle whereas in that of the Earth, the cross is superimposed at the top of the circle. A cross hanging from a circle might appear to a child to be a balloon floating in the air. The distinguishing feature of the three planetary symbols which derive from the circle are an arrow for Mars, a cross for Venus, and a crescent for Mercury.

The circle represents the spiritual essence evolving through manifestation. It shows the wholeness of the latent faculties in man to be developed during the course of his evolution, which finally unfolds his divinity as the Son ascends to the throne of the Father in Heaven. The life-giving principle expressed in the outer manifestation is symbolized by the encircled space. Venus, Mars and Mercury are concerned with this life-giving force. The Venusian impulse is important for generating, preserving and nourishing the various life forms on Earth.

The cross represents the churning of the ocean. When two opposing forces combine together to activate electrical energy, there is much activity and the magnetic field becomes highly charged. In the cross symbol, the masculine energy represented by the vertical line, and the feminine by the horizontal, together represent manifestation. Wherever life unfolds and any form of creation takes place, one finds the interplay of these positive and negative forces. Placed under the circle, the cross denotes the Divine Essence involved in the creative process.

The cross symbolizes intense activity. It is the churning process whereby the unity of the divinity is polarized and immersed into action.

Being the meeting ground of two opposing forces, it creates storms, conflicts and differences. These transform the primeval energy into various forms. The impulse generated by Venus always creates fundamental changes and brings forth new manifestation. The sex impulse produces deep-rooted changes both in the psyche of the individual as well as in the society. But the sexual urge is merely one of the various forces generated by the churning process.

Under the Venusian impulse, the Divine Energy is polarized and immersed into action and the creative process is activated. The influence of polarized impulses — the positive and the negative poles of electricity, the masculine and the feminine nature in man, the Purusha and Prakriti principles in nature — is primarily directed towards manifestation. The cross which represents the meeting of these two forces stands for the war in heaven or the churning process. When the primeval process is weighed down by the cross, the Divine Energy is made to manifest at lower levels of existence. The symbol of the circle with a cross underneath it indicates this process of materialization. The Venusian range of operation extends from the very beginning of creation until the very end. This interaction results in great attraction between different constituents of manifestation. Sociability which is a basic quality of Venus expresses the magnetic influence of the churning operation. The cross has a central meeting point, and each pole discharges the specialized energy so that the opposites attract each other fervently. The creative process itself is the result of this attraction. What the metaphysicians call the Divine Love pervading all forms of creation is in fact the expression of the Venusian impulse. Venus denotes love which leads to mutual attraction. The entire manifestation holds itself together as a result of this attraction.

During the descent of the Venusian influence from the highest level of subjectivity it assumes different modes of expression. The fine sensitivity at the higher planes is known as inspiration, and intuition, while at a lower emotional level it becomes sensuality and sexuality. As a result of intensified sensitivity under Venus, the perceptive faculties of the person are enhanced. The individual becomes responsive to the feelings and thoughts of others. He is able to establish immediate rapport with large numbers of people. He is consciously or unconsciously aware of the common bond of universal energy between all forms of existence. The extent of his perceptive faculties becomes limitless. Wherever there is matter, whatever the level of manifestation, the Venusian impulse enables the individual to establish rapport. The emergence of artistic talents like music, painting, dancing, sculpture, poetry and architecture are produced by this impulse. The divine in the artist under the Venusian impact activates the inner depths of perception and externalizes it at different levels of creation.

The Divine Energy operates in positive and negative ways through both masculine and feminine channels of expression. It can be used for constructive and noble aims or for destructive and base purposes. The cross hanging under the circle is suggestive of the polarized expression of the Divine potential. The cross is the union between positive and negative energy channels, the male and female forms of creation. If the container of the Divine downpour is lined with the emotional or desire sheaths, the impact of the energy received therein produces sensuous feeling and indulgence in sense enjoyments. The individual receiving the impact becomes sensitive to the feelings and thoughts of others but his craving for sense gratification is enhanced making his desires insatiable. He will seek ever greater gratification without reaching any end to his thirst.

The Venusian impulse generally moves downward. In most cases, it rushes toward a greater degree of materialization. The balance is therefore upset. The spiritual component is weakened and the desire for self gratification accentuated. When such a situation arises, there is every likelihood that the individual will become debauched or degenerate. On the other hand, with a strong spiritual influence, he can become a seer with intuitive perception of the complex stages of creative unfoldment transcending temporal and spatial limitations. Such a person can instinctively establish sympathetic relationships with the highest as well as the lowest. He discovers the Divine Energy at both extremes of manifestation.

Shukra in Hindu mythology is known by his patronymic Bhargava, which derives from Bhrigu. He is called Kavi or Kavya, the poet as well as poetry. The planet is variously called: Asphujit, the effulgent one; Shodasavisu, he who has sixteen rays; Maghabhava or the son of Magha; and Shweta or white. Ushana is one of the names of the regent of the planet Venus. In the Vedas, he was given the epithet Kavya because of his great learning and wisdom. He is a well-known writer on civic and religious laws. Such an eminent deity is considered as the teacher of the Daityas (demons), and Asuras which emphasizes the enigmatic character of Venus.

Maghabhava or son of Magha relates Venus to the tenth asterism Magha, characterized by abundant life-giving energy. Under the Venusian impulse, the soul is pushed into the world with much energy and courage. Magha is connected with reproduction. It has an affinity with affluence and comfort, sexual pleasure and luxurious living. Such impulses find great resonance with Venus. The association of the regent of Venus with Magha points to their channeling the same quality of cosmic energy.

Shodasavisu, the deity with sixteen rays, refers to sixteen important cosmic forces. They are the sixteen phases of the Moon, each of which is identified and given a special name. They also refer to the sixteen components of the microcosm or Shodasagana, which consists of the five organs of action, the five sense organs, the five elements, and chitta or consciousness. In Hindu thought, the number sixteen has a special importance and stands for sixteen articles of offerings, sixteen kinds of worship, sixteen goddesses, the sixteen hands of Durga, the goddess of Power, the sixteen erotic sentiments, and the sixteen sacraments from impregnation to death. All these are channels for different celestial impulses. The sixteen rays of Venus are the active potency which energizes them. Even his being called Shweta or White refers to his being positive, not under the influence of any other power. For this reason, Pythagoras called Venus the Sol Alter or the "Other Sun."

The appellation Daitya-Guru indicates the special mission of Venus, but the role of Daityas, the demons, is often misunderstood. Literally, Daitya means demon but this conceals the real nature and function of these mighty beings. Daitya is a son of Diti whereas Diti herself is a daughter of Daksha, the Prajapati or creator specially charged with the procreative process. Diti was married to Sage Kashyapa, one of the primeval seven sages. The Daityas, as this reveals, are not hostile forces trying to retard the evolutionary progress. They are essential counterparts of the Daivic or benign energy assisting and guiding manifestation. The Daityas as sons of Diti merely mean the multitude: the word Diti means "cutting, splitting, and dividing," while Aditya standing for the Sun means wholeness. The numerous forms of manifestation reeled off from cosmic unity represent the Daityas. They have been split from the 'Whole' and have lost their original pure nature. The guardian of these separate beings who are ever struggling to gain (or regain) their inherent status has to possess tremendous wisdom and insight. Only the teacher who understands the nature and ordeals of the Path, can lead disciples correctly and effectively. Shukra, Venus, is attributed to possess the secret of immortality which even Jupiter, the god's preceptor did not possess.

The reference linking Venus to the Asuras who arose from the very first act of polarization of the primeval energy, is important for understanding the chief function of the planet. With the creation of the gods, there arose the necessity of producing a counterbalancing power without which there would be unbalanced growth of the universe. The gods represent unity while the Daityas are the multitude. The Daityas are also associated with primeval giants. Yet the gigantic demons who were brainless and beastly are different from the original Asuras who are the personifications of centrifugal forces. The Asuras whom Venus or Shukra guided were devotees of different aspects of the Divine Trinity represented by Brahma, Vishnu and Shiva. The Asuras obtained powerful siddhis, that is control over supernatural powers as a result of benedictions received from these gods. The primary distinction between the Devas and the Asuras is ahankara, the ego, which the latter represent. But egoism or the idea of the separate self is the root cause of human manifestation. Shukra, as the teacher of egoistic beings like the Daityas and Rakshasas, has the prime task of preserving and nourishing them in an ordered existence. This is only possible by the observance of an ideal code of social behavior, which Shukra laid down as the Dharma Shastra or code of righteous behavior. The planetary impulse from Venus aims at maintaining a well-ordered harmonious interaction between different people.

The *Shiva Purana* mentions that Shukra was born from the vital fluid of Lord Shiva when his passion was aroused by the captivating form of Vishnu which had once subdued and destroyed a powerful demon. The form was so seductive that having seen it Shiva could not contain himself; his creative-fluid came out and Shukra arose from it. The word Shukra in Sanskrit means semen as well as Agni or fire. Shiva himself christened this personification of energy as Shukra and assigned it sway over the Asuras or the multitude to carry out the task of reproduction.

This legend highlights the function of Venus in relation to procreation. Lord Shiva is the supreme creative force and Venus is the personification of his creative fluid. This fluid is ejaculated as a result of its downward movement as opposed to its upward movement, which takes place when the Kundalini is aroused under spiritual discipline. Its downward movement manifests through the sexual urge. It is expressed as an emotional impulse for physical union, while the upward movement leads to the integration of the various principles of the soul. As this movement occurred due to Shiva's witnessing an illusive form of the preservation principle represented by Vishnu, the resulting planetary deity is also credited to produce attraction to the world of illusion or the material world and the urge to get involved in it which is expressed as sex.

The *Hari Vansha* relates that Shukra went to Shiva and prayed to him for a means of protecting the Asuras against the gods. For obtaining this benediction, he performed a painful rite imbibing the smoke of chaff with his head hung downward for thousands of years. In his absence, the gods attacked the Asuras and Vishnu killed his mother. Shukra cursed Vishnu for this murder to be born seven times in the world of men. He restored his mother to life as he knew the mantra to do so. Alarmed that Shukra might accomplish the penance for his desired boon, Indra sent his daughter Jayanti to lure him away from his quest. She waited upon him and soothed him but, undistracted Shukra, accomplished his penance. Afterwards, however, Shukra married Jayanti.

This legend also highlights Shukra's preoccupation with procreation. Lord Shiva is the supreme power who bestows the essence of life-energy to every form of creation, the Asuras as well as the gods. His virgin sons refused to get involved in the process of outer manifestation. Special progenitors 'Prajapatis' were created for this purpose. Bhrigu, the father of Shukra was one such Prajapati. The externalization of the creative energy could only succeed by increasing the number of individuals in the scheme. Bhrigu initiated the process by giving birth to the procreative urge represented by Venus. To produce the required impulse, Shukra did penance by hanging himself upside down. This idea of inversion is often mentioned in Eastern spiritual literature. The Tree of Life, in the *Upnishads* and *Bhagavad Gita*, is compared with Ashwattha tree which has its roots above and branches below. The differentiation of consciousness, mind and matter is symbolized by this inverted tree. It represents the manifest universe rooted in the Unmanifest, the subtlest spirit, and branching down into the realm of matter. The human nervous system, rooted in the brain, also hangs downward. The relationship between the pure subjectivity of the Unmanifest and differentiated life forms is represented by Shukra hanging himself upside down in order to protect the Daityas, i.e., to perpetuate the multitude.

Venus emits the creative impulse. His activities are part of the Divine plan of evolution. He is rooted in the ethereal realm of spirit, but his sphere of operation is below in the material world. The Sun-Moon-Mercury triad functions on the level of subjectivity as the higher triad in the septenary principle, and with Venus begins the journey to the lower quaternary. The Venusian impulse flows from above downwards perpetuating the outer form of the world. The smoke which Shukra imbibed refers to the Vedic Yajña or fire sacrifice for spiritualizing oneself and one's environment. Smoke is a prelude to fire which arises during the ritual. Such an act of spiritual observance is the very antithesis of what Venus is supposed to produce. On the beginning of spiritual aspiration, whether for outer rituals or inner knowledge, the involvement of the person in matter must weaken. Generating the spiritual current represented by the rising smoke helps Shukra achieve his goal. During this time the individual has to encounter much inconvenience and temptation. The Venusian impulse which intitially intensifies material desire, in its deeper nature gives rise to ethical practices and causes one to aspire for the spiritual life.

Vishnu is the preserver. In his strategy to contain the Asuric realm of existence, he killed the mother of Venus, that is, he wanted to stifle the procreative potential of the Daityas. This would have destroyed the plan

of Shukra and ended the course of procreative manifestation. To counteract the effect, Shukra cursed Vishnu himself to take seven births on earth.
This refers to the seven rounds of manifestation. Venus has the power to
restore to life the dead, so he made his mother alive again, that is, he
established his link with the Divine source of energy which provided him
the necessary vitality to restore the mechanism of procreative existence.
Finally, the marriage of Jayanti with Venus indicates the blending of
Venusian consciousness with the Divine urge for creation.

The Venusian involvement in material existence strengthens the urge
for self-gratification, yet its basic impulse is deeply spiritual, channeling
all energy sources for fulfilling the Divine mission. Venus assists the
Asuras but he does so for implementing the Divine plan. This is corrob-
orated by Venus siding with Soma, the regent of the Moon, in Soma's
conflict with Brihaspati for the sake of Tara (see p. 54). Soma was assisted
by Venus in his effort to satisfy the inner aspiration of the soul, represented
by Tara, when outer rituals, represented by Jupiter, failed to satisfy her
yearning soul.

The marriage of Devayani, daughter of Venus, with Yayati, a king in
the Lunar dynasty started by Pururavas, son of Mercury, shows another
important characteristic of Venus. According to this legend, the Daityas,
under the protection and guidance of Venus, defeated the Devas, rendering
them helpless. This happened because the Daityas slain in the battle were
restored to life by Venus by means of the mystic charm of life-giving
nectar, Mritasanjivani, which he alone possessed. The gods resolved to
secure the charm for themselves if possible. For this purpose, they induced
Kacha, a son of Jupiter, to go to Venus, become his student and learn the
secret.

Kacha went to Shukra and became his disciple. While he was learning
the art from him, Shukra's daughter Devayani fell in love with him.
Meanwhile, the Asuras learned the intention of Kacha and killed him
twice to restrain him from obtaining the secret. On both occasions he was
restored to life by Venus at the intercession of his daughter. Thus dis-
traught, the Asuras killed Kacha a third time, burned his body, mixed his
ashes with Shukra's drink and made him drink it. But, this time also,
Devayani begged her father to restore Kacha to life but as he already
pervaded the body of Shukra, it was difficult to retrieve him and restore
him to life without killing her father. Kacha, however, volunteered to
restore Shukra to life if he could be extricated from his body. Kacha was
in a position to do so as he had already learned the mystic charm and had
perfected it. When Shukra accepted, and Kacha was restored to life,
Devayani proposed her marriage to him. Kacha declined the offer telling
her that he regarded her as a younger sister. This enraged Devayani. She

cursed Kacha that the great charm he had learned from her father would be powerless and he would not be able to use it. Kacha, on the other hand, cursed her that she would never succeed in marrying a Brahmin, which she herself was, but would marry a Kshatriya or warrior.

In the course of time, while Shukra was serving an Asura king named Vrisha Parvan, Devayani became friendly with the king's daughter Sharmistha. Once when they went to take a bath leaving their clothes at the shore, the wind god interchanged their clothes. Having dressed, they discovered the change and began to quarrel as to how it occurred. Sharmishtha lost her temper, slapped Devayani in the face and threw her into a well. Devayani, while in the well, resolved to get her revenge. An eligible prince named Yayati found her in the well and rescued her. In recompense, Devayani offered herself in marriage to him. As a punishment for the insulting behavior of Sharmishtha, Devayani demanded that she be made into her servant maid. Vrisha Parvan, out of deference to Shukra, pressured Sarmishtha into this unhappy position.

At her husband's palace, Devayani continually humiliated and ill-treated Sharmishtha. The king, however, became fond of her, secretly established a relationship with her and eventually married her. Sharmishtha had a son from Yayati. The astrologers predicted a glorious future for the child, while Devayani's sons were destined to only a mediocre future. This further enraged Devayani. She banished Sharmistha with her child into exile. She also complained to her father Shukra against her husband Yayati. Shukra cursed Yayati to premature old age. Yayati, however, propitiated Shukra and obtained from him permission to transfer his decrepitude to anyone who would consent to take it on himself in exchange for his youth. Yayati asked his sons but all of them refused to do so. Meanwhile, Sharmishtha's son Puru came of age, heard of the curse and volunteered to give his youth to the king. Yayati accordingly transferred his old age to Puru. Being once more in the prime of youth, Yayati passed his time in sensual pleasures. Thus he lived for a thousand years. But his appetite for carnal gratification did not diminish. At last, he realised the futility of such craving and with vigorous determination and effort renounced his sensual life, returned his youth to its rightful owner, Puru, and making him successor to the throne retired to the forest for a life of meditation.

This legend presents many features of Venus that are often overlooked. Venus possesses a life-giving energy which even the preceptor of gods, Brihaspati or Jupiter does not possess. Venus can restore the dead to life and perpetuate their existence. This special gift to Venus is directly linked with his birth from the semen of Lord Shiva, which is the very fire vivifying the cells of every living being. Procreation and revival to life are both connected with reincarnation. As the Venusian impulse involves the individual in material attachments, the thirst for life is accentuated which leads to rebirth. With every reincarnation, the body of the individual soul is rejuvenated. Because of their state of consciousness, the Devas cannot be subjected to birth and death or to the rejuvenating process which only those involved in material cravings can possess.

Venus is a teacher and as such does not restrict his wisdom to any special category of students. He teaches the Daityas as well as godly persons like Kacha. Anyone who can observe the rules of discipleship can learn from him the secret of life and death. Kacha did it, as did Yayati. Shukra's curse to Yayati was a method of teaching him the secret of life and death, obtaining which Yayati retired into the forest for meditation. Venus is moved by love and affection. Even when he risked his own annihilation, he restored Kacha to life to please his daughter whom he loved. Narrowness and restrictive considerations do not motivate Venus to action but he does not interfere in the working of karma. Though he knew the secret of restoring a person to life even after death, yet he failed, in spite of his love for his daughter, to make her happy.

Devayani, daughter of Shukra and his feminine counterpart, cannot marry a Brahmin, one of the religious class. She can unite only with a warrior. With the blending of consciousness with wisdom represented by the Brahmin class, the urge for sensory gratification is weakened. In association with Jupiter, the Venusian impact declines and the relationship becomes Platonic. Kacha, being a son of Jupiter, knew very well that marriage or the blending together of physical and psychological lives can only effectively take place when both individuals are of the same nature. The thirst for life emanating from Venus and personified in Devayani could not agree with the Brahmin temperament toward renunciation. His curse that Devayani would only marry in the warrior class arose from the same law of affinity.

The asterism Magha, which Venus is named son of, marks the beginning of Tamasic tendencies that relate to the materialization of the Divine Essence in the soul. Devayani represents this temperament. Her union with the Sattwic temperament or the Brahmin class could not occur according to the law of harmony. Devayani, the female counterpart of Venus, could only unite with materially oriented masculine souls represented by the Kshatriya class. The union between the Kshatriya king Yayati and Devayani, the daughter of a Brahmin, could be productive but Yayati was enamoured with his own Kshatriya counterpart represented by Sharmishtha the daughter of a king. Only Sharmishtha's son succeeded Yayati; none of Devayani's were able to do so. Mercury, from whom Yayati descended, was capable of involving himself in matter while maintaining his consciousness at spiritual levels also. Yayati could be productive with both Devayani and Sharmishtha. Venus is productive in association with Mercury but is more so in association with Mars. Venus can make one who is old, infirm, and decrepit young again, but he cannot make him overcome his craving for worldly pleasure. Yayati in association with Devayani could never transcend his desire for self-gratification. Shukra could make him old, could restore his youth and perpetuate his existence, but Yayati's psychological transformation was beyond him. Such a transformation could come only with inner reflection, an attribute of Mercury, and strong mental determination which shows identification with one's higher triad where Mercury operates correctly.

To summarize, Venus is associated with the seminal fluid which represents the Divine creative energy in the materialization process. It functions like a twin sister to the Earth. It is even considered as the little Sun for the Earth. Venus scatters or splits the Divine Essence among the multitude. It guides social evolution and strengthens personal relationships. It functions primarily by accentuating the urge to unite. While leading human beings to procreation, Venus accentuates egoism and strengthens the urge towards sense gratification. Venusian energy does not have much affinity with Jupiter; the latter is concerned with wisdom and protection of the state of balance, while Venus induces the individual to material desires, to take several births and encounter several deaths. It is not interested in leading the individual to liberation, though it is perfectly aware of the secret of it. It produces attraction for physical well-being and social status, but it is also appreciative of spiritual knowledge. It derives its support from the preservation principle in nature: social connection, human relationship, family cohesion, artistic talents, generation of finer feelings and enjoyment of sexual pleasure. Esoterically however, the Venusian impulse shows that mankind and all animal life have fallen from the Divine circle of wholeness into the realm of generation based on duality. Yet it serves, thereby, as an important step in concretization of the Divine Idea.

Blavatsky stated a great truth when she stated that every world has its parent star and sister planet (*SD Vol. III, p. 45*) . She indicated that this Earth of ours is the adopted child and younger brother of Venus, but its inhabitants are of their own kind. There is indeed deep importance in the statement that Venus represents the Sage's sacrifice for the sons of the Earth.

5
MARS
MANGALA

♂

Mars, the fiery planet of the solar system, called Mangala the auspicious, is graphically represented by an arrow jutting out of a circle ♂. Most important in this figure is the arrow, a symbol used sparingly in astrological literature. In the *Upanishads*, the arrow expresses the direction of contemplation towards the supreme goal. An arrow is used as a weapon of aggression either to protect oneself or to attack an enemy. It is used in sports, especially for hunting, to hit a target that is hard to access. Such actions imply effort to reach and subjugate a distant object. Mars as a planet imparts great ambition, the desire to scale the unexplored, the urge to roam far and experience new ways of life. The Martian temperament cannot be easily satisfied. It suffers from boundless thirst for the unknown. The Martian urge to achieve difficult objects and attain distant goals is symbolized by the arrow.

The inner significance of Mars becomes clearer when the figure is considered in its entirety. The circle, as we have seen, represents the Hiranyagarbha, the Golden Egg or unknown depth from which everything has come forth. It indicates the first delimitation of the Divine Energy under the impulse of cosmic evolution. It is the storehouse of all latent energies. For the human being, the circle symbolizes latent faculties which are to be articulated in time. The jutting arrow from the circle indicates the process of this articulation. Whatever is inside goes outward under the impulse of Mars. It is like the breaking of the shell so that the baby chicken can come out. Only after these latent faculties are developed can the individual attain his full stature.

This process of breaking the shell is difficult and often very painful. Disturbing our sense of security, the commencement of the new life creates much unhappiness. In getting dislodged from the mother's womb, the fetus does not feel very happy and the first impulse of the new born baby is to cry. In fact, the arrow on the circle is an expression of the child's exit from the mother's womb, the circle standing for the womb and the arrow indicating the passage from it. The violent effect of Mars, the astrological prediction of accidents, wars, diseases and impulsive actions of all types, is based on this pain of the new born breaking the egg. In this process the fetus must exert tremendous pressure against the surrounding hard crust. On the successful breaking of this veil over its inner potential depends the future life and its evolutionary course. From this one can understand why adjectives such as auspicious are attributed to this fiery and bloody planet. Whatever happens to the individual under the impact of Mars is for his good, his lasting progress and growth.

The circle shows the material limit of creation and the arrow indicates the spiritual potential that material involvements cannot satisfy. Mars always strives after an ideal, a goal which is unattainable, a principle beyond his capacity to accomplish. It directs us to higher levels of existence, heightens the urge to abandon the materialistic way of life and renounce mundane existence to achieve the everlasting spirit. This is the stage of Arjuna on the battlefield in the *Bhagavad Gita* seeking renunciation though he finds himself engrossed in arduous duties.

The arrow projected from the storehouse of Divine Energy signified by the circle represents human effort toward a predetermined, upward looking spiritual goal. The upward direction of the arrow is an expression of the externalizing impulse of the planet. The urge to break open the shell and direct this energy higher (toward nonpersonal goals); that is, the urge to unfold and the direction towards which the unfoldment is guided together characterize the basic nature of Mars. This planet is Divine Energy within limitations, available for a Divine objective relative to the person concerned. Whatever the action induced by Mars, its impact is beneficial and enduring. For this reason, the Hindus called it Mangala, the favorable and propitious.

The two main components of the figure, the circle and the arrow, in their entirety refer to the microcosm, the human being with all his limitations but possessing the potential of the Absolute. The circle refers to bounded potential, which is the portion of the Absolute latent in the consciousness of the incarnating soul. It is this potential which makes man the unknown, whose growth and expansion know no bounds. The energy of the Absolute All is hidden in every individual. As between a spark and the flame, or a drop of water and the sea, there is no essential difference, so no real difference exists between the human individual and his Divine Creator. The circle representing bounded potential refers to the latent faculties of the individual. There is no limit to the growth and expansion of human potential. The arrow superimposed upon the circle suggests the movement of actualizing this latency. The task of Mars is always concerned with making the world better, guiding it toward a more harmonious existence though the efforts involved require enormous sacrifice and courage.

The planet Mars symbolizes arrogance. This impulse is found at the very origin of the planetary deity. In Hindu mythology, Mars is identified with Kartikkeya, the god of war. He is the son of the Supreme Lord Shiva without the intervention of any woman. He is born of Shiva and the Earth. As a son of the Earth, he is called Bhauma, Bhumiputra, and Mahisuta. He is also called Shiva-gharma-ja, born of the sweat of Shiva; Gaganolmuki, the torch of the sky; Lohita, the red; Navarchi, the nine-rayed; Chara, the spy or the animate; and Rinantaka, the ender of debts, the patron of debtors.

Blavatsky states that Adam-Jehovah, Brahma and Mars are, in one sense, identical (*SD Vol. III, p. 55*). They are all symbols for the primitive or initial generative power that works for the purpose of human procreation. Adam is red in color as are Brahma-Viraj and Mars — god and planet. Water is the 'blood' of the earth, therefore these figures are connected with earth and water. She quotes Moses as saying that it takes earth and water to create a human soul. Mars as Kartikeya, the god of war, is born of the sweat of Shiva (the water of the god) and the Earth.

Kartikeya, the presiding deity for Mars, is called Lohita, the red, which also means blood. Blood is the very essence of physical life on earth. The similarity between Kartikeya and Mars points out the essential feature of the planet represented by its geometrical figure: it indicates the urge to penetrate to and unite with the invisible universal existence though its starting point is gross physical earth. Being self-confident of his inner potential Kartikeya abandons even his parents, Shiva and Parvati, and reveals thereby the characteristic arrogance of Mars on the lower planes and imperious will on the higher.

In the *Shiva Purana* the birth of Kartikeya is associated with the destruction of Taraka, a demon who acquired the benediction of Brahma that he could not be killed by anyone except a seven day old child of Shiva (see p. 178). Taraka was thus almost invincible. He oppressed the gods and took control of the universe. When the gods approached Brahma for subjugating Taraka, he suggested that no one could, not even Shiva, because Shiva was a celibate yogi and his having a child was an impossibility. Meanwhile Parvati, the eternal consort of Shiva, had taken another birth and was united with Shiva again. The gods wanted to take this opportunity to destroy Taraka.

Indra called Kamadeva, the god of love, for his support. Kamadeva agreed and when he shot his arrow at Shiva, Shiva immediately saw it, became angry and opened his third eye from which fire came forth. Before the gods could intercede, Kamadeva was burnt to ashes. Having learned the altruism of the purpose, Shiva agreed to restore Kamadeva to life in due course. The fiery blaze that burnt Kamadeva to ashes, however, proceeded further and the universe itself was in danger of complete annihilation. With the consent of Shiva, Brahma stabilized the blaze, transformed it into the form of a white horse and carried it to the sea. He requested the sea to keep the horse until the next Pralaya or Deluge when he would come back and resume charge of it. But, he warned the sea to keep the horse on its surface or he would completely dry it up.

Having known that the effort of the gods to subjugate him did not succeed, Taraka's menacing atrocities increased. Considering the time ripe to destroy the mighty demon, the fiery blaze put in custody of the sea was remembered. The holy river Ganga brought out the child whom the six sisters of Krittikas (the Pleiades) had nurtured. For this reason the six-headed child was named Kartikeya meaning the child of the Krittikas. The war resumed between Taraka and the gods. The Asuras, under the command of Taraka, in their invincible pride challenged and confronted the gods. Indra placed Kartikeya on an elephant, but he preferred his aerial car. During the duel between Taraka and Vishnu, even Vishnu's thunderbolt was blunted and Taraka was not killed. The Divine Voice then announced that Kartikeya was the only force that could subjugate the demon and he should take command. Kartikeya descended from his airship and confronted Taraka. When Taraka saw Kartikeya, he asked whether this small child was the final destroyer of the Daityas. Getting an affirmative answer, he decided to fight him single handed. Deciding to kill Taraka, Kartikeya took his mace, invoked the blessings of Shiva, attacked Taraka and immediately smashed him to pieces. Once Taraka had fallen to the ground, Kartikeya did not attack him again. Later on the gods killed many Daityas and a large number surrendered. After the fight, Kartikeya retired to Shiva and Parvati.

This story shows the origin of Mars or Kartikeya from the upward moving Serpent Fire of Shiva. The power ensouling Mars is the primeval force which creates all forms of existence. It always moves upwards with thoughts of righteousness and serves the benefic creative power. In discharging its duties, it is important for it to recall its objective, the will to achieve, to dedicate itself to the Supreme, and then inflict its mighty destructive energy, its mace that none can resist. Taraka was the son of Vajranga, meaning one whose body is made of the thunderbolt. It also means a serpent. His mother was known as Varangi, which means one with excellent limbs or very pleasing form. Taraka possessed courage, strength, wisdom and venom without any deformity. He had all the qualities anyone could ask for. The boon that he could be only killed by a child of seven days referred to one who was of the earth, who was created, of time. Taraka the material egoist could not be killed by eternal beings, the gods. Kartikeya, being born of the power deposited in the sea for the duration of manifestation, is coterminous with manifestation. Mars does not represent ultimate power, but is an aspect of manifestation suffused in all forms of creation as the ultimate life-giving energy. The horse is the creative energy carrying the potency of Shiva. The solar energy is also carried by horses, as is the energy of the Moon. The horse is the embodiment of Divine Energy in motion. Mars is the energy which carries Shiva's power for the destruction of the arrogant, self seekers who work against the evolutionary force in manifestation.

Kartikeya was born of water and fire, the gods Mitra and Varuna. The solar energy which is the positive force ensouling every form of existence is the fire of Shiva's third eye. Mars has strong affinity with the Sun. The primary difference between the two is that the Sun is the invincible energy, the indomitable force that penetrates all darkness. Mars, on the other hand, represents the same energy but is that part of it which is aroused when some opposition is confronted. When destructive forces are met, the destructive quality of Mars becomes predominant. Mars can arouse fire even in water but also subsists on water. Water, in fact, is the element which provides cohesion in matter. Vishnu, the preserver, is closely associated with water. During the Manvantara, when the manifestation is dissolved, Vishnu as Narayana lays on his serpent-coiled bed floating on water. Fire gives life, while water preserves form. In the human body, blood is the water of life but it is energized by the life-force. So blood in all living forms is the result of the cosmic creative principle represented by fire, and the eternal preservative principle represented by water. Kartikeya is produced by water and fire. As the deity presiding over the planet Mars, Kartikeya controls the blood running in the veins of every living creature.

The six heads of Kartikeya present considerable difficulties in interpretation. Blavatsky has, however, given a clue *(SD Vol I, p. 177)*. She states the number six is regarded in the ancient mysteries is an emblem of the physical nature. Elaborating this idea, she refers to the double equilateral triangle, and points out that the triangle with its apex pointed downwards is a sign of Vishnu in his deeper implications as the god of water, Narayana, who moves on the cosmic waters. The upper triangle is the representation of Shiva, the principle of fire, symbolized by the triple flame in his hand. The two triangles together show that the number six symbolizes both the creative and preservative principles. Mars has a tremendous influence on living beings. It provides the necessary life-force to forge ahead in the world. Six also represents the universality of the life-force. Four heads symbolize the four directions while six heads add above and below as additional directions to these. During the fight with Taraka, Kartikeya descended from his seat in the sky. Whenever Mars has heavenly functions to perform, it can provide the necessary impetus for them, but when it is needed for gross physical tasks where physical valour and strength are needed it can operate on this level as well. But Mars does not always exhibit its courage and strength. When Mars encounters a task and finds he must take it on, then Mars recalls his hidden power and exercises it by his will and uses it invincibly.

The role of Kartikeya in the destruction of Taraka, his basic mission for which he is called the God of War, reveals only one aspect of his personality. Another story is connected with his marriage. Shiva and Parvati had a second son Ganesh, the elephant headed God, who has tremendous intellect and great power to remove obstructions. Kartikeya was the elder brother and Ganesh the younger. Both were friendly to each other and their parents were happy with them. When they grew to the marriageable age, the parents wanted to find suitable brides for them. When the news was broken to them, both wanted to get married first. The parents, however, stipulated that he who could circumambulate the universe first would get married first. Immediately, Kartikeya went on his way while Ganesh, being a fat and chubby child, thought of his inability and tried to think of some way to outsmart Kartikeya.

Ganesh took his bath and asked his parents to take their seats on the throne. He worshipped them, went round them seven times and demanded that he should now be married. He argued that the scriptures had assigned a higher status to his parents than to the entire universe so he had accomplished more than the required journey. Convinced by his argument, they married Ganesh to Buddhi (intellect) and Siddhi (perfection), two eligible girls. Ganesh began to live happily with his family. When Kartikeya returned from his circumambulation he was told of what happened. He became very depressed, felt tricked and went to meditate in the mountains. Shiva and Parvati visited him in the mountains at regular intervals.

This refers to the great attraction of Mars for conjugal happiness generally denied him. He has an uncommon approach to sex and sociability. As the offspring of the upward directed seed of Shiva, expressed as fire which destroyed the god of love and separated him from his wife for several eons, he does not give sexual happiness. Martian people possess a strong sexual urge, but outer conditions are usually not suitable for such union. They try to abide by ethical and moral codes in their behavior but such approaches lead them to greater spirituality rather than to physical and worldly happiness.

Another implication of this story is that the Martian impact is extremely individualistic. Marriage being a symbolic expression of the
blending between two forces or levels, Kartikeya or Mars does not get the
opportunity. In his spiritual pilgrimage, he has to proceed alone to his
higher consciousness (mountains represent higher consciousness) and
become so deeply immersed in penance that even the higher powers, both
positive (Shiva) and negative (Parvati), protect him and provide him the
necessary guidance and sustenance. Mars is self-respecting, self-reliant,
and remorselessly upsetting in his decisions. One-pointedness and confidence in his own power are his two most important virtues, but this is
because Mars is empowered by the cosmic energy which enables the
manifestation to bring forth his inherent destiny.

In essence, Mars is a deeply spiritual planet engaged in articulating
the inner potential on the outer surface of life. The inner potential is
represented by the circle and its externalization by the arrow, the direction
of the arrow showing the destiny according to the Divine Plan of evolution. As the regent of the planet Mars comes from the vital energy of Shiva,
the electrifying fire inherent in all living forms, Mars destroys all restricting influences to Divine fulfillment. It is invincible in its effect. It destroys
the material forces in order to enable the higher forces to sprout and grow.
It is connected with blood circulation in human beings and the electrifying
energy in all forms of existence which makes them vital and alive. It is
attracted towards the opposite sex, but generally does not find fulfillment
in such endeavours. The spiritual approach of Mars makes its influence
unrealistic and unsuccessful as far as common results are concerned. Mars
does not strive to blend its consciousness with others: it wants to wrest
heaven all by itself. Its self-confidence is so great that it does not feel
docile even to the supreme power. It prefers to be at a distance when it
does not agree with those in authority. In matters of the spiritual life, Mars
accentuates the importance of intellectual independence. It has tremendous empathy inherently, however, with the masses and is often ready to
sacrifice itself for others. While working for others, Mars achieves great
success while for himself he brings sorrow and frustration.

Blavatsky summarized the nature of Mars when she stated that "Mars
is the Lord of birth and death, of generation and destruction, of ploughing,
building, sculpture, stone-cutting, of architecture ... in essence, of all
comprised under the English word *Art*." He is the primal principle,
disintegrating into two opposites to produce all things. Mars is the
personification of the power of the Logos.

6
JUPITER
BRIHASPATI
♃

Jupiter is the best benefic of the solar system, the bringer of the cosmic good always engaged in arresting the materialization process and stabilizing the progress attained. In the *Rig Veda* he is described as the bull of men whom none can deceive. He is known as Brihaspati, the deity who personifies the worship of the Gods. Hence, Jupiter represents the materialization of the Divine Grace, by means of ritual and ceremonies, or exoteric worship.

The influence of Jupiter is shown by its geometrical figure; the cross with the arc curving to the right side tucked to its left arm ♃. It reveals the central character of the planet which is to arrest further materialization and promote the spiritualizing energy. There is great resemblance between the figures for Saturn and Jupiter. Both are connected with the form aspect of life. The cross is the central figure around which both the figures are made. Saturn is a cross in which the vertical line is linked with an arc at its bottom, while Jupiter is a cross where the horizontal line is linked with an arc at its beginning.

Birth, death and liberation are the three important stages in cosmic evolution. Death releases the bondage of material existence, but the limitations imposed by consciousness itself continue until one is completely free and attains Nirvana. The cross at the end of the vertical line, as in the case of Saturn, releases the material bondage and begins the process of mental transformation which makes the impact painful for the physical being. The Jupiterian influence is very different. The horizontal line is connected with the form aspect of manifestation and represents Nature. The arc attached to it expresses the spiritualization of matter. The impact of Jupiter is therefore to impart religious satisfaction, contentment, and a sense of fulfillment as physical existence is given a kind of missionary fervor. Under the Jupiterian impact, one desires to live, to do social work, speak and undertake activities in the name of the Divine or truth. Such an individual strives to spiritualize his life and the material components of his existence are gradually transformed. As matter is the base on which such activities are developed, such individuals derive visible satisfaction. They grow prosperous, fructify and multiply. Doing these material activities, they derive the psychological satisfaction of fulfilling a divine mission. Their understanding of the spiritual life may be partial and form-based, while Saturn completely eschews materiality. The realization of death when matter vanishes remains for them a very painful experience.

An important attribute of the Jupiterian influence is its concern for the welfare of humanity. This includes spiritual as well as physical welfare. The two components of the figure, the cross and the arc are given the same importance, while under the Saturnine impulse spirituality is caused by the denial of materiality. The Jupiterian influence gives a positive approach to life and such persons believe that God is in every form of creation. The highest form of spirituality according to this approach is to perceive God in every individual and at every place. The fulfillment of life according to the Jupiterian influence is to work for society and for humanity in general. One can imagine the Jupiterian symbol as spirit embracing matter: it is a kind of very vibrant energy. It stands for the early phase of the Swastika, which is the symbol of active Divine Energy promoting the evolution of the universe.

The left arm of the cross has an intimate relation with the Great Deep. The arc arises from the beginning of arm. The nature of the curvature of the arc expresses the movement of the Divine Impulse from the deepest layer of materiality towards its apex where it gets released into the spirit. Under the Jupiterian impulse one does not completely deny material involvement. The desire to experience the pleasures and conveniences of material affluence is felt. What is sought is the avoidance of undesirable consequences of the material impact. One therefore finds that individuals of a Jupiterian type try to secure material affluence, worldy status, social and political power but are also conscious that these goals are not the ultimate or highest. They wish to be on the side of the Divine and truth. They are willing to propitiate the gods in order to gain all that is good in life. Exoteric religious practices become important for them. Jupiter in its basic energy refers to the need to transform materiality into the spiritual quest by using one's material possessions for humanitarian objectives. Such persons therefore try to gain status both in the realm of matter and spirit.

In the *Rig Veda*, Brihaspati is invoked as a mighty power capable of providing immense protection and great prosperity. Brihaspati bestows so much benediction on his friends that they can overcome any opposition and greatly increase their wealth; their children and children's children will grow in strength. Thus conquest over enemies, expansion of material resources, growth of family members and increase in social status are all received under the benefic influence of Jupiter. The prosperity received through Brihaspati results from good conduct; he enables the good deeds of the past to fructify and favorable opportunities to occur so that the inner qualities of the individual may blossom. Mars destroys impediments, and provides the impetus to fight and to externalize latent qualities. Jupiter, on the other hand, is averse to fighting and bloodshed. He arranges favorable conditions for growth and expansion so that conflict does not arise between opposing forces. Jupiter shows the path for right living and the code of conduct harmonious with the law of nature. He is the teacher of the gods representing harmony and bliss.

From the most ancient scripture, the *Rig Veda*, to the *Upanishads* and *Puranas*, Jupiter has been given various names which emphasize his main attributes. Brahamanspati and Brihaspati have been used alternatively as equivalent to each other. Both derive from the same root as the word Brahma, the god of creation. This root, 'bri', means to grow and to expand. It refers to the wisdom which enables the growth and expansion of the universe. Jupiter is the regent of this wisdom.

Jupiter provides opportunities for the limitless expansion of inner qualities. Its emphasis is on the opportunity for growth: it is like the spring wind which enables seeds to sprout and flowers to blossom. What qualities will attain fruition are not its primary consideration. Jupiter does not restrict; it protects and enables expansion. Hindu mythology often states that the Creator Brahma gave such boons to the demons that made them invincible. Possessing the same primeval nature as Brahma, Jupiter also has the quality of arousing whatever is latent in the individual. But unlike Brahma's boons, even when adverse qualities are accentuated, Jupiter conspires to create a situation where the individual comes to the right path, after receiving the natural justice for the misdeeds committed in his arrogance of power.

Legends relate Brihaspati to Brahma, Angiras, Bharadwaja and other sages. In the *Brihadaranayaka Upanishad*, Brihaspati is called the Father of Gods. He is considered to be the son of the sage Angiras and therefore he bears the patronymic Angirasa. Elsewhere Brihaspati is acclaimed as the father of Bharadwaja, one of the seven primeval seers. The father-son relationship in esoteric literature refers to the transmission of consciousness from one to another. The entry of the life-spark of father into the son is allegorized in several ways. In all such relationships, the basic point to recognize is the identity of spiritual knowledge and wisdom between the two. The wisdom of Brahma that he imparted to Atharvan and which finally reached Angiras, as contained in the *Mundaka Upanishad,* is the knowledge by which everything is known. This knowledge begins by distinguishing the two kinds of knowledge, one which relates to the world of appearances and the other to knowledge of the Self. The lineage represented by Jupiter is concerned with the dissemination of the higher wisdom. The Jupiterian impact aims at providing the direct experience of material involvement. The wisdom inculcated by Jupiter reveals that the scope of the knowledge gained through the outgoing mind, by its inherently limited nature, must be illusory. Realizing the illusory nature of knowledge of name and form, one is led to the higher knowledge, the knowledge of consciousness itself.

The special responsibility of Jupiter is to teach and gently lead his students on the path of truth. This is apparent from the names given to him. He is known as Animishacharya, unblinking preceptor; Chakshusa, light of the eye, teacher of the sacred wisdom; Ijya, teacher of the gods; and Indrejya, one who has subjugated his sense organs. Jupiter is also referred as Guru, which means a preceptor and teacher as well as one who initiates the student into the secret wisdom of the Vedas. One who has established perfect control over his own impulses and does not permit his desires to cloud his perception is a real teacher. The "light of the eye" is a suggestive epithet for Jupiter. The function of the eye is to perceive. It links the object with its inner reality and communicates it to our inner perception. Some great gurus teach their disciples through their gaze alone. Jupiter is ever vigilant, has perfect understanding of the sacred wisdom and is capable of leading the student to the realities of life. Being a teacher, Brihaspati leads one from the known to the unknown, from the periphery to the center, from the exoteric to the esoteric. With great patience and understanding this god of wisdom guards over the welfare of all beings. He is concerned with the harmony, sustenance, growth and expression of the inherent potentials of every form of creation.

Brihaspati is said to be born of the sage Angiras, and to be yellow in color. He sits on a water-lily and has four arms. One arm holds a garland of Rudraksha beads, another carries a begging bowl, the third holds a mace, and the fourth bestows blessings. As the regent of the planet Jupiter, he rides a chariot called Nitighosha drawn by eight pale horses. Yellow is a color of intellect, auspicious for rituals and devotional activities. Red symbolizes valor and courage, depending on its hue. Deep or blood red represents fight, conflict and war, whereas crimson or rosy indicates affection, love and union. Saffron suggests renunciation and saintliness. Jupiter's yellow complexion suggests his connection with auspicious performances, rituals and householders' worship. The impact of Jupiterian wisom does not lead to renunciation and the path of withdrawal; it teaches the individual right performance of duties, and involves him in actions to fulfill the will of higher powers. The water lily is a symbol of the same order. It represents regeneration and unfoldment towards spirituality through beauty and harmony.

Rudraksha means the eye of Shiva. It is the berry of a tree used for medicinal and religious purposes. These berries are made into beads and used for counting mantras. The sages put a garland of Rudraksha beads around their necks to ward off unfavorable influences. Rudraksha has great protective powers and saves the individual from any onslaught of dark forces. Such a garland in the hand of Brishaspati indicates that his consciousness steadfastedly united with the cosmic protective force represented by Shiva. Under the benediction of Brihaspati, no adverse force can harm an individual. That is also the reason why the *Rig Veda* invokes him as "Lighting up the Flame, he shall conquer his enemies: strong shall he be who offers prayer and brings gifts to him."

The begging bowl represents Jupiter as not accumulating material possessions for himself. He is completely unified with the ascending evolutionary force and has surrendered himself to the will of God. Such a renunciation comes only when there is no sense of belonging, no anxiety about the future. Jupiter is not concerned with riches but with equanimity of mind, stability, coolness and balance. His every action demonstrates his interest in the welfare of others. The bestowal of blessings indicates his great concern for the welfare of humanity, for the progress and evolution of the universe. In spite of such renunciation, Jupiter has a special status among the celestial beings. He wields tremendous force. He holds the manifestation together by his great wisdom. The possession of this power is represented by the mace he holds in one of his hands. His goodness is not to be mistaken as weakness. The authority that he holds is sacred due to his possession of wisdom and his unity with the Divine Will. It has been bestowed on him in recognition of his spiritual merit.

The chariot is the vehicle which carries Jupiter on his Divine mission. It is a symbol of authority, signifying his status in the planetary hierarchy and special importance in the kingdom of the gods. It is complementary to the mace that he holds. The chariot also emphasizes his dynamism. Nitighosha, the name of his chariot, reveals the special quality of the vehicle. 'Niti' means propriety as well as the science of morality, ethics and moral philosophy. 'Ghosha' means thunder as well as proclamation. The chariot of Jupiter announces the arrival of righteousness personified. It thunderously announces the law and code of truth and right action. The eight pale horses yoked to the chariot represent the eight perfections in latency.

These are:

1. **ANIMA** — The power of becoming as small as one wishes.
2. **LAGHIMA** — The power of becoming as light as one wishes.
3. **PRAPTI** — The power of obtaining anything desired.
4. **PRAKAMYA** — The power of the irresistible will.
5. **MAHIMA** — The power of becoming as large as one wishes.
6. **ISHITWA** — The attribute of Supreme Greatness.
7. **VASHITWA** — The capacity to suppress one's desires and passions.
8. **KAMAVASAYITA** — The ability to fullfill all one's desires.

These are the powers at the command of Jupiter which carry him on his desired mission, but they are not very apparent. They are pale horses: they lie latent within him and can only be activated in case of real need.

In essence, Brihaspati or Jupiter is a teacher with full possession of the sacred wisdom. He works from the outer to the inner and leads students from the known, the exoteric, to the unknown, the esoteric. He protects the virtuous and establishes harmony. He transmutes materiality into spirituality. Jupiter is more concerned with ritual, perpetuation, growth, development, and imparting knowledge and wisdom rather than releasing the individual from bondage to ignorance and bestowing Nirvana or Liberation. Jupiter is Jiva, the principle of life or vital breath. He is concerned with the individual soul enshrined in the body and imparts to it life, motion and sensation, enabling it to blossom toward its fullness.

7
SATURN
SHANI

ℏ

Saturn is the most dreaded of planets, the great malefic. Its geometrical figure, half a circle hanging from a cross, has something intimidating about it ℏ. The symbol for the earth resembles that of Saturn but has a circle instead of an arc. This difference is vital. As far as the earth is concerned, the ever active whirlwind of the cross is linked with the wholeness of the Divine impulse represented by the full circle. The earth emblem indicates the wholeness of manifestation under the constant sway of polarized forces. It shows a Divine purpose in earthly manifestation. In the case of Saturn, the cross with an arc below it indicates a Divine pressure on the evolving individual to move from the gross material environment to his spiritual goal. The arc curving to the right points to the path of return in the soul's pilgrimage. The linkage of the cross with the arc symbolizes the beginning of the spiritualization process. This is the basic feature of the Saturnian impulse.

Saturn produces psychological limitations. The urge to experience greater freedom on various planes of existence is intensified under Saturn. However, if the physical sheaths are not yet ripe enough to satisfy the urge, the individual discovers his limitations. This produces conflict and the individual feels tortured. There is turmoil in the psyche and the mind is agitated. During this churning process, the cross has its full sway. When this experience is understood by the soul, there comes quietude which gives direction to the spiritual journey of the individual. This state is represented by the arc hanging below the cross. Redemption from Saturnine affliction lies in understanding the limitations imposed upon the soul during its incarnation and its need to function within the given parameter.

The process of spiritual growth certainly involves suffering and all spiritual aspirants have to confront it as their inevitable ordeal. In the case of Saturn, however, there is a significant difference from other forms of strain. The limitations imposed by Saturn arise from the crystallization of the material sheaths. There is very little flexibility in the objective realm where the individual has to reap the consequences of the Saturnine influence. It does not permit any kind of adjustment. The soul's urge to spiritualize and to regain its natural freedom invokes the redemption of past karmas.

The urge towards freedom is met by opposition from material conditions in the form of personal difficulties such as physical illness, environmental disturbances, psychological suffering, financial shortages leading to feelings of helplessness, and even the complete destruction of one's dreams. The sense of restriction experienced during the influence of Saturn arises from these factors. The emerging spirit seeking liberation from the trammels of material existence gets stifled by the physical and psychological sheaths. There is much emotional pain and intellectual frustration. Saturn produces a radical reorganization in the various sheaths of the individual. The necessity for such change is felt as pain and suffering. The life seems torn by conflicts and a feeling of crucifixion arises. Under the influence of Saturn we are forced to carry our cross in life.

The semi-circular arc at the bottom of the cross links the lowest point of materiality, which also stands for death, with the highest point of creation, liberation or immortality. It is taken from that portion of the circle which represents the journey of the soul from the deepest layer of materiality back to the highest point of liberation (see p. 27). The urge to transcend materiality comes voluntarily. It arises when a dam is put up against the growth towards materiality. The impediments to material enjoyment are experienced as frustration. Saturn destroys the person's illusions. It burns up that which is transitory. When our deepest fantasies are destroyed, there is intense pain. After psychological reorganization, there comes tranquillity and an experience of one's inner strength. Saturn destroys the illusory and the transitory to let the individual gaze into eternity and to impart on him enduring strength.

Saturn acts deeply and extensively. It affects the highest and the lowest aspects in our nature. Its impact can be endured only when the individual has the necessary strength and determination to bear it. Saturn is not a teacher who imparts his training gradually after preparing the student for the lesson. It wants results. But to obtain the required results, Saturn can wait indefinitely. Yet whenever there is any possibility of the individual growing in the process, Saturn takes a chance. It is very determined in achieving its ends. Both the components of its symbol, the cross and the arc, represent the dynamic interaction of different forces in nature. When the individual fails to understand the lesson, which often happens, it appears as a great calamity. The individual may become reactionary. Psychologically he may become very negative. The experience learned during this period of frustration in the long run serves to develop strength. In the short run, the individual may become anti-social, immoral, and unspiritual. All of these are important aspects of Saturn.

The arc placed below the material cross shows that the spiritual unfoldment under Saturn is shadowed by the weight of material experience. The essential feature of this Saturnine impact is that the life-style of the person affected must change externally either for the better or the worse. Internally also, there must be a change in attitude. Saturn imparts a deeper understanding of the materialistic nature of existence. This understanding is closely connected with the trials and tribulations we meet in life. The wisdom produced by Saturn arises from confronting the difficulties in everyday life. This wisdom is necessary to strengthen the soul so it can complete its upward journey.

Saturn is known as "Shanishcharacharya," which means a teacher who moves slowly. Saturn has the slowest movement among the visible planets, but this is not the only reason for the appellation. Slowly occurring events are generally imperceptible. From the moment of our birth we are imperceptibly drawn towards our end, death. The movement toward death, the natural process of physical decay, is so slow that it passes almost unnoticed. Even the growth of the personality experienced as the blossoming into youth and adulthood is, in fact, a subtle movement towards annihilation. The trouble and the wisdom produced by Saturn are so hidden from direct perception that they are attributed to other causes. Saturn acts slowly because it operates on the soul nature of the person, on which alone such actions can make an imprint. Saturn's interest in the outer or physical nature of the human being is superficial. Saturn is a deep acting planet concerned with the permanent nature of the soul and unveiling its original capabilities.

In order to eliminate the illusory veil on life, Saturn does not resort to short-cut methods. Saturn is linked to the Sun and is considered as his son. He possesses the deep acting method of solar operation. There is rhythmic movement to the Sun; its periodicity is marked. The maturity and understanding occurring as a result of the solar impact take place as a matter of the natural sequence of events. The maturity resulting from the solar impact is not measured in the number of years one has lived but in terms of the maturity and depth of insight one has gained. Saturn also imparts wisdom of the same order. The wisdom gained under the Saturnian impulse depends upon the power of our struggle in life. It depends upon deep contemplation of the various forces affecting life. Meditation, penance, contemplation, and release from desire and material attachments require a long duration to mature and fructify. Such results can be obtained only when the teacher has patience with his disciples and works incessantly with their psycho-mental shortcomings. For obtaining enduring results, it is necessary that there is no hurry or immediacy of purpose. Keeping these goals in view, we can appreciate why Saturn grinds slowly, surely, producing long-term enduring results. The arc under the cross of the Saturn symbol indicates the result obtained under the Saturnian impulse, while the appellation Sanishcharacharya refers to the mode of obtaining the result.

In Hindu mythology, Saturn is the son of the Sun. The daughter of the celestial architect is married to the Sun but finds his effulgence too oppressive for her. She returns to her father for relief from her arduous duties to her overly bright husband. For the period of her absence, she keeps her shadow Chhaya, whose name literally means shadow, to take care of the Sun to prevent him from learning of her absence. Saturn is born of this union between the Sun and Chhaya. This allegory suggests that Saturn is the projection of solar radiance through the veil of matter, which alone is capable of casting a shadow. The casting of a shadow denotes that the pure radiance of the Sun has been obstructed by matter. Saturn is also named Asit, Surya-putra and Manda. Asit means black and dark blue, and a black serpent. Surya-putra means the son of the Sun. Manda means slow or dull.

The various mythological children born to the Sun represent different combinations of solar light with feminine creative forces. The resulting children become special creative powers furthering the Divine mission that is the sole purpose of the solar light. Some of these children are: Yama, god of death; Manu, father of the human race; Sugriva, the monkey king friendly with the demons but who sided with the gods to help conquer them; Jatayu, the vulture who gave the great hero Rama knowledge about how his wife Sita was abducted; the Ashwins, great healers with tremendous rejuvenating powers; Karna, a hero of the *Mahabharata* born of Kunti; and Savarni, a daughter of the Sun. All these offspring of the Sun have the common feature of carrying further the Divine mission of the light, the victory of the spiritual force over materiality.

Saturn does the same thing but in a special way. Saturn spiritualizes but not by arousing an inner urge to discover the real Self. This comes as an after-effect. Saturn causes frustration with the material world. It creates sorrow first. It accentuates the nature of the 'shadow' and makes the veil covering the soul's real nature more prominent through its restricting influence. Saturn does not show us the ultimate goal at first but confronts us with the limitations of the veil. Then follows the urge to liberate oneself and attain one's real nature.

Another name for Saturn is Saptarchi, which means "he who has seven flames or rays." The Sun has seven rays, or seven channels of the life current. These are the seven flows of the celestial river Ganges, or the seven flames of the fire. They are the basic differentiation of the life-current which results in the seven human temperaments. This categorization depends upon the seven paths on which souls evolve. It not only influences temperament but affects our life conditions. The special path each soul must follow to unfold its basic nature depends upon the special ray contained within it. The basic characteristics of the seven channels has been classified under the seven Rays. These show the underlying impulses which guide all activities of the individual during both the unconscious and conscious stages of cosmic evolution. These are:

1. **WILL**   Working on the Self Principle in the individual.
2. **WISDOM**   Working on the intelligence.
3. **ACTIVITY OR THOUGHT**   Which arises from the activization of Mahat or cosmic intelligence.
4. **THE SEARCH FOR TRUTH**   Which results in scientific pursuits and at times makes a person agnostic.
5. **RELIGIOUS ATTRACTION**   Which draws individuals to rituals and ceremonies in order to spiritualize and purify themselves.
6. **ARTISTS**   Who endeavor to merge themselves in the universal life by cultivating the fine arts in their pure forms.
7. **MYSTICS AND VISIONARIES**   Who find the same spirit pervading everywhere, with differences being only a matter of expression.

While souls confront their trials and tribulations, they are conditioned by the special conditions of the past and their basic Ray. As we have seen, Saturn affects a person by working through the veil of illusion surrounding him. In fact, any influence flowing from Saturn has, at the very outset, to traverse the veil of the shadow. Before it can begin its operation, it must pass through the illusory world surrounding the manifestation. The illusory veils are also of seven kinds, so when the Saturnian rays percolate through these veils, they also get influenced. They appear as seven darker rays. Saturn as the son of the Sun has the same basic effect as the Sun in arousing the inner nature of the soul. The quality of the Ray emitted remains the same but from Saturn it is darkened. Its actual impact depends upon the underlying Ray of the individual. Unless this special feature of Saturn is recognized, the Saturnian action generally confuses the student.

The various names given to Saturn highlight special features of the planet. The description of Shani as given in Hindu spiritual texts describes the nature of the planetary deity ruling it. It is said that Saturn is black or dark blue in complexion, has four arms in which he holds an arrow, a javelin, a bow, and with the fourth hand bestowing blessings, he rides a vulture. It is noteworthy that Shiva, Vishnu, Rama and Krishna who are considered very benevolent deities also have the same dark blue complexion as Saturn, the god of death and destruction. The darkness that surrounds Saturn represents the denial of all attributes, an existence beyond the planes of material manifestation which cannot be expressed. Being of the nature of the Ultimate, Saturn can have no form. Absence of objectification or externalisation is regarded in popular conception as darkness. The mother's womb is dark. The unknown, the timeless, the future, and eternity are all considered to be dark. The beginning of cosmic ideation is described in terms of darkness: "Darkness alone filled the boundless all, for Father, Mother and Son were once more one, and the Son had not yet awakened for the new wheel, and his pilgrimage thereon." This darkness is, in fact, dark blue for it contains all colors. It is the Ultimate from which there is no reaction.

Every form of manifestation on its final merging with the Ultimate mingles in this dark blue. All colors represent different kinds of reactions that arise in the realm of manifestation. Beyond the realm of manifestation there is neither color nor reaction. The nature of this reactionless, colorless, state of existence is Bliss. Perfect poise and rest without any anxiety and agitation can be experienced in that blissful depth of the Ultimate. Pure harmony prevails there. Social status, distinction, class consciousness and all discriminatory ideas are completely absent. Attainment of this everlasting harmony is however a very disturbing process. It takes away all that is known, all that has been accumulated, and all that can be perceived. The different kinds of attributes with which one is associated during the eons of incarnations are completely dissolved in this realm of darkness without any hope of their retrieval. The state of nothingness is psychologically very disturbing. It resembles what Jesus felt on the cross. It is like death. The painful experience of renouncing everything that we associate with living makes us compare Saturn with death.

The dark blue complexion represents the death-like situation which is the great illusion that surrounds everything. It is the mighty ignorance which arises from one's separation from the Real. Saturn is not darkness and does not really reside within darkness, it is beyond darkness, beyond illusion and ignorance. When the light of Saturn reaches the mortal individual, it comes through the veil of ignorance. This veil of shadow creates difficulties in comprehending the true nature of Saturn. This veil, from the standpoint of the experiencer, creates confusion, obscurity and the feeling of isolation.

The trials arising from the experience of great loneliness that Saturn brings are like surgical operations meant to end the ailment of attachment to the material world. In it there is inevitable pain. Whenever the individual is weaned from his long-lasting attachment, he feels pain. Often the heart bleeds. But this is an inevitable process, without which there can be no clarity of vision and true rending of the layers of illusion which blind the individual. Because the dark rays emitted from Saturn inevitably draw the individual to the path of realization of truth, pain is a necessary concomitant of its influence. Saturn is, therefore, a dreaded planet. This fear is accentuated because Saturn is the Ultimate, the formless, where there is nothing to hold on to and feel secure. This Ultimate is like a perpetual motion which never ceases, never slackens nor increases its speed — not even during the interludes between creation. It is the Ultimate beyond which there is nothing. In its cosmic sweep, this perpetual motion is Duration, it is the Great Womb but is formless. In this formless Duration where even time is not, what color and attribute could be found? The dark blue complexion of Saturn represents its true nature as the Ultimate in its most objective aspect: there is nothing beyond *it*.

The operation of this Ultimate takes place by the invincible instruments of the arrow, javelin and bow held in the hands of Shani. These are special instruments of attack. The arrow establishes direct contact between the archer and his object, whether the object is a victim to be killed, or a teacher at whose feet out of respect the arrow is to be shot. In the case of Saturn, the arrow is shot at the victim to relieve him of karmic debts that fetter him on the path of enlightenment. It is done in order to enable him to effectively approach the Ultimate. The arrow is also the aspiration by which one can rise to one's higher Self. The arrow shot by Saturn creates psychological turmoil and churns the psyche so that hidden problems and potentials are externalized, and the reality is known. Having perceived the hidden nature of oneself, one often gets bewildered, but in the long run, the perception of one's inner weakness arouses a deeper sense of spirituality. This spiritual perception of oneself provides the motivating force toward the Ultimate Reality. Saturn's arrow rends the veil of ignorance, uncovers the hidden Self, externalizes the inherent evil as well as beneficial potential, and gives an insight into the true nature of the Self.

The javelin is a kind of dart which pierces its victim and kills him. The difference between an arrow and a javelin lies in the contact point. An arrow is shot from a distance. The archer may even be invisible. The arrow shot by Saturn has these characteristics. Often the action precipitated by Saturn is not discernible: it is not immediately known how or from whom the assault has come. But the individual suffers the pain and is psychologically disturbed, even though he may not be aware of the direction from which the shot was fired. To pinpoint the source of trouble created by Saturn is difficult. It is especially so when deep pain is inflicted. In the case of the javelin, the assailant is in close contact with the victim. There is a direct relationship between the two. Saturn is not afraid of its victim. It does not always remain hidden or elusive like a thief. Sometimes the impact of Saturn is clearly identifiable. Disease, injury, untimely loss of support and status in the society are the short and quick actions represented by the javelin in his hand.

The bow represents the psychological foundation made by Saturn for the spiritual unfoldment of the individual. The bow is the base from which the missile is shot. Much inner and outer reorientation is imperative for the growth and blossoming of spiritual consciousness. Only on a carefully prepared foundation can the Divine aspiration represented by the arrow succeed. Saturn is the most spiritualizing planet in the sense that it effectively prepares its students for inner awakening. Often this means denial of all material comfort, but sometimes by granting the conveniences of life and freeing the individual from mundane care and anxieties, Saturn enables the individual to explore the deeper levels of his nature.

Surgical skill, expertize in medicinal herbs for healing complicated ailments, as well as insight into Divine mysteries are produced by Saturn. Like a good surgeon, Saturn is more concerned with the long-term welfare of the individual rather than short-term palliation. It is concerned with curing rather than covering the ailment. How Saturn brings about this preparation for spiritual unfoldment is hard to see, but it provides it in the most effective manner so that the eradication of material attachment is lasting. Saturn is not concerned with enabling the individual to see the ultimate destiny awaiting him, rather it pushes him in that direction so that his onward journey is made possible and becomes unavoidable. Even if the individual is not aware of the necessary adjustments made in his psyche it does not matter for Saturn as long as it has prepared the strong foundation from which sliding back is difficult.

The bestowal of blessings emphasizes the benevolence of Saturn. Confidence in Saturn and surrender to him are the two most effective means of securing his benediction. Saturn is ready to bestow blessings even during periods of arduous preparations and unbearable pain. By reposing confidence in the benevolence of the deity and surrendering oneself to the will of the planet, much pain is relieved and the unfoldment process is quickened.

The vulture as the vehicle of Saturn has the obvious reference to death through the dead bodies on which it subsists. However the feathered tribe, of which the present day vultures are descendents, has a deeper significance. The vulture or bird of prey is present as a symbol in many ancient teachings like the Zoroastrian, the Gnostic, the Egyptian and the Vedic. In Hindu mythology, this feathered tribe of birds takes birth from the Sage Kashyapa, one of the seven progenitors of the universe. In some legends he antedates even Brahma, the cosmic creator. Among his forty renowned sons, Garuda is the most important. Garuda became the vehicle of Vishnu, the preserver of the universe. Garuda was an elder brother of Aruna, the charioteer of the Sun, and in some legends, Aruna is another name of the Sun.

The tribe of the vultures has a close connection with the Sun. The two sons of Garuda, Jatayu and Sampati are renowned for trying to fly up to the Sun. In the process, Jatayu got his wings burnt and fell down to earth where Rama and Lakshman met him on their search for Sita. They learned from Jatayu about his fight with Ravana to free Sita, and finally they did his last rites as he died. Speaking of himself to Rama, Jatayu says, "It is 60,000 years, O King, since I was born," after which, turning his back to the Sun, he dies. The various allegories about the vulture make him the emblem of the Great Cycle, the Maha Kalpa, coeternal with Vishnu, one with Time and the Sun. The vulture as the vehicle of Saturn alludes to the eternal that vultures symbolize.

These vultures belong to the race of the Indian Phoenix, the emblem of regeneration and periodicity. During the process of cosmic manifestation, there is a cyclic movement of expansion and contraction. This movement is said to be of various durations, each of which has special names. The manifesting souls continue their pilgrimage during these cycles. Saturn sends his seven dark rays to these souls to draw them toward their ultimate destiny and make the unfoldment of their potential quicker and easier. In this exercise, Saturn requires the assistance of time. Saturn can wait indefinitely if it is required for the end in view. Saturn is not impatient. To the outer vision, vultures are birds that eat dead bodies and reduce them to nothing. To the inner vision, they represent duration, Time, and the Great Cycle during which the material sheaths of the person are periodically born and destroyed until they are able to merge back into the perpetual motion.

Blavatsky mentions another significant point about these birds *(SD Vol. III, p. 256)*. She states that Garuda, the king of the feathered tribe subsequently descended from and is of one stock with the reptiles, the Nagas who subsequently became their mortal enemies. In the course of evolution, birds which evolved from reptiles eventually turned on those they issued from in order to devour them, perhaps prompted by natural law, in order to make room for other and more perfect species. The relationship between vultures and serpents is described in various myths.

Legends state that Vinata, wife of the sage Kashyapa, and from whom Garuda and Aruna were born, had a dispute with Kadru, another wife of Kashyapa and mother of Kapila from whom the Nagas, the serpents, were born. The dispute was about the color of Ucchaishravas, one of the horses of Indra. Kadru defeated Vinata and in accordance with the conditions of the wager made Vinata her slave. To purchase her freedom, Garuda brought down, not without a hard struggle with Indra, the heavenly nectar, Amrit, and Vinata was released. It must be remembered, however, that the nectar was taken away by Indra from the serpents in the first place, who became the enemies of Garuda. The legend further states that this mythical bird eats up the serpents who are mortally afraid of it.

Immortality of the physical sheath, through which the incarnating soul gains experiences and casts them aside when they are no longer necessary, would be harmful to the end sought after by Saturn. The soul encased in these sheaths is always immortal and therefore not in need of the nectar. The Nagas or serpents who wanted the nectar are denied it. Indra will not let them have it. The Nagas are highly evolved occult beings but they are not gods. Hence, their gaining the everlasting bliss and immortality which the celestial nectar produces would be injurious. As Kadru is the mother of the serpents who are also said to be fathered by Kashyapa, immortality to serpents would not have been helpful. The serpents are deceitful, and treacherous and attack at unsuspected moments. Perpetuation of such psychological traits is dangerous for the working of the natural law of evolution which Saturn directs to its goal. The hostility of Saturn's vehicle, the Vulture of Garuda, against serpents or Nagas alludes to the prevailing illusion and ignorance through which the evolving entities must successfully emerge. Saturn aims at dispelling darkness and inculcating wisdom in the most practical manner. This can happen when the evolving soul understands the nature of ignorance and the limitations imposed by the encasing sheaths. Saturn also aims at destroying and dissolving these sheaths, which causes the death of the human body. The allegory has other meanings. Nagas are wise men or seers. Garuda as the vulture represents the cycles of time and conscious unfoldment through which the soul is lead to enlightenment. Saturn reaches its goal by the evolutionary method. This explains the role of the vulture as his vehicle.

The Sanskrit word 'Gridha', which stands for vulture, also means greed and a covetous nature. When a person strives greedily after material objects and passionately longs for their possession, Saturn makes them frustrated and gradually turns them away from these desires. Saturn arouses discontent and thereby directs the individual to that which is enduring. The vulture refers to the psycho-physical process of destruction and disappointment in the material realm that finally leads to spirituality. Vultures fly toward the Sun and Saturn is the son of the Sun; Garuda as a vehicle enables Lord Vishnu to have perfect control over Time so that final dissolultion in Eternity is possible. Garuda's relationship with both Vishnu and Saturn suggests a similarity in their task of preservation of the cosmos at an earthly level.

In Western thought, Saturn is represented as an old man with a sickle in his hand. The Hindus consider him either as a Yama, the god of death, or as Shiva, the Supreme God of the Cosmos. Whatever status is assigned to Saturn, the references to him esoterically emphasize that he loves mankind and was placed to guide it toward its higher destiny.

8
RAHU
THE NORTH NODE OF THE MOON

☊

The importance afforded the lunar nodes is a special feature of Vedic astrology. However, very little information is given in astrological texts to explain their meaning. In Hindu mythology and Vedic spiritual literature, however, many references can be found to them. Through this can discern their true nature and understand why they are so powerful in spite of the fact that they have no concrete form.

The ancient seers were aware of several invisible planetary influences and called them "shadowy planets" (chhaya grahas). The astrological sage Parashara refers to seven visible and five invisible planets *(BPHS Chapter IV, Sloka 5–8, pp. 21–22)*. These invisible planets are named Rahu, Ketu, Dhuma, Parivesha and Indradhanus. They are considered to be malefics or productive of harm. This is because they externalize certain deep-rooted faults in the individual. They produce unfortunate conditions in order to eradicate personality weaknesses and instil the strength to face the ordeals arising in the spiritualization process. This is based on the fact that the individual in his incarnations accumulates many harmful influences which have to be dissolved before a new spiritual orientation is possible. Such a cleansing operation is neither very pleasant nor simple.

Rahu is the name given to the ascending node of the Moon. It is also known as Ahi, which means a serpent, the Sun, the demon Vritra, a thief, a scoundrel, or a cloud. Vritra, symbolically a serpent or dragon, is considered to be the personification of darkness, as well as a mountain. The demon Vritra was destroyed by Indra, the king of the gods. The serpent, as the great power of Nature, represents the basic law of creation on which depends the orderly progression of terrestrial existence.

Explaining the power represented by Ahi, Blavatsky relates it to the mighty Dhyan Chohans, the collective groups of spiritual beings *(SD Vol. I, P. 111)*. These are the same as the angelic hosts of Christianity and the Elohim or "Messengers" of the Jews — all of which are vehicles for the Divine or Universal Thought and Will. They are intelligent forces which give to, and enact in Nature her laws, while they themselves act according to laws imposed upon them by yet higher powers.

Rahu and Ketu, the descending node, are important cosmic agencies. Their primary function as messengers of higher powers is to destroy the asuric or demonic tendencies within us. Rahu is described as a mountain and as darkness because materialistic proclivities must be aroused to their fullness, like dark mountains, before they can be destroyed. Yet Rahu is not simply darkness; it accentuates darkness so that it must be effectively eliminated. Rahu is considered malefic because it produces disenchantment with material attachments and physical well-being, the most coveted aspects of human life.

Being a shadowy planet, the effect of Rahu is felt primarily on the shadowy counterpart of the human body, the psychological and psychic sheaths. The concretization of the Divine Spark in the physical casement is the main function of Saturn, which acts both to shape and to change the form. Saturn operates primarily on the physical plane. Saturn and Rahu are similar in many ways, but Rahu affects more one's thoughts, feelings and reactions to things. Under adverse conditions, the reactions aroused by Rahu are unconventional, even perverse. Whatever the final outcome, whether in the mental realm, or on the psycho-somatic composition of the being, Rahu's effect is aways indirect. There will be a primary impulse at a psychological level which, interceded by something else, creates perversions, derangements, psychological imbalance or physical ailments.

Much of Rahu's effect can be understood by the serpent which symbolizes it. In all ancient religions, serpents are important objects of worship. Saturn, giving his advice leading to Adam's fall from the Garden of Eden, was represented as a serpent. In some religions the serpent is worshipped as God itself.

Yet actual snakes are different from the Nagas, the serpent gods who are highly evolved Divine powers, the sages who hold the reins of Divine manifestation. The Nagas are snake-shaped but they do not creep; they stand erect and move. This is allegorical but it serves to distinguish the ordinary reptile from the adepts symbolized by serpents. It explains why the *Puranas* call Rahu "snake-shaped" rather than a mere snake. Geoffrey Hodson indicates that serpents are a symbol of both wisdom and the wise (*HWHB p. 124*). He states that the Nagas of Hindu mythology are none other than the ancient seers, the great Rishis. As the rationale for chosing the serpent as a symbol for wisdom, he points out that it glides secretly, and for the most part unseen, on the surface of the globe just as wisdom does. Like wisdom, the serpent is a concealed power potent either to illumine if rightly employed, or to destroy if misused. The smooth sinuosity of the snake and its movement aptly portray the harmonious and rhythmic self-expression of wisdom. Men of wisdom are not perceived by the world at large, and they often prefer to live an obscure life, like the snake that is hidden.

Another reason for the serpent symbolizing wisdom is because it is born of an egg *(SD Vol. II, p. 79)*. In this way it becomes the emblem of the Logoi or self-born. True wisdom can never be imparted by another. It has to be self-born. This wisdom sustains manifestation by providing the basic energy for cohesion and binding interrelationship. According to Hindu mythology, Vishnu, who sustains the universe, rests on Ananta-Naga or Sesha-Naga meaning "the Infinite Serpent." He sleeps on it until the next dissolution when everything is once again withdrawn into the Absolute. The serpent as the vehicle for Vishnu implies that it provides the basic channel for the preservation of the universe. This august status is assigned Vishnu's serpent, as he is considered to be the embodiment of wisdom.

The couch of Vishnu is formed by the seven coils of this serpent, Sesha-Naga. It indicates infinite time and space that contains the seed of creation and periodically throws it off, the efflorescence of which becomes the manifest universe. The serpent is a universal symbol of cyclic manifestation. The serpent is itself the undulatory, electric, triply polarized creative force in the cosmos, on all planes and in every vehicle of man. The cosmic preservation principle is supported by the wise serpent that represents the very force which makes the manifestation possible through its rhythmic expansion and contraction.

Rahu as a serpent has another revelation to make. This is indicated by the fact that serpents represent time in space. Serpents have the energy and wisdom to carry out the Divine plan of manifestation. Because this wisdom is coterminous with time, it also represents immortality which is suggested by the serpent's sloughing its skin whereby it rejuvenates itself. The serpent stands for psychic regeneration and immortality. It is this kind of wisdom, which is radically different from the impulses of other planets, that makes Rahu unique. The proper harnessing of Rahu's energy is considered necessary for acquiring control over nature's finer forces and for the arousing the Kundalini or Serpent Fire.

Rahu itself is compared to a poisonous black serpent. Such serpents are considered both wise as well as deadly. These are the two sides of the same natural quality which is explained by Hodson as follows *(HWHB pp. 124–130)*. He mentions that the reptile, despite its seasonal change, is unchanging and appears in a new and glistening covering. So wisdom, he says, while remaining the same in essence, is self-manifest in ever new forms, none being able to hold it permanently. The serpent's tongue is forked or bipolar, so is wisdom, as it is susceptible to degradation into low cunning when employed for selfish purposes or to elevation into lofty intuition when employed according to unselfish ideals. Snake venom can destroy as well as heal depending upon its use and dosage. This is true of wisdom as well. Degraded, it poisons the soul, while rightly used it operates as an antidote to all ills. Similar dual effects of Rahu, for beneficial as well as malefic results, are expected depending upon conditions.

In predictive astrology, Rahu is also connected with poison used for both destructive and regenerative purposes. The wisdom effect of the planet is expressed by its providing the individual with the direct experience of the hard realities of life, the truth of which once realized becomes a permanent part of the psyche. Whatever is the result of Rahu, it is liable to affect us in both ways, for good and for ill. It is said that Rahu's presence in the ascendant exerts an unpleasant influence while in the Tenth house it bestows excellent results giving better professional prospects, especially in association with foreigners. Rahu in Ninth, Tenth and Eleventh houses, along with its ruler well-placed and strong, gives very favorable results. These predictive possibilities of Rahu emanate from the bi-polar effects of the planet. Rahu gives deep acting results. Acting both ways, like wisdom and poison, Rahu gives spiritual attainment, regeneration and enlightenment with regard to Eternal Truth, as well as downfall in one's status, affliction with malignant diseases, poisoning and decay. There is nothing in this illusory objective world of ours that cannot be made to serve two purposes — good or bad, help or harm *(SD Vol. V, pp. 284–130)*. This is a universal law well expressed by Rahu. But like natural law, Rahu's hold is so firm that, whatever its effect, it is extremely difficult to extricate oneself from it.

In the Vedas, Rahu is invoked as a demon named Svarbhanu, who devours the luminaries to cause the eclipse. Acording to the *Aitareya Brahmana* on New Moon days, the Moon comes into a condition where Svarbhanu can devour both the luminaries and cause a solar eclipse. After the eclipse the Moon is reborn, having emerged from the Sun's body. The war in heaven when the gods and the demons fought terrible battles for power over the universe also refers to the same relationship. In this story, Vasuki, the ruling deity of Patala, the nether-world, represented as a great snake or Naga, serves as the rope which is tied around Mandara mountain to obtain the Amrita or nectar of immortality. These allusions refer to the process of spiritual awakening and to the ritual of Initiation which mirrors it. This leads to the inner unfoldment of the individual and bestows the fruit of immortality and the secret knowledge of nature's mysteries.

The regeneration of the Moon after the solar eclipse indicates the regenerative power of Rahu. In our objective universe, the Sun is the symbol of the life-giving beneficent deity. In the subjective, boundless world of the spirit, it has another significance. It refers to the power of initiation, the light of knowledge, which leads the seeker through the hall of mysteries and guides him into eternal life. In this process the consciousness of the seeker is linked with the immortal spirit and his eyes are opened to reality.

Blavatsky explains the relationship of the planets and the importance of the luminaries by stating that the Sun is the manifestation of the seventh principle of our planetary system *(SD Vol. V, pp. 154–55)*. The Moon is the fourth principle, shining in the borrowed robes of her master, saturated with and reflecting every passionate impulse and evil desire of her grossly material body, the Earth. The whole cycle of Adeptship, Initiation and all its mysteries is connected with and subservient to the two luminaries and the seven planets. Spiritual perception derives from the Sun; all psychic states, diseases and even lunacy, proceed from the Moon. From this we see that Rahu's obscuring the luminaries and the Moon emerging from the Sun are allegories of the fourth principle in man, uniting with the highest or Atmic principle and again coming out of it in rejuvenated form. Rahu radically changes the inner core of our being.

It is significant that a mountain is mentioned as the central rod around which the serpent Vasuki was tied as a rope to churn out the nectar. This central rod is also referred to as the precious tree in Indra's garden. In esoteric texts *(HWHB p. 127; C)*, the tree or the central rod represents "the spinal cord and canal or the etheric and superphysical channel in its center passing from the root of the cord in the sacrum along its whole length, into the medulla oblongata and brain." The gods and demons represent the two opposing forces of spirit and matter. In this context we should recall that Rahu always exists in relation to Ketu, both of which together form one serpent, though they function as two.

In the process of awakening the Kundalini the role of these two serpents is very crucial. Rahu and Ketu together symbolize the apparently opposing and hostile pairs in the world. They embody the idea of dualism, the struggle between good and evil, spirit and matter, light and darkness, gods and demons, saviours and serpents, and so on. The struggle for awakening, symbolically the trial of initiation, arouses the pure wisdom of the Kundalini, which is both creative and destructive. By bestowing wisdom it gives insight and patience and aligns the personal consciousness with universal awareness. The success in this struggle for mastery depends upon physical purity and psychological preparedness, freedom from the karmic past, a peaceful environment, and favourable planetary influences. The devouring of the Sun and the Moon and the role of Rahu and Ketu — Svarbhanu — refer to the great drama played for the spiritual regeneration of the individual and the Earth.

The war in heaven also refers to the terrible ordeals in store for the seeker of Truth — the struggle between himself and his personified human passions, which he must slay or fail in the quest. If he overcomes these illusions and temptations he becomes the Dragon-slayer, and a "son of the serpent." He becomes a serpent himself, having cast off his old skin and reborn in a new body he becomes a son of wisdom and immorality in eternity. With this new awakening, the physical sheath of the individual is also rejuvenated. Because of psychological purification, his aura completely changes its hue. The old adverse karmas being purged out, the individual gains the vitality of the cosmic life.

Such trials occur even in the ordinary course of human life under the impact of Rahu. The obscuration of the Sun and the Moon, the luminaries which represent the True Man, leads to psychological restrictions which cause excruciating pain. When the eternal aspect of one's life represented by the Sun is obscured by Rahu, it portends a karmic fault, in which relationship the karmic restriction is worked out and the equilibrium reestablished. In the process the individual, having suffered great psychological frustration, becomes aware of the wider extension of life. This whole operation takes place on an invisible, subjective plane, on the psychological and psychic level. Rahu is a shadowy planet and its impact is directly felt on the shadowy or the invisible aspects of the individual and only indirectly experienced on the physical plane.

The Sun is the Atman, the Soul, whose obscuration envelops the individual in complete darkness, isolates him from the eternal energy-source and confines him in the psychological and psychic realms of manifestation. The Moon is related to the psyche, the channel through which consciousness flows to the Atman. When the Moon is afflicted by Rahu, the individual fails to establish rapport with his higher nature. Consequently, suicidal temperament, ambivalence, emotional storms, extreme likes and dislikes, sudden fits of depression and drug addiction caused by psychic disturbances become the main traits of the person. These personality imbalances caused by Rahu's affliction do not easily respond to any physical therapy. They arise at psychological and psychic levels; the healing influences must be directed to these levels to be effective. Often these diseases have a karmic origin. Rahu as an agent of the law of karma accentuates them in order to bring forth karmic rectification. In the event of obscuration of the Sun and Moon, the will-force flowing from the Sun is weakened, and the mental balance resulting from the benefic effect of the Moon is absent. As a result the individual fails to maintain his conscious control over outer disturbances.

Hindu mythology describes Rahu as born of a lioness and black in color. He rides a lion and has four hands. In his three arms he holds a scimitar, a spear and a shield, while from the fourth, he bestows blessings. The sages thought that the birth of Rahu from a lioness and his riding a lion are analogous to the allegory of Vijaratana *(SD Vol. III, p. 380; Vol. V, p. 154, 284)*, which described his usurping his father's kingdom. In an important way, this allegory also refers to initiation rites or the process of awakening. Even in Alchemy mention is made of a lion devouring the Sun. One has to recall that in such references the Sun represents the cosmic creative and regenerative principle, as does the lion. The initiatory rites that represent the unfoldment of the human mind to cosmic truth are mystically depicted as the Sun entering into the body of a lion, or even as the shearing of the effulgent solar rays.

In order to discover the influence of Rahu in the process of spiritual awakening, we have to go deeper into the details of the allegory. Blavatsky mentions that the root or seed of all future initiate-saviours is called Vishwakarman, the "Father" Principle, who is beyond the comprehension of mortals *(SD Vol. V, p. 154)*. In the second stage it is called Surya, the "Son" who offers himself as a sacrifice to himself. In the third stage it is called the Initiate, who sacrifices his physical to his spiritual self. It is Vishwakarman, who became virtually Vijaratana, the "son shorn of his beams," who suffers for his too ardent nature and then becomes glorified by purification. This refers to spiritual awakening achieved by sacrifice and purification.

Being the son of a lioness, Rahu has the nature and consciousness of the lion. Rahu represents the active or male potency of Shakti, the female reproductive power in nature, Durga, the feminine counterpart of Shiva, also rides a lion. As a serpent, Rahu pervades the entire body of Shiva who controls the gods and demons alike. Rahu was used by the demons as well as the gods in the churning of the cosmic ocean. Rahu also has a special relationship with the Moon, whom it devours in order to regenerate it and thereby rejuvenate the manifestation. The Moon rests on the crest of Shiva, the great enlightener and bestower of all siddhis or perfections, the destroyer and regenerator of the cosmos. Such a close association of Rahu with Shiva emphasizes the mystic nature of Rahu working for the bestowal of inner knowledge.

The four hands of Rahu indicate the instruments with which it manifests itself. A scimitar is a short sabre with a curved, sharp edged blade broadening from the handle, while a spear is a long, pointed weapon used in fighting and hunting. A shield is a broad piece of armour that protects or defends. One cannot attribute cruelty to Rahu, though astrologically it is considered a first-rate malefic. Rahu is however capable of inflicting injuries sharply and suddenly. It can attack from a short distance as well as from a long one. In every form of attack, Rahu precipitates mortal effects depending upon the vigor with which the attack is made.

Astrologers have realized that the results produced by Rahu are generally permanent though their cause is not usually recognized. Rahu produces important changes in everyday affairs. These changes are brought on with great suddenness. Under its influence all calculations and expectations are completely upset and go awry. The individual is not able to do what he expected, or in the way he planned, or cannot meet the persons whom he wanted to meet. Complete dislocation is the astrological effect of Rahu. These results are characterized by its various weapons of attack and protection. But Rahu does not only shield his devotees from undesirable influences, he also bestows blessings on them. This is why hymns eulogize Rahu as always ready to bestow on his devotees wealth and abundance and as being always friendly and loving.

The *Puranas* describe Rahu as "half-bodied, immensely powerful, a trouble-maker for the Sun and Moon, born of a lioness, having a huge body like a mountain, of lamp black color, snake-shaped, terrible mouthed and the devourer of the Sun and Moon." This description makes Rahu more powerful than the Sun and Moon who give life to all. Being a 'messenger' of the great cyclic law under which all other laws operate, even the luminaries that provide life for the entire universe are ineffective against Rahu. As the law governing the cosmic manifestation, Rahu does not have any objective personification and as such is half-bodied, Ardhakayam: it has no physical body to work through, though it has non-physical existence.

Together with Ketu, its counterpart, Rahu forms the complete serpent. Though complementary to each other, the two nodes have distinct characteristics of their own. The epithet "half-bodied" emphasizes the subjective nature of these planets. They are shadowy, without any objective, physical, or visible counterpart. Being of a shadowy nature, difficult to detect, Rahu's effect is subtle and elusive. The sages were aware of the churning effect of Rahu and its importance in bestowing control over the subtle powers of nature. But considering the excruciating pain and great psychological isolation experienced under these trials, which cut the individual off from the life-force supplied by the Sun and Moon, Rahu is a trouble maker.

The mountain symbolizes the archaic character of the law operating under Rahu. Mountains are often described under the same evolutionary process that created the universe. The universality and ancient nature of the law, represented by the difference between the black and blue colors, arises from two considerations: Rahu's function in the process of spiritual awakening, as symbolized in initiation rites, and its involvement with the materialization process. The blue color, as mentioned in the Vedas, is that of the universal beneficent spirit, while black stands for the demonic nature. In Hindu mythology, as we have noted, most of the gods and avatars from Shiva to Rama are described as blue, while the demons are black. Blue represents universality, the ether or Akasha, which is the subtle, supersensuous, spiritual essence that pervades all space. In many teachings, including the *Upanishads,* the Akasha is the all directing and omnipotent deity. The Akasha is also known as occult electricity, an aspect of Kundalini.

Immense power used for benevolent purposes is the key-note of the gods. The influence of Rahu that is ultimately good for the individual comes under its dark blue color. In this regard, Rahu annihilates the egoistic, self-centered, demonic nature in man. Lord Shiva destroys in order to create anew. Lord Krishna kills demons and destroys asuric tendencies. Lord Rama slays the great asura Ravana. So too, dark blue Rahu destroys all materialistic desires of the human individual. The huge mountain of blackness attributed to Rahu points to its gigantic dimension. The realm of its operation stretches from the lowest physical to the highest spiritual. In order to create the necessary effect, Rahu is almost demonic in its operation. Its long-term impact is to spiritualize the individual. The determination in carrying out its objectives is symbolized by the three arms of Rahu holding various weapons. When Rahu strikes, it is ruthless. Yet when Rahu shields a person, none can harm him. The strength of Rahu in giving protection is supremely godly, but its savageness in the attack is intensely demonic as well.

Vedic hymns invoke Rahu as "adorned with sandal paste, flowers and an umbrella, of blue color, armed with a sword and shield, seated facing south on a throne and surrounded by all siddhis." Naga or serpent is also one of the names of Rahu, and the name in the Hindu pantheon of the Dragon Spirit who inhabits the nether-world, Patala Loka. He is an ever wise deity endowed with extraordinary magic power. He is the presiding spirit of the god of the five regions (the four directions of the compass and the center as the fifth point). The principal function of Rahu is to arouse spiritual awareness by making the individual aware of his immeasurable latent faculties. Until this understanding dawns the individual is troubled by the influence of the planet.

In order to produce the spiritual power that bestows wisdom and enlightenment, Rahu functions under the command of the spiritual hierarchy, which in turn functions according to the guidance of Dakshinamurti, the sage who resides near the Tropic of Capricorn in the south. Rahu facing south refers to its constant contact with this seat of spiritual power from which derives its spiritual influence to bestow on those it favors.

Rahu rides on a chariot drawn by eight horses that are black in color and eternally yoked to it. Rahu has thirty-two sons called Ketus, implying thereby that they are like comets. This description of the shadowy planet presents it in its creative role. The chariot represents the whole personality of the being as an expression of the aura radiating at the super-physical level. The chariot is a status symbol of the being who rides it, and in the same way the physical body of the person is an expression of the soul within it. The soul is royal, as is the rider in a chariot. Rahu being the person seated in the chariot refers to the inner planetary ruler affecting the inner man. Rahu seated in the chariot signifies the important position it is assigned among the planets. A similar status is indicated by assigning to it an umbrella of protection by higher forces. But the chariot symbol adds something more than the umbrella. It gives Rahu an active role, moving in a special direction to carry out a pre-determined mission. From this we see that the influence of Rahu, whatever it may be, is always purposive. Even when it causes some apparent sorrow, it is intended to develop and externalize some hidden potential of the individual or to rectify karmic faults from past lives.

The significance of Rahu's eight horses is found in Hindu mythology where similar allusions are made in regard to cosmogenesis. Shiva is the Supreme Creator from whom all other creative powers arise. There are eight incarnations of Shiva to enable the cosmic manifestation to proceed on the right course. They represent the eight aspects of creative energy. They are: Sharva, meaning to go or to kill; Bhava, meaning birth or acquisition; Rudra, which implies dreadful; Ugra, the fierce or violent; Bhima, the formidable; Pashupati, the herdsman or the owner of cattle; Ishana, the ruler or master; and Mahadeva which is the Supreme Shiva himself.

These aspects of the Supreme Lord form earth, water, fire, air, ether, the indwelling soul and the Sun and the Moon, which are also eight in number and constitute the manifest existence. Shiva in his cosmic creative role is assisted by eight Bhairavas or terrible ones who are said to be frightful, horrible and formidable, who are his different limbs. They are: Shiva, Bhaya (fear), Bhayanaka Rasa (the fearful dramatic mood), a specific river, a special musical composition, a special rhythm in music, a jackal, and a specific mountain. All these Bhairavas represent the eight horses of black color that draw the chariot of Rahu.

Rahu and Shiva are thus alike in several ways. Shiva is engaged in the regeneration and remanifestation of the universe, and Rahu functions under his direction in a similar mission. In this task of cosmogenesis Rahu

begets thirty-two sons. These are the twenty-seven Nakshatras or asterisms and the five planets. The asterisms are important cosmic powers
assisting the formation of the universe. They are associated in their
workings with the five planets, excluding the two luminaries. The reference to their comet-like form alludes to the stage of their early formation
when they were in the process of concretization. Through Rahu, the
embodiment of eternal law, the asterisms and the planets (excepting the
Sun and Moon) produce their results in consonance with the law of
evolution and the law of karma. The nature of these agents of astrological
results can be better understood in the light of what Blavatsky states about
them *(SD Vol. I, p. 141)*. She mentions that before our globe became
egg-shaped, a long trail of cosmic dust, or fire-mist, moved and writhed
like a serpent in space. These trails of cosmic dust are the sons of Rahu;
and the father and sons are eternally engaged in the cosmic process of
regeneration and rejuvenation according to the great cyclic law of manifestation. These aspects of Rahu are indicated by the geometrical symbol
assigned to it.

Emblematically, Rahu is represented by two small circles linked by
a larger semicircle curving upwards. The circle represents the wholeness
of the being, the entire potential contained within the person. It stands for
the Divine potential apportioned during the course of an incarnation for
its actualization. The two circles included in the emblem of Rahu represent
two successive lives. If we orient the emblem considering east (or astrologically, the First house) as the top of the figure, both circles occupy the
positions of the Fourth and the Tenth houses in a horoscope. These two
houses represent the two sides of the horizontal arm of the celestial cross.
The left circle stands for past lives from which what the individual must
become has to be carved off. The right circle stands for the life to come,
the final destiny of the person.

The larger semicircle linking these two circles passes through the
houses of the horoscope that indicate the working of Rahu. The sweep of
the arc covers the Third house which stands for valour and courage, the
Second house which represents death, and the Ascendant which indicates
the conditions of present birth. The arc then sweeps over to the Twelfth
house which represents the waters of Lethe or forgetfulness that rejuvenates the person. After this, the circle covers the Eleventh house standing
for the results of one's efforts and then it enters the circle standing for the
future life or the Tenth house. This vast sweep indicates the various phases
through which the soul has to traverse in order the attain its future destiny.
It represents the law under which life operates for the individual.

According to this symbol, Rahu represents the great cyclical law
related to the rejuvenating and regenerating process. This diagram links

the present restrictions and opportunities of the individual with his past actions. Acting as the 'messenger' of the great cyclic law of manifestation, Rahu works under the direction of a still higher law, a mission in which it functions ruthlessly but with the assistance and cooperation of many cosmic forces. The important point to note is that this shadowy planet functions as an agent of a higher law of manifestation according to which all other planets and many finer forces of Nature work.

9
KETU
THE SOUTH NODE OF THE MOON
℧

Ketu, the descending or south lunar node, forms an integral part of the serpent. As mentioned earlier, Vasuki, the ruling serpent of the nether world was used in the churning operation as a rope tied around the central rod formed by the mountain Mandara. Upon retrieval of the nectar from the ocean, the gods did not want to share it with the demons. Vasuki surreptitiously sneaked among the gods and partook of a portion of the nectar but was soon detected. The gods became angry and Vishnu hurled his discus at the serpent but as it had already partaken of the nectar it could not be destroyed. It was merely divided in two. The upper portion of the serpent became Rahu and the lower Ketu. Outwardly, they began to function as Rahu and Ketu, but together they continued to represent the great cyclic law of manifestation that sustains the universe.

Basically, Rahu and Ketu represent karmic retribution. They link present restrictions and opportunities with past actions. They arrange events in such a way that harmonious balance ultimately prevails. A long time may be needed before this result is achieved, during which period the individual may experience much frustration and sorrow. But the nodes will finally achieve the needed results.

The ultimate harmony requires a radical reorientation in one's life pattern. This situation is reached when the individual is exasperated in his helplessness. As a result of insurmountable misfortune he begins to look within and turns his gaze heaven-ward. In the process he begins to explore the natural laws operating in life and a new consciousness dawns within him. Then he begins to harmonize his everyday life to establish an equilibrium between himself and the universal life. When the inner thought process is awakened, the individual may develop his intuitive perception and find the right course of living without first being drawn into the vortex of personal calamity. Whatever the impetus to reorient one's life pattern, a basic restructuring of one's thought and action is essential for achieving harmony between the individual and the universe. This impetus is given by Rahu and Ketu.

Ketu is invoked in Vedic hymns as follows: "Decked with silk, flowers, garlands, sandal paste and an umbrellal, of variegated color and seated in a divine chariot, you travel around mount Meru. Born of Jaimini's family under the Abhijit star may four-armed, deathless, effulgent Ketu, seated facing south on a throne, make us ever happy with wealth and abundance."

The high status assigned to Ketu is evident from such epithets as "decked with silk, flowers, garland, sandal paste and an umbrella," and "seated on the throne." Ketu is adorned with sandal paste and is seated to the south, which reveals the deep involvement of this planet in spiritual awakening and imparting inner knowledge like Rahu.

In spite of the two nodes having the same origin and many similarities, the Vedic seers have highlighted their distinguishing features. Rahu is dark blue in color while Ketu is variegated. Analogous to Rahu, Ketu is linked with darkness but possesses a mysterious ray of light and splendor. Furthermore, Ketu has a star on its head, even though it has serpent's body.

Ketu is said to belong to the celebrated family of the sage Jaimini, the founder of the Mimamsa school of philosophy. This philosophy is mainly concerned with the correct interpretation of rituals and the settlement of controversial points in regard to Vedic texts. Belonging to this learned seer's family, Ketu relates to the wisdom born of contemplating the nature of creation and the significance of different religious activities for attaining final liberation. The esoteric nature of wisdom and the understanding of the hidden laws of creation fall within the domain of Ketu. Ketu brings about the dawn of an intuitive comprehension of the essential nature of things and of the primeval cause of all manifestation.

The mysterious splendour of Ketu refers to the unification of the individual consciousness with the primeval essence of manifestation. The universe shines with the radiance of the Absolute All. All the splendor in the cosmos reflects the light that shines in Brahma, the cosmic creator. The unification of the individual mind with the primeval source of energy illumines it and gives it radiance. Under the impact of Ketu, empathy is established with the universal creative life force that bestows wisdom and insight into the working of nature.

Such a comprehension of the secrets of nature does not descend on the individual without any effort. The strange ray of light surrounding Ketu is born of strenuous effort exerted in order to acquire spiritual knowledge. Like the alchemists, Ketu makes an individual explore the innermost recesses of the human psyche. It makes the individual perceive the subjective reality behind the veil of objective manifestation. When the influence of Ketu is predominant, it activates the thinking principle. The cause of this process may be any real or imaginary dissatisfaction, or the seed of some unresolved philosophical thought. When such a situation arises, the individual becomes fully absorbed in the problem. If it occurs at an early age in life, his hair may turn grey, his face may become haggard, and generally he will be isolated and left out of the main current of his age. Under Rahu, on the other hand, the dissatisfaction directly affects the psychological state making the individual brooding, depressed and unbalanced.

The ancient seers gave to Ketu such epithets as Tamas, Dwaja, and Shikhin, which reveal his basic character. Tamas is one of the three basic attributes of nature, and ordinarily means darkness. The nature of darkness associated with Ketu is that of avarana shakti, the veil that conceals the real nature behind the manifestation *(CJW verses 344–350)*. By casting an illusory or Mayic covering, this power gives us a wrong view of reality. Ketu conceals the real light of divinity. In its original nature, Ketu is blended with the primeval light, but it looks out at the manifestation under the shadow of the great illusion. It thereby radiates a strange illumination born of its understanding of the illusory character of creation. Such an awareness is quite uncommon.

This mysterious illumination that arises from the influence of Ketu is similar to the famous smile on the Mona Lisa. One does not understand the mysterious expression of the portrait. One wonders whether the enigmatic smile reveals the detached delight of a mature woman or her concealed involvement with the external world, but it clearly distinguishes the inner person from the external surroundings. One can similarly imagine the enigmatic splendor of Ketu arising from its understanding of human nature wrapped in the great illusion. Under this situation, the individual has a detachment born of understanding the reality beyond the illusion but is still involved in the illusion. Such an expression arises from recognizing human ignorance and the possibility of acquiring the greater wisdom that common human beings so light heartedly neglect. The Jaimini element of Ketu makes the individual a serious student who comprehends the vastness of the subject of inquiry and the limitations of the inquiring mind. Such a comprehension of inner realities does not however completely dissolve the individual's attachment to the illusory world.

The word Shikhin can be interpreted in several ways, each of which reveals a different aspect of the planet. It means an arrow, a horse, a bull, a lamp, a tree, a religious mendicant and a peacock. Shikhin represents something pointed, well directed and serving as a fulcrum. Basically the word signifies the sharp penetration of an arrow. An arrow is directed toward a target, which relative to Ketu refers to the understanding of the process of Divine manifestation. When such an understanding dawns, the

Shikhin does not leave the individual purely intellectual. He orients his life in the light of the new understanding. Such an understanding under the impact of Ketu induces the individual to work for the Divine plan.

This aspect is suggested by a horse, a bull, and so on. When the creative energy is directed towards manifestation, the mindstuff is vivified so that the subjective understanding affects objective forms. In this process the Ketu impulse functions as the fulcrum symbolized by a tree trunk around which various activities of the individual revolve. A religious mendicant, without desiring anything for himself except bare physical requirements, wanders from place to place sowing the seeds of religious thought among people. The epithet Shikhin suggests that, surrounded by the darkness of the veil of ignorance, Ketu arouses the thought process which rends the veil, and acting from within works like a horse or a bull for carrying out the Divine mission. In this enterprise the individual works like a religious mendicant desiring nothing for himself except that the will of God be done.

The word Dwaja, which ordinarily means a flag or an emblem, has many other connotations. It symbolizes an eminent person, the organ of generation, and a house situated in the east. The individual under the impulse of Ketu has the impression that he himself is the cause for its fructification. This is not true. The individual under this impulse works but what he does is for someone else: he carries out the order given by a higher power. A flag is an emblem of something higher in whose name and under whose authority the person carrying the flag operates. Similarly, the generative organ does not procreate, it merely carries the seed from the male to the female. Ketu provides the channel for creative energy.

One may note in this regard that Ketu is analogous to the Fire-Mist which forms the basic material for the concretization of the universe. Similarly, mindstuff is the basic constituent of all forms of objective manifestation. By impregnating nebulous matter with Divine creative energy, Ketu assists in the externalization of the Divine plan. Ketu does not involve itself in the physical or material realm, as it is fully aware of the transient nature of existence. It functions from the mental plane. It externalizes the wisdom concealed in manifestation so that the material entity is induced toward spiritual unfoldment. Ketu's influence acts as a catalytic agent to link the manifestation with its inner reality. In this process Ketu functions as pure intelligence.

Ketu is born under Abhijit. This asterism was used mainly during the Vedic period and relates to the bright northern star Vega. It occupies the sign of Capricorn under which the universalization of the individual takes place. The guiding motto of this asterism is in consonance with the planetary impulse of Ketu: both aim at carrying out the will of God. The quality of Abhijit is Sattvic and its presiding deity is Brahma, the Creator himself. Capricorn is intimately connected with the southern direction, and spiritual guardians like Dakshinamurti who are responsible for the evolution of life on earth. Ketu's relationship with the spiritual hierarchy is highlighted by its being born under Abhijit. Ketu's birth in Jaimini's family under Abhijit stands for regenerative mental processes under inner guidance that allow for the spiritual evolution of humanity. The epithet of a house situated in the east refers to the same spiritual nature of the planet suggesting that Ketu heralds the advent of new ideas and new thoughts, which usher in new and higher aspects of life.

The Vedas also describe Ketu as seated in a Divine car, analogous to a chariot, that goes around Mount Mandara, also called Meru. According to the *Bhagavad Gita (X, 23),* Meru is the peak of the mountain with which Lord Krishna, the incarnation of Vishnu, identifies himself. Meru represents the magic mountain, consisting of gold and gems, around which all the planets are said to revolve. This suggests that Ketu operates as an agent for Vishnu, the preserver, and assists the gods and demons in the churning of the ocean. The allegory stands for the stresses and strains in human-life that lead to psychological mutation in order to externalize the Divine nectar. During this churning process many jewels came out of the sea. In the life of an individual, such changes have a great destabilizing effect but enable him to externalize his latent powers. Such an impulse on the cosmic plane leads to great cataclysmic changes. While these changes take place and the ocean is churned, Ketu along with Rahu continue to assist the opposing forces to further their Divine mission of generating the nectar, the most precious essence of existence diffused throughout the universe

The emblem of Ketu is a downward curving semicircle linking two small circles placed on either side above it. The two circles represent the Fourth and Tenth houses in the horoscope, as indicated under Rahu, while the midpoint at the bottom of the larger semicircle becomes the cusp of the Seventh house. Both small circles stand for the actualization of the individual's destiny. They symbolize the innumerable past and future incarnations through which the soul's growth to perfection is realized. They also mark the Nadir and the Zenith points in the chart. The inmost essence of the being, which is indicated by the left-hand circle, is linked by Ketu to the acme of one's manifestation in the right-hand circle, the highest achievement possible for the soul in the specific incarnation. This actualization occurs through several phases of development represented by the houses which the semicircular arc traverses.

The arc begins with the Fifth house and terminates with the Tenth. The Fifth house represents the creativity of the person, while the Sixth shows outer reactions to one's creative efforts. These are expressed as the many obstacles that must be overcome in order to develop one's latent perfections. Then the individual descends to a point of balance and begins looking toward the spirit. The attraction for material existence and the pleasures of the senses have not yet been destroyed but are beginning to be cast away. When the stirrings for spiritual development begin to sway the mind after the experiences of the Sixth house, the balance of life established during the Seventh house impulse leads him to the exploration of hidden truths. The Eight house gradually opens out the secret store of knowledge and reveals the inner truth to him for his own direct perception. This leads him on the path of spiritualization and strict adherence to higher principles. The Ninth house finally links him to the universal life force and the individual is able to realize his true Self.

The downward curving semicircle represents the full course of life's struggle during the various phases of the soul's unfoldment. Finally, when the individual merges into the universal consciousness and his mind is dissolved into pure subjectivity, the soul learns its lesson. It perceives the truth and falsehood of the outer world. At this stage it also acquires the "mysterious illumination" with which Ketu is imbued. The individual begins to drive his chariot around Mount Meru and becomes one with Vishnu, the prevesever.

Ketu is the counterpart of Rahu. Both nodes always function together. United they bring out the hidden potential of the individual. Rahu works from the material side; it externalizes the ego and accentuates materialistic urges to such an extent that their realization and fulfillment become impossibile. As a result of this heightened craving, dissatisfaction and frustration ensue. Ketu, on the other hand, produces introspection. The deep thinking induced by Ketu reveals the illusory nature of material objects. With such disillusionment, there is certainly discontent, the characteristic result of the Ketu-impulse.

Rahu is a planet of karmic retribution, while Ketu is one of spiritual humiliation, but whatever they do, they always do well for their devotees. Rahu and Ketu both were worshipped by the Vedic seers for bestowing riches and plenty, wealth and abundance to their devotees. It is not material abundance that is indicated here but the fullness of a consciousness that has gone beyond illusion. They both produce their results by a churning operation; that is, by creating psychological storms and strains. They produce psychological destabilization leading us gradually towards the exploration of the hidden recesses of our being so that we may discover our secret immortality, which is liberation. In the terrestrial existence, the nodes bring cataclysmic, seismic changes so that the Divine spark can find the appropriate field for its expression. The same churning operation continues on the cosmic plane as well, along with the great cyclic law of manifestation represented by the Rahu-Ketu nexus.

The churning of the ocean, with which Rahu and Ketu are connected, is a pervasive phenomenon. Its application to the cosmic origin of manifestation is merely one of its meanings. Blavatsky notes that the war in heaven, in which Rahu and Ketu assist the gods and the demons in fulfilling their duties, also refers to the evolution of intelligence in man. She states that the relationship between the churning of the ocean and the war in heaven is a long and abstruse subject *. In its most general aspect, this war is going on eternally. So long as differentiation exists, there will be the war of opposites in heaven and on the different levels of human existence so that ultimate harmony and equilibrium can be achieved.

Emphasizing the significance of differentiation and arriving at the equilibrium between contraries, the *Secret Doctrine (Vol. I, p.148)* describes the process allegorically. "The Father-Mother spin a web whose upper end is fastened to the spirit — the light of the One Darkness — and the lower end is fastened to its shadowy end, matter; and this web is the universe spun out of two substances made in one, which is Svabhavat." The lowest end of the web is represented by Rahu, the very embodiment of matter, while Ketu, the mysterious illumination of Spirit, represents the upper end fastened to Spirit. Both these nodes together spin the web to produce the universe. This function of the Rahu-Ketu nexus is indeed a stupendous task. In it Rahu has the task of materialization and Ketu that of mental and spiritual regeneration. Rahu wields the scimitar and spear, while Ketu is associated with the arrow. Rahu works from without, while Ketu looks from behind the veil of ignorance. But both bestow abundance, and both are seated facing south, taking their orders from the same Divine Intelligence that guides the destiny of the universe. Taken together, the nodes personify the great law that is the very foundation on which the cosmos rests and which alone preserves its cohesion and equilibrium.

---

* H. P. Blavatsky, *Transactions of the Blavatsky Lodge*, The Theosophy Co., CA, 1923; pp. 109–110.

III

THE
SIGNS OF THE ZODIAC

THE SIGNS
OF THE ZODIAC

The symbols of the signs of the zodiac originated from a careful observation of Nature and of the Cosmic Man who expresses himself through her. Many processes must be described to show the subtle variations in energy from one level of manifestation to another, to indicate the growth of the soul from one stage of consciousness to another. From the purely subjective state of unmanifest existence to the concretization of the highly complex human organism, the soul undergoes many transformations, all of which are significant for an in-depth understanding of life's unfoldment. In order to describe them in all their nuances and variations, different geometrical symbols supported at times by mythological allusions are necessary. In order to decipher the basic qualities of different zodiacal energies, such symbols and mythologies should be considered as merely indicative. The ancient sages in assigning these symbols show their keen observation of Nature and reveal their profound knowledge of the subtle forces acting in cosmic evolution. In order to comprehend these various zodiacal impulses for predictive processes, one has to transcend the written word and grasp the inner sense using intuition, insight and knowledge.

1
ARIES
Mesha
♈

Aries is symbolized by a vertical line divided in two at the top with branches moving outward like two arcs of a circle ♈. The simplicity of the symbol can be misleading. It is a profound representation of the pre-cosmic stage of existence. The basic vertical line in the symbol stands for the Spirit or 'Purusha', the positive creative impulse. It is the consciousness aspect of the manifestation process. It is the aspect of Divine unfoldment which is self-reliant; it requires no support for its growth and multiplication. It reflects the characteristic of the gods or 'Devas', by which they shine in their own light casting no shadow. Standing alone, moving on its own to its creative pilgrimage, it decides to become two, to bifurcate. Polarization results from this decision. The Puranas mention this first stage of cosmic evolution when Brahma, in deep meditation in order to continue the creative process, decides to divide himself into two. Thus he becomes 'Brahma Viraj' and 'Vacha Viraj', one male and the other female, the former representing spirit and the latter matter. This division into male and female is not a reaction to any external stimulus. It is induced from within. This initial impetus which divides itself into two to begin the creative process is represented by Aries.

Aries, whose symbol also appears like the sprouting of a seed, is a powerful impulse which contains within itself great potentials as well as enormous responsibilities. It marks the beginning of the cosmic process. It initiates the drama of cosmogenesis and anthropogenesis. At this stage, the creative illusion, known as 'Maya' in Vedantic philosophy, arises from the veiling power of the Supreme and becomes active. This impulse is expressed in the materialization process under which the subjective essence is transformed into an objective form. Aries stands for this process of transforming the subjective non-existence into the objective material existence.

The urge to grow, represented by the sprouting of leaves, signifies the unfathomable energy contained in this sign. At this stage, the cosmic creative impulse, the positive force in nature, represented by the vertical stem, shoots out the first two leaves which in the course of time will grow into a mighty tree. These seemingly tender leaves contain an immeasurable potential of expansion. This immeasurable potential is concealed in a simple atom as a result of the veil cast by the illusory nature of the "veiling power." The subjective consciousness, objectified as an atom when on the move, is the point which becomes the vertical line in the figure. The First Creative Act contains within itself in an embryonic form all subsequent stages of emanation.

An important feature of the first creative impulse is its own sacrifice at the altar of matter so that the subsequent stages of manifestation can be made possible. 'Prakriti', material nature, can never exist without Purusha, the inner spirit. Once the Purusha has become externalized, Prakriti pervades it so extensively as to merge its identity within it. Consciousness is impossible to perceive in its pristine state. Its existence can only be felt and recognized subjectively, but not cognized physically. This aspect of manifestation is expressed by the vertical line representing the spirit-on-the-move culminating in division and becoming the two arcs of the universal manifestation. Astrologers often overlook the self-sacrificing nature of Aries people which enables their progeny to blossom and grow in the objective world.

The symbol of Aries also resembles a drooping Tau cross. It can be compared to the forked tongue of a serpent as well as to the two horns of a ram. All these reveal important aspects of the sign.

The first urge of the cosmic creative activity is a primordial motion. However it can fructify only when there is polarization. Ambivalence, swinging between opposites, and fullness of creative vitality are basic characteristics of this sign. Those who are born under the influence of this sign are highly creative but have much duality in their nature as they go back and forth between extremes. They have intense love as well as deeply rooted hatred. They are extremely energetic but lethargic and lazy at the same time. The polarized energy of the male and the female principles represented by this sign give a tremendous attraction for the opposite sex. Aries born are ardent lovers but not exploiters. Their urge to unite is spontaneous. They are generally guided by altruistic motives. In such experiences, however, they discover themselves, their inner motives and powers and their path of inner growth.

The Tau cross represents the path of unfoldment of the divine energy. The first zodiacal impulse produces the basic undercurrent of divinity as well as the path of its unfoldment. The first blades of grass or leaves of a tree have to exert tremendous force in the sprouting process. This characteristic is very true for the Aries person. They have to struggle hard in life.

Only after strenuous efforts are their inner capacities externalized, but when it occurs, it is a joyous moment, an enthralling experience. Their life is never easy and restful. They are like Sinbad the Sailor, moving from one place to another in search of new experiences and developing new faculties.

The resemblance to a serpent's tongue also emphasizes the dual nature of Arian energy. The tongue of the serpent is associated with its venom which can be used for curative as well as destructive purposes. Depending upon the situation and the quantum of venom used, the dose can be lethal or can counteract the most deadly poison. In the same way the impact of Aries can be highly creative or can destroy instantaneously. It is not the thought aroused by Aries which precipitates such a result but the basic impulse of Aries expressed as emotion and passion.

The two spreading arcs, or wings of the vertical line, link the sign with the material plane of existence. It does not imply that there is no urge towards spirituality. The two arcs, as two newly formed leaves or two horns of the ram, suggest the presence of both the urge towards materialization and that for the release from it. One arc represents the origin from the primordial source and the evolutionary course that immerses itself in material existence. It corresponds to the first quarter of the circumference of the circle that represents the divine impulse moving toward materialization (see p. 27). This arc as a part of the Aries symbol shows that the materialization impulse generated by Aries almost ceases when its energy begins to concretize in an effective way.

The second arc starts from the level when the urge towards liberation becomes irresistible. It represents the fourth quarter of the circumference. The two arcs taken together represent Aries. Together they indicate that Aries can lead one to deeper layers of materialization as well as to the tremendous exertion needed for release from material bondage and reabsorption in the source.

Ascending from the planes of materialization, the life force released under the impact of Aries meets the central shaft of life and light, merges in it and again emerges from it, with the downward course showing repeated immersion into matter. This is the spectacle presented by the symbol when viewed in its wholeness.

The release from bondage for the Aries born is never complete. The thirst for life at a higher level of manifestation is never satisfied. Aries marks the stage in one's evolutionary pilgrimage when one cycle of experiences ends and another begins. This is evident from the fact that though Aries types are skilled in many ways and have deep insight into many situations, they are often confronted with radically different situations where their skills are of little avail. The Aries individual is frequently confronted with new circumstances where his old achievements are not of much use and where he has to learn new lessons in order to succeed. There is always an unconventional nature to his life and a newness in his approach. Aries gives rise to explorers and adventurers in the realm of science, philosophy and new frontiers of knowledge. This display of dauntless spirit is an expression of the thirst for new discoveries which is basic to the sign. As the first sign of the zodiac, Aries signifies new beginnings, a new way of life, a new approach to problems, all of which require courage, initiative, and the ability to confront life alone, unaided and without any clear-cut guidance from outside sources. The newly sprouting blades of grass have to face such a situation. Aries has to exercise tremendous power to succeed in its goal of externalization.

Aries is assigned the animal symbol of a ram. The ram is an emblem of freshness, innocence, purity, agility and beauty. It appears in one form or another in all the religions of the world. The ram represents the latent goodness, the unmanifest reflecting in itself the primeval root matter (Mula Prakriti), which contains all creation latent within it. This symbol refers to the fragile man, a babe so to say, who one day under favorable conditions must come to express all the splendor and glory of the divinity residing within him. Considered in this light, the ram is almost divine, an atom of life which is not yet contaminated by the touch of the acquisitive tendencies of materialism. It is pure and full of joy in its innocence. It is happy and frolicsome. It is always eager to jump and play oblivious to any impending danger that may lurk on its way. The ram is an image of the pure spirit, enjoying the expression of its latent energy. The body of the ram is covered with wool showing that the Aries born are warm, passionate and generous.

From the standpoint of the supreme unmanifest, all creatures, unless soiled by materialism, are playful entities, innocent and frolicsome like a ram. The spirit of purity, newness and the eager impulse to express latent possibilities, the courage to cooperate in the Divine mission of manifestation and reabsorption into the One, are the primary urges of Aries. In fact, in this beginning is contained all that is required by the pilgrim on his cosmic mission. The two wings attached to the vertical line stand for the sprouting of Divinity in man which takes the evolving soul through the different phases of materialization and eventually releases it from its shackles. The sign represents this entire process in seed form.

2
TAURUS
BRISHABHA
☉

Taurus is the bull of the zodiac. Geometrically, it is represented by a circle with a circular arc at the top ☉. It resembles the symbol for Mercury without the cross hanging from it. In Hindu mythology, Shiva, the Supreme God of creation, has as his vehicle a bull called Nandi. Shiva's bull is worshipped by Hindu women who desire children. Nandi is Shiva's vehicle for travel. He is intimately connected with the basic urge represented by Taurus.

Taurus succeeds Aries. Aries represents the struggling energy eager to express itself and experience the newness of manifestation. The second stage in cosmic evolution is the activation of creative energy. At this stage the energy eager to express itself must immerse itself in the process of materialization. There is a subtle difference between the two forms of creative energy of Aries and Taurus, which radically alters their modes of expression. The energy with Aries is a vague urge. Its action is not well directed, its goal nebulous. The second phase imparts a specific goal. Taurus has an object towards which the energy has to move. Unlike Aries, Taurus is neither undirected passion, nor purposeless emotional upsurge without expectation of result. Yet this does not give it the impulse for immediate production so much as the the general desire to unite. At this stage desire is more important than action.

Under Taurus, the basic impulse is to strive for creative union. Divinity is essentially an impulse for externalizing the latent faculties of our being. This externalization involves a process of creation. When a father engages himself in the act of reproduction, he externalizes a bit of his inner essence. In this way the creative urge assumes the presence of the Divine Essence which seeks externalization. In the symbol for Taurus, this Divine Essence is represented by an enclosed circle. During the process of creation, the urge connects the innermost subjective essence with its blossoming forth. The act of blossoming involves the materialization process.

This phase of the soul's pilgrimage is represented by the second and the third quadrants of the circumference of the circle. The first half shown by the second quarter represents materialization while the third stands for the beginning of the process of release. The circular arc curving downwards represents this phase of the change. The absence of the cross from this emblem shows the condition anterior to the soul's involvement in polarization. The circle with a circular crest, symbolizing Taurus, is essentially the Divine creative *urge*. As such, Taurus refers to one-pointedness, the direction of which is evolutionary involvement with a view to achieving perfection and ultimately the release of the spirit hidden within. Taurus represents the potential and the readiness to jump into the fray.

The bull as the symbol of Taurus shows the psychological characteristic of this sign. A special feature of the bull is its utter disinterestedness with everything that does not concern it. It approaches a cow only when she is ready to bear another calf. The bull's mission in life is not to waste its energy but to be purposeful. For the assigned task, Taurus has immense vitality and strength. But this energy is not dissipated without a definite goal. The Taurus born only work when they want to attain a certain object. It is like a vulture pouncing upon its prey once it is in sight. Such an attitude often seems selfish. Outwardly, such a person appears listless but once their desire is aroused, whether for sex, money, or social status, they approach their object with all their power.

Indian womanhood stands for motherhood. Mother Nature is the Hindu ideal. Nature is the passive component of the creative process. The positive force flows from the spirit. When the Indian woman cherishes the benediction from Nandi, the bull of Lord Shiva, it symbolizes her readiness to receive the Divine flow of grace so that his creative mission can be successful. Cooperating with such a Divine mission is a reward by itself not withstanding the tremendous hardships that have to be undergone in discharging the ensuing responsibility. The cherished goal of Indian womanhood is to achieve fruitful motherhood through cooperation in the Divine mission of carrying out the evolutionary process. Therefore Hindu women greatly venerate Nandi, Shiva's bull.

Taurus represents the stage of cosmic evolution when the Divine Essence is not overflowing in all directions as happens during the initial Aries phase, but when the direction of its movement is established. In this downpour of Divine influence there are various subtler phases which alter the expression of Taurus from one person to another. During the early stages of its expression, the impulse is passionate, self-seeking and almost demonic. The mind becomes subordinate to basic physical urges. It is like a meteor penetrating the earth's atmosphere. It is the forceful penetration of energy that is important. This makes the psychological structure either highly devotional or extremely self-seeking knowing nothing other than what it desires. This phase is represented by the early slope of the downward moving arc. In time, intelligence dawns and the soul gains maturity.

The Moon's exaltation in Taurus relates to the second stage of development within this sign. Having penetrated the material veil, the soul realizes its limitations and responsibilities. With clarity of the mission ahead and awareness of the power at its command, the soul functions like a responsible parent. At this phase creativity as a Divine mission is emphasized. The vision of its immense possibilities arouses in it the will to be a divine servant. Such a person enjoys his social status, wealth, power and above all his family and serves them. The circular crest and the circle touch one another at this phase.

Once this stage is over egoism develops in the individual. The arc leaves the circle and moves upward. The sense of I-ness makes the individual creative but not satisfied with the given situation. The restless mind moving from one pleasure to another, from one material involvement to another, enables the soul to fathom various aspects of its inner potential. Having done so, it becomes impatient, feeling that the opportunities in life are inadequate to develop all of its qualities. This is the final phase of the Taurus impulse, when the soul is ready to proceed further to receive another downpour of Divine influence.

Basically, Taurus is creative potential, but in saturating the soul with this impulse it carries it through subtler transformations. From pure emotional energy directed towards procreation, it gradually makes the individual recognize the fullness of the drama and his part in it. Soon he understands the limitations of this involvement and begins to express *his* true self. Subtle transformation in the creative urge occurs during this phase of cosmic ideation.

3
GEMINI
MITHUNA
♊

The third zodiacal impulse represented by Gemini is very complex. It indicates the end of the androgynal state and the division of the sexes. Yet this simple description fails to convey all the important changes that take place at this stage. The Hindus have described it as the manifestation of Mahat or cosmic intelligence, the first and guiding principle of Nature. This term, found in Yoga philosophy, stands for 'the great principle' from which the other principles (tattwas) or essential constituents of the manifested world originate. Intellect is one of these derivative principles, whereas intelligence, which is the nearest English equivalent of the concept Mahat, is its producer. From this intelligence arises the thinking principle known as Manas, which further leads to Ahankara or egoism, the feeling of "I am this." Gemini represents the impulse which enables cosmic intelligence to manifest and through which further differentiation takes place. It begins the actual process of the one becoming the many.

Spiritual intelligence represented by Mahat possesses tremendous energy. In it lies the energy which polarizes the self-contained state of balance and throws it into the whirlwind of creative activities. From it arises the positive and negative or subjective and objective aspects of existence. As a result of such polarization, there arises passionate attraction between the different forms of existence. After Adam created Eve out of his rib, this led them into a passionate embrace that drove them from the Garden of Eden. At the Garden, their existence resembled that of Indra's court in heaven wherein beings maintain their balanced unity not yet disturbed by the act of polarization. Only when duality comes into existence can the manifestation really develop.

The third sign of the zodiac does not represent merely the act of polarization but its subsequent expression of triplication. The three primary attributes of Nature — Rajas (activity), Tamas (Inertia), and Sattwa (harmony) — which enable the expression of the numerous levels of life and form arise at this stage. Having aroused the necessary condition for the triplication of the Divine energy, the Gemini impulse basically remains uninvolved thus preserving the central feature of cosmic intelligence.

Symbolically, Gemini is represented as a man and woman in sexual embrace. Sometimes it is depicted as a man and woman in a boat or as a pair of human beings, one carrying a harp, and the other a mace. Greek mythology also describes it. The two stars of this sign, Castor and Pollux, are born of the same mother, Leda, but have different fathers. Castor was born of Leda's union with Tyndares, a human being, while Pollux was conceived when Zeus seduced her in the form of a swan. Helen was also a child of Leda, whose seduction by Paris led to the siege of Troy. These references emphasize different forms of dualistic energies in action. The child of a human being is considered male, while the child of a god is important for its feminine qualities. The mace is a symbol of the masculine nature while the harp represents the feminine. The boat as a vessel is symbolically the same as a sexual embrace. All these allegories refer to polarization of the cosmic energy between masculine and feminine aspects which are also represented by Psyche and Cupid. Mind or intelligence is an ever active expression of the Divine Energy. But the mind is activated by the mutual interaction of its polarized components.

The geometrical figure for Gemini is two vertical lines whose top and bottom points are crossed over by horizontal lines Ⅱ. The vertical and the horizontal lines refer to two sets of human beings fully polarized between positive and negative aspects of manifestation but united together as a pair. The juxtaposition of these lines and their shape, especially that of the upper line with a slight upward curvature and of the bottom line with a downward slope points to the relationship between masculine and feminine forces in one's constitution. It arouses mutual attraction, dependence and involvement in creative activity. The shape and position of these lines shows the harmonious blending of the two dissimilar counterparts: the similarity between them could have caused tension and friction. The vertical lines being delimited by the horizontal ones expresses the restrictions imposed on cosmic intelligence whose primary quality is unbounded freedom. These restrictions suggest that only a portion of the unbounded Divine energy has presently been apportioned to the zodiacal influence. Out of the whole, only a limited portion is taken out for some specific purpose.

The two vertical lines represent the Spirit or 'Purusha', the male aspect of manifestation, while the two horizontal lines suggest Nature or Prakriti, the female or material component. The curvature on the horizontal line shows the attraction towards materiality in the lower horizontal lines balanced by the spiritual aspirations of the upper line. The horizontal and vertical lines taken together do not form a cross. These lines are not phallic in expression either. But there is a deep rooted conflict arising from such developed intellect.

The Gemini impulse is characterized by much activity on the mental plane. Its great attraction for the opposite sex is not produced primarily on the physical plane. It is important to note that this impulse is originally asexual. This stage of cosmogenesis is described in Hindu literature in terms of certain 'Prajapatis', the mighty cosmic beings who refuse to do their assigned task of creation because they consider it impure. Astrologically also, Gemini is not considered conducive to human fecundity. The preference for meditative practices by the Prajapatis at this level finds its reflection in Gemini types who are more adjusted to intellectual harmony than physical relationship. On the cosmic plane, it is signified by the development of the mind principle and expressed as the recognition of space and time, which are the result of thought. Time and space are abstract principles that do not have any objective existence of their own. They are produced by the mind of the person. But in this realm of illusion, every form of manifestation exists and fructifies. The third zodiacal impulse is therefore also described as the Creative Illusion or Maya.

Another way of visualizing the Gemini symbol is to consider it as two Tau crosses, one of which is inverted, and both joined by the attraction of opposites. The movement can be either in the realm of spirituality, where the standing Tau is important, or in the realm of materiality, when the Tau is inverted. This situation makes the Gemini born either very interested in spiritual problems or much involved in materiality as, for example, becoming a successful businessman. As egoism is an important aspect of the inverted Tau, such persons can be so full of pride that they can consider themselves as powerful as the Divine itself. In cases where the standing Tau is predominant, there is empathy for fellow human beings and identification with the universal life can be experienced. The growth of sensitivity, sympathy and human feeling is the radiating impulse between these two extremes.

The Gemini symbol expresses the complex transformation resulting from the differentiation of male and female principles and their unification. Through this emotion and thought, along with egoism and selfishness arises. At this stage pure intelligence is manifested and provides adequate possibilities for the expression of spiritual as well as earthly attainments.

4
CANCER
KARKATA

෨

Cancer, the fourth sign of the zodiac, is represented by two small circles joined by two curved lines ෨ . Under its impulse, the soul scans the dizzy heights of heaven leading to perfection, and looks down as well at the dismal depths of the inferno that contains all human passion and material desire. During the course of this impulse, the spirit develops superb intuitive faculties or the most depraved behavior. The impulse operates over the seven higher as well as the seven lower worlds. The four levels of consciousness*, the four directions of space, or the four heads of Brahma, the cosmic creator, all relate to the sign of Cancer. They cover the entire subjective and objective manifestation stretching from the eternal past to the eternal future. The two circles express that the two different aspects of existence which all creation has to manifest remain united under this impulse, though maintaining their separate identity.

Cancer is ruled by the Moon. The Moon relates to the human psyche, to mind, intelligence and the flight of imagination. The radiation from this planet sustains life on Earth. This sustenance is provided to physical, psychic as well as higher levels of existence. The Moon has the power to induce the development of spiritual faculties as well to give powers to perform black magic. The curved lines in the Cancer symbol represent the quality of this basic urge. The upward bulging line expresses the possibility of developing the finer feelings emanating from the depth of one's inner being, while the downward bulging line shows the material cravings which involve the individual in the search for power. Cancer thereby is associated with much mystery.

Cancer is symbolized by a crab. This ten-footed crustacean is a very insignificant looking creature and like the emblem representing this sign

---

*   Jagriti (wakefulness), Swapna (state of dreaming), Sushupti (deep or profound sleep) and Samadhi (profound, abstract meditation or Turya).

does not appear at first glance to be a profound insignia of cosmic evolution. Both these symbols, however, succinctly express the great depth of this impulse.

A crab dwells in water as well as on land but is neither found in deep waters nor far from the shore. It has ten feet. It sheds its hard crust when it grows too large for it. It is shy by nature. All these have a close resemblance with important characteristics of the fourth sign. The ten legs stand for the ten sense organs; the five sense organs operating on the subjective plane and the five motor organs functioning on the objective. The development of a wide field of action occurs with the fourth cosmic impulse. The life on earth corresponds to the physical level of the individual, and the watery condition of the crab's life corresponds to the emotional, the psychic or the subjective aspects. Human beings while functioning on these planes do not move very far to explore the spiritual depths. The continuity of the individual soul through various incarnations is symbolized by the crab shedding its shell. Man by nature is also very shy like a crab, reluctant to come into close contact with the denizens of the spiritual world.

Cancer makes the manifestation of time and space possible on the objective plane. It creates heaven and hell and bestows on man appropriate vehicles to continue his journey. Continuity in evolution through reincarnation is provided under this impulse of cosmic manifestation. The ten feet of the crab also refer to the number ten*, which in occult terminology stands for perfection. The purpose of all physical and psychic experience through the mechanism of reincarnation is to carry the individual to his archetypal perfection. It also points to the fact that perfection is the inherent nature of all things. It is this inborn quality of perfection that assures the success of the gradual unfoldment of one's potentials through the course of cosmic evolution.

For predictive purposes also, the symbol of the crab is suggestive. Cancer born persons are generally shy. The crab is sensitive to the slightest noise or movement in its vicinity. Cancerians are nervous, sensitive and impressionable. The crab is not poisonous, it is even edible. Human beings under this sign are seldom violent in temperament. They will even sacrifice their lives for their cause. The shining eyes of the crab remind us of the gracious nature of the Cancer born personality.

---

*   See Capricorn. Cancer is closely related to Capricorn; both are counterparts to each other.

The aquatic nature of the crab suggests that this stage of manifestation has not yet severed its connection with its original element, that it still maintains the purity of its nature. It acquires power to adapt itself while maintaining its continuity of consciousness. In spite of the crab residing also on land, the predominance of its aquatic nature suggests that evolution here has not yet reached the stage where it can function effectively on a fully differentiated physical level. It still has its repose in the great receptacle of human souls, 'Hiranyagarbha'. Differentiation has reached a stage of universalization expressed by the medieval concept of Anima Mundi, the World Soul, but the individualization necessary for the production of separate human egos has not yet occurred.

The fourth zodiacal impulse bestows a unique quality: it imprints the different forms of manifestation with their future possibilities and ultimate destiny. Cancer stands for all latent potentials as well as the ultimate goal of every form of creation. It induces the gradual unfoldment of all the different states of consciousness and dimensions of existence. The shining eyes of the crab gazing at distant objects points to the connection between the latent depths and the ultimate goal. One generally observes that Cancerians have a vision. They give more attention to what could be rather than to what is. This is true with regard to their approach to human relationships as well as practical situations.

The circle on the left of the Cancer symbol represents the latent potential of the individual while the one on the right stands for its ultimate flowering. The evolutionary journey of the individual enables his latent faculties represented by the fourth sign to finally reach their archetypal form indicated by the tenth sign. The course of evolution from the fourth to the tenth signs, which weaves through several zodiacal impulses, is represented by the unity of the two circles with their curved lines. The linking arcs represent the impulses which connect the two circles that themselves show the duality within the total evolutionary journey of the individual. The Golden Egg, or Hiranyagarbha of Vedantic philosophy, itself the seed and the goal, appears through the symbol of Cancer.

The left circle emerging from the top, proceeding to the right and curving downward represents the energy contained in the Cosmic Mother's womb from which the evolutionary journey begins. The downward curvature at its end indicates that all experiences derive from the consciousness which guides the soul towards the realization of its ultimate destiny indicated by the circle on the right. The left circle contains the faculties to be developed. The inherent attraction of the latent faculties for their archetypal perfection shown by the circle on the right determines the evolutionary path. The archetype is always sending impulses to the incarnating soul to guide it on. The circles symbolize perfection, rhythmic movement and wholeness. The fourth zodiacal impulse as well as the tenth are associated with wholeness and the rhythmical movement of the cosmic manifestation in a special manner. The right circle is linked with the arc touching it from the bottom suggesting that the residues of experience during the process of their transmutation into the Pure Essence, have to pass through a series of changes bringing the entity into deeper layers of materiality.

The two circles of the symbol show that Cancer represents a mini-world of creative energies. At this level of manifestation there exists concretized duality as spirit and matter, form and consciousness, latency and full blossomed potency. Cancer has the unique quality of extending its realm of operation from the lowest depth of human experience to the highest bliss attainable. It is the stage where intelligence has polarized, duality has become manifest and the outward evolutionary journey into the realm of time and space has begun. In actual life, one finds that the Cancer born person has a wide range in which he can function. No attainment is too high or no degradation too low. Cancerians can feel at ease in the realm of matter, physical action and social relationship. At the same time they can operate in the psychic world, the plane of thought and emotions, and on the spiritual plane as well.

5
LEO
SIMHA

$$\Omega$$

The fifth sign of the zodiac, Leo, is indicated by a lion, which is the meaning of its Sanskrit name 'Simha'. Emblematically, it is represented by a circle connected with an upward curving arc at its right top corner which tapers downward with a slight twist to the right Ω. The lion and the emblem for the Leo stand for the stage of individualization. The roaring lion indicates the individual soul separated from Anima Mundi or the world soul. It roams around the forest of chaos, the Great Illusion or Maya, and ultimately accomplishes its destiny by realizing itself. These symbols refer to the root of the divine creative impulse. Leo enables the inner being to manifest on the outer plane. This externalization of the subjective essence is the outcome of the Divine creative impulse. Several stages have to be crossed before its final result is achieved.

At this stage in cosmogenesis, the Divine essence assumes a creative aspect like the vital cosmic electricity named Fohat in occult literature, the thread of primordial light. During its operation, it enters the labyrinth of chaotic matter and runs through various planes of manifestation, tying itself into knots and moving in spirals, establishing various force centers to finally emerge as the universe and Man. This is a long pilgrimage during which much change occurs between the primeval potential and its appearance on the mundane level. In predictive astrology, as a result of the fifth cosmic impulse, the child takes shape in the mother's womb, ideas in an author's mind concretize on paper, and the artist expresses his inner inspiration in outer form.

In occult literature, 'Fohat' is the active (male) potency of the 'Shakti', the female creative power in nature. In this context, the relationship between male potency and female reproductive power can be approached a little differently. According to the Hindus there is a bi-polar expression of the primordial energy, one side of which acts on the other to produce creation. The Hegelian thesis, which interacts with its antithesis and results in synthesis, is a reflection of the same cosmic creative process. The passive form of energy is as important for creation as is the active one.

The passive energy, known in Yoga philosophy as Prakriti or Nature, is the means of expression for the active energy, Spirit or Purusha. Prakriti in Hindu mythology is the mother of all men. The goddesses in their different names and forms are aspects of the passive cosmic energy. They are the creative agents of mother nature. Such important Hindu Goddesses are Uma, Durga, Kali and Yogamaya. Several have a lion as their vehicle. The incongruity of feminine power, the embodiment of delicate feeling, associated with a fierce animal, the lion, the king of the forests, reveals the relationship between Fohat and the feminine cosmic energy. The lion as the vehicle for the Goddess refers to two special responsibilities entrusted to the feminine energy in nature, power and grace in the creative process.

All ancient religions give great importance to the lion and emphasize its regal splendor. It is not merely the graceful curves of the fierce animal which attracted the ancient seers to it. The spiritual power capable of transforming human nature into something divine was associated with the lion. The lion has a highly sensitized natural force which has a tremendous impact on the psyche. The lion possesses great courage and electrical energy concealed within it. This inner vitality makes it the ruler of the forest. The power concealed in the physical form of this medium sized animal enables it to command allegiance of even the largest animals. The lion in relation to the cosmic creative power refers to the latent energy in Hiranyagarbha or the primordial egg, which requires the impact of the primordial light for its activation. Leo, as the fifth zodiacal impulse, represents this primordial light which works on the individual to arouse him to the state of creativity. The inner immortal ruler residing in the sacred cave of the heart is the real source of creativity by churning his eternal depth.

Much of the characteristics of Leo can be understood relative to its animal symbol. The lion does not waste its vital energy or virility. It copulates rarely and only for reproductive purposes. Leo Ascendants are generally less sexually active than others but when they are it commonly results in impregnation. The external form of a lion is often dirty and smells unpleasant. The animal is self-centered, but inwardly, it is active, attentive and energetic. Considering the human being in totality, his external nature is ordinary, imperfect and impure, quite different from the inner being who is ever shining, the true Self beyond time and space. The lion represents the individual whose external self resembles the unattractive form of the lion while the inner Self corresponds to the lion's inner power.

The geometrical representation of Leo indicates its essential features. The circle stands for wholeness, for the Golden Egg, the Hiranyagarbha, containing the totality of the evolutionary potential. At this stage of cosmic generation, the hard crust of the individual egg breaks and the energy contained within flows out. The individualized energy capsule, or soul which materializes itself, is symbolized by the downward curving arc of the circle. The purpose of involvement in matter is to gain experience. For this the soul undergoes a series of births and deaths and finally returns to its source. The last phase of the journey, when the pilgrim turns his gaze homeward and begins the path of return, is symbolized by the upward curved arc at the right of the symbol. The symbol as a whole represents the entire pilgrimage of the soul. The fifth zodiacal impulse thereby contains within itself the course of the soul's journey from beginning to end.

The Leo emblem shows the relationship between the manifestation and its original source. The circle is perfection, fullness, the totality of latent possibilities. The evolutionary impulse is depicted by the upward jutting of the descending arc. The outer crust of the Golden Egg is broken by the creative impulse of the individualizing soul. With the breaking of the circle, which also implies the destruction of its pristine perfection, the evolutionary pilgrimage begins. The initial phase of this movement is involvement in matter. During the successive phases of the materialization process, the life force represented by the arc moves deeper into matter until the urge to return to the source dawns on the soul. The outward turned hook at the end of the arc shows that the ultimate goal of all manifestation is its return to its original source.

Leo born individuals have a great creative urge. Its level and form depends upon the influences impinging on the individual. Often, the urge to create is just for its own sake and not directed to a specific goal. If the creative impulse functions on the physical level, there will be procreation. If the impulse is on the mental plane, there is emotional and intellectual creation.

Leo shows the tremendous *urge* to concretize that so far has been unmanifest. This concretization of the universal life force is linked with the process of human individualization when the human soul is separated from the group soul. At this point, one stage of evolution is differentiated in a radical way from another. This is symbolized by the single circle contained in the emblem with a loop at its top, as if the life force is coming out of the wholeness of the circle. Astrologically, one finds that Leo ascendants usually feel good, right and happy as long as they are involved in creative activity, whether for themselves, their family or society.

6
VIRGO
KANYA
♍

Under Virgo the soul becomes deeply involved in matter, which is necessary to accelerate the evolutionary movement. However, such an involvement produces physical hardships. The sixth sign produces difficult conditions in order to externalize the latent attributes of the soul. At this stage, the feminine creative principle differentiated during the previous zodiacal impulse is given a direction to follow. The new task requires the material cross to be borne with a sense of dedication and commitment. It thereby leads the inner being to experience limitation in its functioning. Virgo thus represents the crucifixion of the cosmic man. Under the Virgo impulse, the being of time, Kala Purusha, is nailed to the cross of matter. Material attachment creates a strong physical bondage, but in the inner nature, the manifesting soul is aware of the possibility of liberation from them. At the sixth zodiacal impulse, consciousness is fettered but possesses an awareness that the bondage can be removed by understanding of the relationship between spirit and matter. This understanding often makes the individual born under Virgo sorrowful. Such a person feels helpless and craves to find a way out of the labyrinth in which he finds himself.

Virgo is represented by a virgin. Its diagram shows three vertical lines joined at the top by an undulating line which resembles a serpent with a cross tucked to its tail ♍.

In world religions, the symbol of the Virgin is common. Hindu mythology describes the celestial virgin as the earth, Aditi (celestial space) and Parvati (the consort of Lord Shiva). As such, she is worshipped as the universal Mother, Jagadamba. In Greek mythology, she is Pallas Athena who springs from the head of Zeus full grown and armed. The Romans knew her as Minerva, the goddess of wisdom and the arts. The gospels of St. Matthew and St. Luke consider that the Virgin Mary conceives Jesus by the power of the Holy Spirit. No less significant is Sita, the wife of Rama, the hero of the *Ramayana* and incarnation of Vishnu. She was born fully grown to King Janaka while he was performing his yearly ritual ploughing of a field. These allusions refer to the Virgin as of immaculate birth. They are connected with Divine knowledge and the personification of the wisdom hidden in nature. All these figures undergo much suffering in order to assist the working out of the Divine Plan.

It is worth noting that Virgo is the only human symbol among the various signs of the zodiac except that for that of Gemini. Gemini represents a twin which is more an abstraction and is also, like Virgo, owned by Mercury, the planet of intelligence and intellect. As the third sign, Gemini is tenth from the sixth sign, Virgo. This implies, according to Hindu astrology, that the fructification of Gemini representing the mind is made possible by Virgo. Such a relationship shows the importance of Virgo. Bestowal of a human form to the sixth zodiacal impulse implies that the manifesting soul has now acquired the various human sheaths with their dual purposes of protecting the inner man and enabling it to express itself. By providing this special instrument to the manifesting consciousness, the Virgo impulse while accelerating the materialization process provides it adequate resources to establish control over its various faculties.

Virgo refers to a maiden, not a married woman. The impulse flowing through this sign represents the feminine aspect of nature unalloyed by other influences. The impulse at this stage produces an electrified field with a special kind of power which is neither active nor passive. For the activation of latent faculties, the influx of an active agent is necessary. For any kind of reproduction, the mother must be associated with the father. The primeval female energy unmixed with any impact is known in Yoga philosophy as Prakriti, nature. She is worshipped as the virgin whose pure potential allows for the fructification of all human perfections. In order to maintain her pristine purity, the Virgin Nature or Virgin Mother has to conceal herself in several layers of materialization. She has to acquire the different sheaths that surround the human being and the manifested universe and thereby must suffer and forego her inherent freedom. These conditions make the sixth zodiacal sign produce sorrow for the manifesting soul from the outer or the physical standpoint.

In the manifest world, Virgo points to the divine energy lying deeply entrenched in matter. As a result of the relationship between the outer sheath of matter and the inner nature of purity, the balance between inner and outer conditions for those of Virgo Ascendants is very important. If the harmony between the two is disturbed, which is usually the case during the involutionary course of the individual, disease arises on the physical level and enmity in social relationships. If balance between the inner and outer counterparts of the individual is established, it gives power over the six primary forces in nature*. Virgo, in its role of the celestial virgin, has to bear tremendous suffering for the mistakes of her worldly children, but in her divine status she has enormous gifts to bestow on them as well. The Virgo impulse makes us unhappy in the external, physical life, but can also grant great healing or spiritual powers if we direct our energy towards helping others.

The character of this sign is described in its diagram. The geometrical symbol for Virgo consists of three parts; the three vertical lines ♍, the serpent-like undulating line at the upper left ♍, and the cross attached to its end (bottom right) ♍. The vertical lines refer to consciousness and the masculine principle in nature. They show the positive aspect of creative energy which is the dynamic, direct, active agent. Yoga philosophy describes the nature of these active agents as Rajas (activity), Tamas (inertia), and Sattwa (harmony), which we see in the three vertical lines. These three lines also refer to the three states of non-physical consciousness as dream, deep sleep, and pure consciousness transcending all changing states (turiya or samadhi). By establishing control over these states through a perfect understanding of their workings, one becomes liberated.

The undulating serpent-like line on the top of the vertical lines depicts the incongruity in the nature of Virgo, which is evident from its anxiety and psychological complexities along with its inner serenity and purity. The serpent is an ancient symbol with many meaning. In general, it is a symbol of both wisdom and the wise. It stands for the universe of manifestation as the ever present electric energy within it. When stretched out, the energy operates in time and space affecting both involutionary and evolutionary processes. The serpent biting its tail represents eternity. The serpent stretched out expresses the ceaseless destruction and reformation of matter. On the top of the three vertical lines in Virgo's symbol, the serpent describes the rhythmic changes of forms and swelling of latent capabilities. Together, the serpent and the vertical lines stand for Siddhis (perfections) in different realms achieved as a result of subjugating and disciplining the six kinds of energies. The serpent stands for both destructive and constructive energies. In the case of Virgo it shows the harnessing of latent masculine creative forces. This attainment can make the individ-

---

*   Parasakti (the supreme power generating light and heat), Jnanasakti (the power of knowledge and wisdom), Ichhasakti (will power), Kriyasakti (the power of thought and volition), Kundalinisakti (the serpent fire) and Mantrasakti (the power of mantra aroused by letter, speech and music).

ual an agent of death-like destruction, but properly directed, it can unlock the secret wisdom of nature which is productive of immense goodness.

The tucking of the cross at the end of the serpent's tail refers to the limitations of this sign. The cross is an insignia of matter. The cross in this symbol refers to materialization and the submerging of the primeval consciousness under the physical sheaths. This extensive nature of matter is the greatest sorrow of the Virgin, Mother Earth. Under Virgo, nature's finer forces can become veiled. The primeval purity can be lost, and the destructive and unspiritual side of nature become prominent.

The sixth zodiacal impulse produces materialization of the cosmic electrical power. It is manifest as the natural law of motion, of action and reaction, which acting on the life principle becomes the law of karma. Properly regulated, this impulse is capable of harmonizing the various forces in nature, both subjective and objective. It enables the individual to attain various 'siddhis' and thereby material limitations are transcended. The serpent over the vertical lines, implying transcendence over the various levels of consciousness, can give the knowledge of nature's secrets. But there is always a strong tendency resulting from this impulse to be weighed down by one's material propensities as the serpent above the vertical line is pulled down by the cross tucked to its tail ♍.

Under Virgo, nature's finer forces are placed deep under the various levels of manifestation. When the human mind develops creativity as a result of the fifth zodiacal impulse, it penetrates deeper into the environment in which it is placed. In the process, it acquires knowledge and power of the hidden sides of things. The serpent in the symbol points to this unsuspected spiritual aspect of life. The difficulties experienced under the Virgo impulse are due to the fact that all actions have equal and opposite reactions. As the individual affected by this impulse must be intensely creative, it is necessary to encounter such reactions. Such reactions however will be according to the level of intelligence functioning at the moment. Creativity, materiality, dedication to spiritual goals and resulting personal sorrow are the chief traits of Virgo Ascendants. Virgo is in fact the materialization of the cosmic electrical power and the expression of the natural law of action and reaction, the law of karma, which manifests through it.

LIBRA
TULA

Libra is universally represented as a balance. In Sanskrit, several names are given to it: 'Tauli', one who weighs; 'Vanika', the merchant; 'Yukta', what is joined; and 'Tula', a scale. Its diagram is formed by a double horizontal line, the upper line with a semi-circular bulge in the middle ♎. At this point in evolution the Divine Spark becomes fully entrenched in matter. The first six signs of the zodiac involve the immersion of the spirit in matter, known as involution. The second six give the involved soul the task of breaking through its bondage to matter to return to the pure spirit, or spiritual evolution. As Libra stands at the crucial juncture separating the materialization trend from spiritualization, it is said to be a kind of balance. It joins the involutionary or outgoing path with the evolutionary or ingoing path.

Those who have seen Indian dance note that the dancers must often balance themselves in difficult positions. The cosmic dance of Lord Shiva as Nataraja and the yin-yang symbol of Chinese philosophy display this delicate balance. The legend around the dance of Shiva is very profound. In this dance stance (mudra), Shiva, with flames raging all around his body, puts his feet on the Goddess* who represents the passive cosmic energy, and becomes completely still, as if stunned, though inwardly remaining highly alert. This standstill posture of Nataraja represents the stage of manifestation when the powerful cosmic energy, flowing outwardly without seeking anything for itself, is activizated to such a high speed that it takes the appearance of complete stillness. As a cosmic dancer, Nataraja is engulfed in radiant flames. Essentially, fire is the

---

*   Virgo, the virgin, is a synonym of Goddess or 'Devi'. Virgo produces Libra. This suggests that in Shiva's dance when he, as the embodiment of cosmic prime energy, places his foot on the Goddes, then Virgo's impulses are over and he begins to radiate Libra's impulses.

life-force manifest in the different forms of existence, at all levels from
the subtle to the gross.

As a symbol for Libra, Nataraja denotes the complete submerging of
the divine essence in matter. Aries denotes the primeval subjectivity prior
to the manifestation whereas Libra represents the stage when the primeval
essence is completely absorbed in materiality. In Aries, spirit is pronounced and materiality is subordinate to it, while in Libra matter is
predominant and spirit subordinate to it.

Nataraja at this stage of the cosmic dance puts his right foot out to
crush the dwarf, the symbol of ignorance. At the same time the sacred
Ganges, the personification of divine knowledge and life sustaining water,
flows down. Ignorance symbolized as a dwarf arises from materialism.
The various impulses generated so far immerse the soul in deeper layers
of matter causing greater degrees of ignorance. This involvement is
greatest under Libra. From this level the upward movement begins.
During this phase of metamorphosis, three main currents flow. The first
makes the individual like a pig in the mud, in complete ignorance of the
supremacy of spirit over matter. In the second, the individual is attached
to materiality and the pleasures of the senses are dominant, but as his
intelligence is aroused and he becomes aware of his lost purity, he
becomes thirsty for his spiritual goal as for the pure water of the Ganges.
The third brings about the downpour of pure wisdom. Libra represents
both ignorance and wisdom, the former in completion and the latter in its
beginning stage. At this stage, materialism is waning and spiritual awareness waxing.

The Chinese yin-yang symbol expresses the balance between the two
opposing forces driving forward the evolutionary pilgrim. The two sides,
black and white, are so balanced that one drives the other in constant
motion. Under Libra, individuals irrespective of their geographical, ethnic
or social differences, experience momentous events in life which destroy
their attachment to matter and awaken their spiritual knowledge. Yet if
the soul is not ready, material pleasure is bestowed on them so as to
saturate their craving and help bring it to an end. In either case, the final
goal is the turn to the spiritual quest, so that the limitations of the dwarf
are well recognized.

Libra stands for dynamic balance. At this stage, external stillness is
counterbalanced by inner movement. As the symbols indicate, perfect
balance exists under Libra despite the action of opposing forces. This
principle has wide implications. It represents the balance between day and
night, hot and cold, black and white, the clouds and the Sun, all beautifully
poised in the circular disc representing the evolutionary course of manifestation. It is not that the opposing forces are completely neutralized, but

both are in readiness for action and equally powerful. For this reason, it is difficult to predict whether Libra born persons will pursue the paths of materialism or spirituality. They can slide towards the enjoyment of worldly pleasures or they may proceed onward to the realization of their inner purpose. Libra is the stage where the thirst for material indulgence is the most intense. At this point, the materializing spark has reached its deepest point. Depending upon the experiences gathered, the soul may linger at this point dwelling on the delights of matter, or it may take the next step and begin its return journey. There is no greater material depth to which the soul can sink.

The Libra diagram is a double horizontal line, the upper line having a semi-circular bulge in the middle. As we have seen earlier, the horizontal line describes the negative or Prakriti aspect of manifestation. The lower line shows complete submergence in matter. Whatever interaction of this impulse with the external world, the basic substratum is that of materiality represented by the horizontal line. Even in the Nataraja dance, the dwarf supports Nataraja, thereby emphasizing the foundation of materiality for all the activities of this stage. The upper line with the spiritual bulge gives a balance to this line. It is the outflow of the Ganges from the locks of the Lord Shiva and represents the spiritual urge. The upper line symbolizes the volcanic fire inside the being. External tranquility accompanied by internal strife without losing psychological composure is expressed by this geometrical representation. Librans have a deceptive external composure in which a fire burns creating turmoil on the psychic level. Even the spirituality aroused at this stage is based on some kind of thirst or reaction.

From an occult point of view, Libra has great importance. Material and spiritual forces finely equipoised has the possibility of easy distortion if the individual can somehow influence them. To avoid such an eventuality, the various features of this stage of evolution have been concealed. The geometrical symbol has also succeeded in deflecting the public gaze. The perfect straightness of the horizontal line contains within it the possibility of arousing all the powers latent in nature. It stands for the electric energy in its septenary differentiation. The seven planets, the seven life-breaths (Pranas*), the seven flames** from which arise the seven rays of human temperment, the seven colors of the spectrum are all contained in the horizontal line. The spiritual bulge shows its susceptibility to the slightest human effort. The right impulse leads the individual onward, but any wrong step will create a retrograde movement or sliding back in evolution. Such a fall from the spiritual possibility has many times been spoken of as descent into the blazing inferno. The extrication of the soul from such an infernal fire is described as almost impossible. The seventh zodiacal impulse provides one of the most powerful and at the same time most dangerous possibilities to mankind.

---

*   The seven Prana Vayus are: 1) Aavaha or Ugra, 2) Nivaha or Bhima, 3) Udwaha or Dhanta, 4) Samvaha or Dhuni, 5) Wivaha Sasahwa, 6) Pravaha or Abhiyugwa and 7) Parivaha or Vikshita. They are associated with different deities and have differentiated functions.

**   The seven flames of fire are named 1) Karali, 2) Dhumini, 3) Sweta, 4) Lohita, 5) Neela-lohita, 6) Suwarna and 7) Padma-raga. These flames are also known by other names.

8
SCORPIO
VRISHCHIKA
♏

Scorpio shows Divine potential. The cosmic creative energy, which has become entrenched in the material sheaths, begins to realize its capacity for expansion as the material sheath begins to be rent asunder. With this realization comes the desire to unveil its essential nature and its original glory. Having crossed the Libra stage of cosmic evolution where the Divine Spark is immersed in the deepest level of involution and the two opposing forces of materialism and spirituality are blended, the soul now experiences the inner urge to break the material encasement to enjoy its inherent freedom. Several important changes take place in the basic nature of the evolving soul. It begins to reshape its reaction to the world itself. It begins to weaken its material sheaths. It starts to cognize its latent possibilities, and experiencing new powers being developed, a feeling of arrogance may arise. In all such changes, the basic factor is the craving to regain one's primeval glory and the ensuing struggle between opposing forces which are readjusted in the process. The equipoise is disturbed and a new alignment in a spiritual direction becomes important. In the process, many psychological problems and conflicts arise as the birth pangs of a new awakening. These complex factors are difficult to describe. The ancient seers thought it appropriate to depict them by the symbol of a scorpion. The geometrical emblem for this sign is more explicit than the visual symbol of the scorpion.

In lower latitudes, the stars of the sign Scorpio appear like a big question mark or like the spinal cord. The resemblance of this cluster with a scorpion is very close. Both the spinal cord and the scorpion refer to the concealed power which when rightly developed bestows tremendous power. They represent the Divine potential, yet unmanifest but requiring suitable conditions for its expression. In yogic literature the activation of the Kundalini located at the base of the spine brings about such transformation. Traveling through the various chakras linked with the spinal cord, it gives psychic power and changes the nature of one's consciousness.

The scorpion is like a reptile which resides in secret holes and is found mainly in warmer parts of the world. It has a long, narrow, segmented tail that terminates in a venomous stinger. The Serpent Fire, which is full of dangerous possibilities if aroused by the unwary, is also located at the base of the spinal cord. A special characteristic of the scorpion is that the male scorpion, on finding female, engages itself in a kind of primitive courtship consisting of grasping the hands of the female with his own and rubbing her tail against his. After copulation, the male is often attacked by the female and devoured unless he manages to escape.

Whether we consider the scorpion or the emblem of Scorpio, we find ourselves in the realm of the occult in order to discover the nature of the impulse flowing through this sign. Scorpio is also associated with a hole. Whenever we come across the symbol of a deep opening in the earth, a cavity, a hiding place, or hole there is reference to the mystic power concealed in every human individual. These references suggest the possibility of unveiling the subjective reality concealed within the objective covering. The energy dwelling in such a cavity, whether represented by a serpent or a scorpion, is the vital energy which ensouls every form of creation. The mythological dweller of the hole is Vasuki, the Serpent Naga, used in the churning of the cosmic ocean. The churning was carried out by the gods and the demons, implying the interaction of positive and negative poles of diffcrentiated energy. It is also the interaction between Yin and Yang. The prime object of this churning process was to obtain divine nectar of immortality. Once this nectar was obtained, or when this vision of cosmic unity or truth hidden in every form of creation is realized, there is no more immersion in materiality or ignorance. Once this nectar of immortality is partaken of, the individual attains perfection and the highest siddhis. It bestows perfect control over the powers of nature. This power is desired both for altruistic goals as well as personal ends. The difference between the Gods and demons depends upon this difference in their motivation.

Libra represents the urge of the individual to explore the inner recess of his being in order to attain and wrest out the latent possibilities in him. The seventh zodiacal impulse arouses aspiration while under the eighth impulse begins the active quest. The churning of the ocean begins at this stage. The individual's life is in turmoil. The material existence, though one indulges in it, no longer satisfies. The female scorpion, though she succumbs to impregnation by the male, rebels against this situation and wishes to destroy the cause of her immersion in materiality. Scorpio brings a kind of storm, a terrible war within oneself. In this process, no one can with certainty predict the final outcome. The venom or the nectar are both possibile.

Libra stands for the storage of the primeval spark at the lowest strata of the material sheaths of which the cosmos is composed. Scorpio refers to the recognition of the Divine Spark, 'the precious jewel' hidden within oneself and all forms of manifestation and the strife to uncover it. Often a serpent is considered a symbol of this impulse. The undulatory character of the line above the vertical lines is suggestive of a serpent. The arrow at its tail indicates the spiritual aspiration for obtaining the serpent fire, or the wisdom of the inner teachings. The precious jewel of wisdom is concealed in every individual at the root of the spine or tail of the scorpion. As this jewel is guarded by divine powers very jealously, aspirants endeavoring to obtain it face the mortal danger of being stung. The secrecy about the jewel and the place of its location make the scorpion symbol for the eighth zodiacal impulse more suggestive. The anthill, the cavity and the secret places symbolized by this sign as well as the scorpion and the serpent refer to the caves and hideouts where great teachers prepare their disciples for initiation which bestows on them control over nature's secret powers, or the nectar of life.

The geometrical emblem of Scorpio is much like the one for Virgo ♏. The main difference is that Scorpio has an arrow attached to the serpent-like line instead of the cross as in Virgo. The difference between an arrow and a cross reveals the characteristic features of the two signs. The energy nailed at the cross expresses the nature of Virgo while the same energy struggling for its release is Scorpio. The arrow at the tail of the serpent points to the urge for spiritual development. It refers to the energy for the soul's onward journey. The serpent with its restless urge for liberation implies that the fire located at the base of the spine is ready to commence its upward course. During this sojourn the Kundalini must traverse the seven chakras to reach the crown chakra so that the individual consciousness is merged in the universal life-force and the separate self returns to the All. The winding course which takes the Kundalini through these seven summits finally releases the individual from material bondage. The restlessness to commence this pilgrimage is denoted by the arrow.

As this path is full of danger, the activated Scorpio impulse, if not accompanied by adequate spiritual preparation, altruism and self-discipline, can be very destructive. The strong urge towards liberation and the occult path induces the individual in a direction which ultimately fulfills his natural destiny. This is possible when the full splendor of the power concealed in the cavity is released, and the Kundalini reaches its final abode in the thousand petalled Lotus of the head. When the impulse is strong for attaining this goal, it induces the person towards purification of the various sheaths and the cultivation of austerity. When these virtues become natural, one becomes an ascetic. Oherwise, under the strong impulse of Scorpio the development of these attributes takes place through a difficult path whereon one suffers disappointment, frustration and an unhappy personal life.

Scorpio by itself is concerned with arousal of the urge towards spiritual freedom. Other situations make the sign, for predictive purposes, pleasant or trying depending upon the purity of the sheaths covering the individual soul.The eighth zodiacal impulse by itself is neutral. It refers only to the movement of the power concealed in the individual and the earth center. If the sheaths are not yet crystalline and translucent, the release of these hidden energies may give intense selfishness, an exaggerated sense of pride, much personal aggrandizement and intense destructive proclivities. Release of the secret power is directly linked with annihilation of personal self, which is a kind of death. Therefore, the eighth house is considered to be the house of death. The eighth impulse to a great extent produces death for the individual enmeshed in matter, but with the death of the material nature is the birth of the cosmic man and universal consciousness. Under the Scorpio impulse, the cosmic man struggles to arise from the material debris where he has been buried to begin his resurrection.

9
SAGITTARIUS
DHANUS
↑

Sagittarius, the ninth sign of the zodiacal, is represented as a Centaur — a horse with a human head — shooting an arrow. The diagram for it is an arrow pointing upward with a cross tucked to its lower end ↑. Its Sanskrit names are 'Dhanvi', an archer; 'Chapam', a bow; and 'Sharasanam', an arrow shooter. These symbols indicate the transformation of matter into spiritual consciousness. Such a consciousness arises from the activation of the chakras or subtle spinal centers.

The ninth impulse is concerned with transformation. The psyche of the individual is weighed down by material desires, past 'samskaras'. The cross tucked at the end of the arrow represents these attachments. These are called 'loka vasana', the attachments that arise from attraction to the outer world and distort our true nature. The Sagittarius impulse works to dissociate us from such attachments and make us aspire to the higher goal to which the arrow is aimed. In the process of rising above the thraldom of matter toward the goal of spiritual purity, the nature of man must be radically transformed. This aspiration towards the unknown releases an outpouring of nature's finer forces which produce the required change. It is this downpour of energy which enables the sprouting plant to break the hard crust of the seed*, or the embryonic chicken to break its covering shell. This impulse is essential for the successful completion of the cycle of destiny whereby the life-spark embedded in every form of manifestation is able to come forth. The symbols assigned to Sagittarius describe how this impulse operates.

The Sanskrit word Dhanvin stands for Arjuna, the archer, the hero of *Mahabharata* who had Lord Krishna as his charioteer during the battle of Kurukshetra. Arjuna symbolizes the aspirant for enlightenment. He is considered the very embodiment of humanity endeavoring to raise itself

---

*   Sagittarius is auspiciously related to Aries, representing primeval birth.

to divinity, though still beset with the confused feelings and temptations of the material world. His relationship with Krishna is that of family, friend and guide. This refers to the Divine ancestry of the human soul. The Supreme is always friendly to us and ever guiding us. The discovery of our spiritual goal and the recognition of the ever present divine guidance within us happens simultaneously. With this understanding the psychology of the individual is changed and his life becomes spiritually oriented. The epithet of Dhanvin was given to Arjuna when Krishna manifested his Divine nature to him to induce him to strive for his higher destiny. The dawn of this recognition is signifed by Sagittarius.

Chapam, the string of a bow, represents the physical and psychological tension which an individual experiences at the dawn of spiritual illumination. Inwardly, he finds a link with divine consciousness, but physically he remains immersed in material duties. This contradiction is very disturbing. The flash of the cosmic vision wherein the individual perceives his universal nature intensifies this conflict. Yet the aspiration towards this vision provides the energy to bear the hardships on the path of self-discovery. Modern psychology also recognizes that such 'peak experiences', which may last for no more than a moment, can radically alter the individual and his whole pattern of life. The experience and following readjustment to everyday life make the individual very tense. His feet are on the ground besmirched with mud, but inwardly his emotion and aspiration are aroused to attain the highest purity. Such psychological tension is like the string on the bow from which the arrow is to be shot to the distant goal. Under the Sagittarius impulse, the individual strives to fulfill his spiritual obligations in order to gain this inner goal.

The symbol of a Centaur expresses the same characteristic of Sagittarius. Centaurs in Greek mythology are a race of beings part horse and part man, who dwelt in the mountains of Thessaly and Arcadia. They are either engaged in drawing the car of Dionysus, the Greek god of creativity, of the mystic wine and drama who represents the creative activities of the higher life, or they are bound and ridden by Eros, the god of lust, of drunkenness and sensuality, who represents the creative activities of the lower life. Their living in the mountains alludes to their connection with the realm of higher consciousness. The tension on the bow, or the preparedness of an archer, are psychological states created due to the conflict between the lower and higher forces. The Centaurs Pholus and Chiron, who dwell at the foot of Mount Pelion, are famous for their wisdom and knowledge of the healing arts. This indicates that the centaur operates under two opposing forces: one represented by drunkenness, inhospitality and slavery to passion, and the other by helpfulness, creativity and fine sensitivity. The Greeks attribute to the centaur both the wantonness suggestive of its feet being in the mud of material attachments and the finer sensitivity of artistic and spiritual awareness, like Arjuna shadowed by doubt in spite of the divine guide being with him. These symbols for Sagittarius do not merely show the interplay of the two opposing forces of materiality and spirituality, they are also important as a transmuting impulse. The horse in man is the libido, which as creative energy immersed in ignorance, expressed as animal passion, needs transmutation.

The arrow aimed towards the spiritual heights is the most revealing feature of Sagittarius. The arrow stands for the urge towards radical tranformation. This urge which alters the nature of the centaur and makes it like wise Phobes and Chiron requires the sublimation of sexual passion into universal love and the direction of the yogic perfections, siddhis, attained under Scorpio toward the good of all. This transmutation begins with Sagittarius.

In the emblem of Sagittarius, an arrow with a cross attached to its base, the cross stands for matter, and materialization of the creative energy which brings material affluence and the pleasures of life ♐. The cross attached to the arrow refers to the urge towards liberation from the thraldom of this involutionary immersion. When material pleasures exist inwardly while one is attracted towards the higher goal, there is great dissatisfaction. The intensity of the struggle increases as the aspiration for the Real deepens. This impulse leads the individual on his spiritual pilgrimage. As a result of it, there is an upward movement. On this path, the material propensities entrenched in the individual psyche begin to unfold their spiritual content. This heralds a new beginning, a new way of life based on a different understanding of the significance of life. In this upward movement and unfoldment of new intelligence is an inner change which takes the individual closer to perfection, which is often considered as occuring through the grace of God.

How the urge towards liberation is aroused depends upon the maturity gained by the soul and the experiences undergone by it. But, once the vision of the Ultimate Reality has been received, the aspiration toward the final goal becomes irresistable. Following such peak experiences, the individual reorients his efforts towards this realization. This is the stage represented by the shooting of the arrow. It indicates the transformation of the physical, libidinal man into a spiritual entity. At this phase of the divine pilgrimage, a bridge is made between the lower quaternary of the physical, etheric, astral and concrete mental bodies and the higher triad of the *inner Self* (Atma), *intelligence* (Buddhi), and *abstract mental parts of the soul*. At this stage, there is the union between the concrete and abstract, the actual and the ideal, between the objective and subjective counterparts of the being.

Such a transformation vitally affects the life of the individual. At this phase of the soul's growth and development, the individual cannot remain peaceful. Superficial aspects of life, the attainment of material affluence and pleasurable sensations, no longer satisfy the individual. There arises a great discipline in whatever he does. Austerity in every sphere of life becomes his guiding principle. This austerity is the life of penance, 'tapas', under whose fire everything is transformed into a spiritual reality. The complexity of this impulse, unfolding itself in a special way for each individual, makes its description difficult. Transcending the physical indications of the symbol to its psychic implications, this impulse can be expressed by a few key words. These are penance, fire, aspiration, dissatisfaction, perfection, spirituality, discipleship and entry into the secret or inner knowledge.

Anything which leads to the transformation of matter into spirit is within the zone of operation of this sign. Its extensive scope made ancient Indian astrologers relate the Sagittarius impulse with the nine planets, nine jewels, the nine geniuses in the court of the great king Vikramaditya each of whom represented a special human quality, the nine treasures of Kubera, the God of wealth, the nine emotions as expressed in poetic composition, nine poisons, nine energies and the nine 'Prajapatis' or Creators especially those connected with human evolution. These nine-fold aspects of different areas of life point to the transformation that occurs under the ninth zodiacal sign. Sagitarrius transforms matter into spirit, human limitations into human perfections, and sexual love into healing art. The Sagittarius influence is a great protector and sustainer capable of arousing the finest feelings and aspiration in mankind and the universe.

10
CAPRICORN
MAKARA
$$\text{V}\!\text{S} — \text{ち}$$

Capricorn is generally seen as a goat but other symbols are also assigned to it. As a unicorn, a horse-like creature with a single horn in the center of its forehead, it symbolizes chastity and purity. In Hindu astrology, it is known as Makara which literally means "a crocodile." This word, however, has many implications. Geometrically, this sign is described by a complicated diagram. Of the two emblems related to it, one is a horizontal line terminating with a downward moving arc ending with a loop having an extended arc ち, and the other has a V-shaped beginning whose downward arc convexing to the right VS. Neither of these are simple figures which can easily be interpreted. In predictive astrology also, one finds that Capricorn persons are exceptional in many ways. They are complicated individuals who cannot be easily categorized.

Both the goat and the unicorn reveal the austerity inherent in this sign. The unicorn with a horn in the center of its forehead is a mystic creature. The importance of the activation of the pituitary gland in connection with yogic development is well known. When the sexual energy is transmuted into spiritual power, when the Kundalini in its upward movement reaches the pituitary gland, the yogi attains great psychic powers. Such a development becomes possible due to unification of the personal consciousness with the universal life-force. Under the Sagittarius impulse, the divine vision of the cosmic unity has flashed on the individual and aroused the urge to realize it. This is the transformation of the animal nature into true human qualities. The next impulse under Capricorn provides the bridge between man and the superman. The development of the pituitary gland establishes this link.

In yogic practice, the aspirant attempts to activize this gland deliberately. But, in order to do so, one has to follow strict disciplines. These austerities give great importance to Brahmacharya. Brahmacharya does not merely mean control of sexual functions, but includes the observation of ethical principles. In this regard, the reference to a goat relative to this sign is quite meaningful. The goat is a herbivorous animal with simple habits, symbolic of purity of life. Many ancient sages were compared with the goat. The humility or meekness of a goat is proverbial. Under Capricorn, the qualities of self-sacrifice and renunciation are developed. The goat, seemingly a meek and a weak animal, has tremendous courage and self-confidence which enable it to balance sure-footedly even on precarious mountain precipices. All the austerities under Capricorn are directed to the development of the pituitary gland which leads to direct perception of spiritual reality.

The Sanskrit name Makara reveals the spiritual significance of this sign more pointedly. Makara stands for the crocodile, which is considered one of the most precious treasures of Kubera, the god of riches and the regent of the northern quarter. The hold of the crocodile is so powerful that none except a god can counteract it. The impact of the tenth zodiacal sign is also great, and very little can be done to overcome it or deflect its influence. The Capricorn impulse is so intimately linked with nature's finer forces that the deeper levels of the soul are stirred under its impact, which the outer or the physical being is unable to resist.

The crocodile as a symbol of Capricorn has another meaning. The fourth sign Cancer, represented by a crab, is directly related to this tenth sign opposite it in the zodiac. The crab is an aquatic creature, as is the crocodile. The difference is that the crocodile emerges out of water and generally stays on the bank of a river or sea, while the crab dwells primarily in water and comes to land only occasionally and for a short time. Cancer is connected with the life-force emerging in spiritual evolution to get concretized. In Capricorn this process is reversed. The individualized entity dwells increasingly in the universal life-force. Gradually, he returns to the world soul, anima mundi.

The significance of the crocodile symbol has been discussed in length by T. Subba Rao, the great Indian occultist of the late nineteenth century *(EW pp. 6–15)*. According to him, Makara does not simply refer to the crocodile. It signifies creative intelligence restricting its boundary of operation, thus holding every particle within the manifested universe in its arms so to say. According to him the impulse from the tenth zodiacal sign makes the cosmos and the human being fulfill their destiny. The ultimate goal of the individual is to consciously cooperate in the divine plan of evolution.

The word Makara derives from the same Sanskrit root from which comes such words as Maya, creative illusion; Ma, mother; Manas, mind; and Mahat, cosmic intelligence, each of which relates to the process of forming and holding together the individualized particles of the manifest universe. The second syllable of the word, Kara, refers to the hand, the organs of action, and the idea of holding. Numerically, the value of Ma, the first syllable of the word, is five, corresponding to the five elements of which the cosmos is composed. The word Kara is also a synonym of Bhuja, which means the sides of a triangle and indicates the quality of inscribing an area within its boundary. The five organs of action or five elements hold the particles of the manifest creation within a specific limit thus protecting the cosmos from dissolution.

According to Subba Rao, the word Makara (Panchakaram) stands for a pentagon. This implies that the sign represents "the faces of the universe," which are bound by the pentagon. Continuing with this analogy, he states that the material universe has the figure of a Decahedron, a ten sided figure, for which Sanskrit writers used the word Dashadisha meaning ten directions. The real world of the noumena, the soul of the visible universe, which is the hidden world represented by an icosahedron, a twenty sided figure, is mysteriously related to the visible universe represented by the decahedron. The tenth zodiacal impulse includes within its scope the unified field of the subjective-objective universe, in which human beings must operate with a Divine purpose.

Blavatsky, examining the crocodile symbol of Capricorn, gives further spiritual meanings to it *(SD Vol. IV, pp. 147–151)*. To her also the Sanskrit word Makara does not simply refer to a crocodile but "to a mysterious order of beings known as Dhyanis." Dhyanis are highly evolved beings engaged in deep meditation in order to assist the ideational process of cosmic manifestation. These Dhyanis are connected with the crocodile and their abode is Capricorn. These mystical references relative to Capricorn reveal the immense depth of its influences which exoteric astrologers find difficult to explain. According to Blavatsky, Dhyanis and Makara are convertible terms. The Dhyanis are regarded as the secret guardians of this universe, so Capricorn refers to those guiding influences which hold the universe together and guide it to its destiny. The function of the pituitary gland is also to establish contact with subjective reality and comprehend its expressions as phenomenal attributes.

The two diagrams assigned to this sign approach it from different standpoints. The one beginning with a horizontal line ending in a downward moving curve looping towards the end ♑ indicates that Prakriti or Nature, the feminine aspect of manifestation constituting matter and form, having reached its terminal point is again put to trial. The journey is not finally concluded. It has to continue further, form another realm of manifestation and transcend it. The horizontal line carries the individual and the universe to the goal by merging in divine intelligence and establishing unity with the Dhyanis ♑. On reaching this stage of manifestation, further progress still has to be made. The goal is no longer individual progress, but the will of the spiritual hierarchy. The purpose of life changes. The individual does not strive for personal attainments but for the good of nature, to further the cause of cosmic ideation in an impersonal way. The end of materiality has been reached, as signified by the termination of the horizontal line.

From the terminating point, the arc moving downward reminds us again of the creative process until the wholeness of the circle is reached. Having reached perfection, energy has to be directed to the externalizing process once again. The entire symbol represents the stage of attainment and the further task to be accomplished.

The other symbol begins with a V-shape angle followed by a small horizontal line tucked with a small circle and ending with a downward arc convexing to the right ♈. It shows the downpour of divine energy for further working out the Divine plan. The V-shape is a funnel describing the special benediction, guidance, and association of higher beings with the world of manifestation. Materialism at this stage gets spiritualized. The figure continues with a small horizontal line indicating that the benediction is for undertaking further manifestation of the plan, according to special assignments represented by the small circle. The right hand convexing arc points to the evolutionary action following this task. From both these figures we see that the individual manifestation is over and divine guidance for impersonal work is bestowed involving yet greater difficulties and struggles.

11
AQUARIUS
KUMBHA

~~
~~

The word Aquarius, derived from Latin, refers to a water carrier, the symbol of the eleventh sign of the zodiac. The Sanskrit name is Kumbha, which means a pitcher. This word is associated with Kumbhaka, which signifies the retention of the breath in yogic practices. It also relates to Kumbhaja, meaning born of a pitcher, a name for the great sage Agastya, one of the great seers, who brought the Vedic teaching to south India and one of the primary guides of this world-age. In its geometric diagram, the sign is represented by two wavy lines ~~. All these relate the sign with water.

Almost all systems of astrology — Indian, Chaldean, Assyrian, Egyptian or European — have made the pitcher the most common symbol of this sign. It is often represented as a pitcher with water is flowing from it. As a symbol, water represents the cosmic life-force, the universal solvent. It quenches all thirst and absolves the individual from all sins. A dip in running water or a holy river purifies the individual and spiritualizes his heart. In Alchemical symbology, water purifies base metal, the worldly man, before it is transmuted into gold, or restored into his natural state of innocence. In Hindu mythology, Aquarius is related to the great God Indra, who rules over the heavenly world where souls dwell as a result of their good karma. Before creation begins, Vishnu, reclining on the serpent Naga, was floating on the ocean of pure essence. The Ganges, the heavenly river, falls from the head of Lord Shiva. The churning of the ocean symbolizes the manifestative process of the cosmos. From such a wide use of water in spiritual literature, Aquarius as a pitcher with water flowing from it must be related with the cosmic life-force in an important way.

This symbol, arising from the importance of water, relates to many other mythologies. In Greek mythology, Ganymede was carried from the earth by Zeus to make him his "cup bearer." In the Hebrew religion, Lamech, the father of Noah, inaugurates a New Era, or a period of fresh regeneration after the deluge (Pralaya of the Hindus), implying thereby that life emerged from the Great Depth. Aquarius also relates to two aspects of the creative process, complete annihilation of the past evolutionary course, and the birth of a new race or beginning of a new way of life. Aquarius stands for a radical transformation involving the purification of the dross, accumulated as the result of materialistic desire, giving a new spiritual direction to life. The impact of such an inflow of cosmic life-force, in everyday life, is experienced as a thorough shake-up at first, followed by the dawn of a new consciousness in which the general welfare becomes more important than personal gain.

A great importance to transformation, mutation so to say, is given to the Aquarian impulse because the psychological orientation received under Capricorn must find an outlet. This is possible only under an entirely different milieu and new approach to the problems of life. This is emphasized by the symbol of water related to this sign. Moving water has been given great importance in the manifestation of the cosmos. The creation began with water, the various changes in manifestation owe themselves to water, the evolutionary pilgrimage of purifying and spiritualizing one's nature takes place as a result of water, running water. It is only when the life-force energizes us from our inner side, or when our subjective nature is activated by the divine impulse, that we become able to transcend selfish desires in order to dedicate our efforts to the cosmic good. At this stage, the drop moves out to mingle in the ocean.

The pitcher, standing for the mortal tabernacle, must release the water, the life-force contained within it, in order to experience the supreme bliss. The individual energy has to merge in the universal or cosmic energy to attain its ultimate goal. This mingling occurs under the Aquarian impulse. But, the pitcher must be broken for success in this effort. Under Aquarius the individual, while maintaining his separate identity, is merged in the universal life-wave. This process, however, is not necessarily pleasant. The pitcher, or the individual consciousness, is always a hindrance and source of unhappiness.

The association of Aquarius with Kumbhaka, retention of breath and regulation of Prana or the life-force indicates that the Aquarian impulse has an invigorating effect, which can rejuvenate the individual. The way this renewal takes place has been expressed through various allusions. The life of Ganymede, the object of lust personified, is changed by making him the cup-bearer of the gods. This refers to the abandonment of all material attachments and dedicating oneself to the Divine will. The father of Noah is the saviour and precursor of a new civilization. He arouses those creative impulses which are Noah-like, which carry the divine essence, the seeds of a new civilization. The ocean on which Visnu, the creative energy, floats provides the foundation on which future creation can take place. Similarly, the churning of the ocean provides the various jewels, the precious possessions of the cosmos. Thus, we find that water in the Aquarian context expresses the creative purpose. It symbolizes the great impulse under which the Builders, the Dhyanis, and Demiurges, the great architects assisting Brahma, the cosmic architect, are engaged in objectifying the subjective images slumbering in the Alaya, the unmanifest or the Great Depth.

The impulse from this sign, however, is concerned with both the pitcher as well as the water contained in it. The pitcher is the sheath and the water the life-energy dwelling within it. The Aquarian impulse activizes both, but which impact is perceived depends upon the aspect of life predominant in the individual. When affinity is greater with the material component of manifestation, there is greater attachment to the outer forms of manifestation. In this case the emphasis on the pitcher makes the individual materialistic and self-centered. But in case his affinity is with the energy-content radiating from it, then the Aquarian impulse moves him towards promoting the universal good. Which aspect will manifest in an individual is difficult to guess, therefore this sign is considered one of the most enigmatic.

The diagram of this sign is a double wavy line ♒. The wavy line represents movement in water, and also reminds us of the changing moods that one feels under its impact. The significance of water and the dual nature of the impact of this sign is highlighted by this emblem. The individual under its impact is subjected to fluctuating moods, which must be overcome before reaching the next stage on the evolutionary path.

12
PISCES
MINA

⚏

Pisces is one of the most auspicious signs. It brings great satisfaction to the individual born under its influence, especially during the last portion of his life. Such an impact is natural to expect after the individual shell of personal considerations is broken and the new universal consciousness has arisen seeking the good for all life. When "Not My, but Thy will be done" takes hold of the person, it gradually realigns him so that his old material tendencies are dissolved and washed away, either due to their satiety or due to understanding their insignificance in life. After a tropical storm, there comes a calm which gives rise to peace and tranquility. At this stage, the individual, while maintaining full consciousness of the trials and tribulations undergone during his pilgrimage — starting with the fragmentation of the spark from the fire and ending with the final merging of the drop into the sea — becomes part of the universal life. This finality is depicted by two fishes placed in opposite directions, one above the other. Its diagram is by two arcs of the circle, one convexing to the left and the other to the right, which are joined together by a horizontal line that runs across them in the middle ⚏ .

The fish symbolizes fertility, prosperity and regeneration. The Hindus consider that it is an auspicious omen to see a fish at the beginning of any journey or any important mission. When the creation first began, Vishnu, who sustains life, appeared in the form of a fish. This manifestation of the Lord is known as Matsya-avatar, the fish avatar. The primary objective of Vishnu's fish incarnation is said to be to save life and to regenerate the seed preserved therein. In other religions, the fish is given similar importance. The Babylonians had a fish God and messiah called Dagon, the Man-Fish. Dagon was the Chaldean man-fish Oannes, the mysterious being who arose daily out of the depth of the sea to teach the people. The Babylonians were aware of wisdom as the savior needed for guiding everyday life and the fish symbolized this life-sustaining wisdom. The similarity between fish Gods is obvious, all which represent the life-sustaining cosmic energy. Even the Hebrews designated the messiah as Dag or the fish, because he was considered an instructor to humanity and giver of the blessings of eternal life. The connection between Christ and the fish is also quite promiment.

Early Christians believed in the complete dissolution of matter and its at-one-ment with the universal life-force and in the necessity of a spiritual teacher to lead humanity on this evolutionary pilgrimage. For this purpose, they assigned to their savior the symbols of the lamb, the fish and the good shepherd. These forms suggest the universal and beneficent source of the Divine creative impulse. Such teachers or saviors channel the divine energy, draw down the supramental spiritual force and direct it for the cosmic good. So doing, their personality remains completely poised in the universal consciousness. To express this, the Chaldeans wore hats like a fish's head, a practice which continues even today among the papal hierarchy. They also had a shadbelly coat, which represented the body of a fish. The symbol of the fish was important to them because their priestly duties and secret wisdom were connected with the savior who himself was conceived as a fish. Such significance for the fish in ancient thought that it could not leave astrology unaffected. The symbol has prevailed as an emblem of survival, wisdom and divine benediction.

Astrologically, the twelfth sign of the zodiac has the distinction of signifying the end of one cycle, the preservation of the seed and its regeneration. The fish is an aquatic creature, but is different from a crab which represents Cancer and a crocodile associated with Capricorn. The crab and crocodile inhabit both land and sea, while the fish cannot survive out of water. The Pisces impulse absolves the individual of all materiality and produces a kind of life which can prevail only when the individual and the universal have become one. The fish represents the seed, the symbol of progeny itself. It is also an emblem of prosperity and the fulfillment of desire, while the water in which fish reside represents Bythos, the great unfathomable depth that exists in silence and infinity.

Two fish clinging to each other's tails expresses the balancing of two polarities. The opposite poles of electricity at this point cease to exist in their duality. The positive and negative fuse in each other. The impulse of manifestation and the various forms manifest stop under their own self-generating power. At this stage, polarization ends. The cosmic quietude prevails once more. Those born under the influence of Pisces often experience the universal consciousness impinging upon their psyche, which makes them feel very different than other people.

This balancing of duality is achieved by several changes. Three stages are represented by the three important aspects of the symbol. The two fish are placed in the sea. The sea represents cosmic stability. There is the feeling of oneself merged in eternity. Direct experience of this state often produces tremendous fright. Though the fish is capable of maintaining itself in perfect equilibrium in the sea, yet there is a difference between the two. This difference causes several psychological problems, which are mentioned in various spiritual teachings. Even Lord Buddha had to undergo great psychological trials before attaining final liberation. Pisces has as one of its aspects the cosmic stability represented by the sea.

Its second aspect is the unveiling of wisdom. The fish by itself is a symbol of wisdom. In the understanding of Truth which liberates the individual from bondage there is not necessarily the cessation of turmoil. But this understanding provides that strength which enables one to bear fear of the unknown. Having known the secret of nature, whatever happens in life is quietly borne. This aspect of Pisces is represented by the symbol of the fish. The shape of the fish in the Pisces symbol, their formation indicating that the mouth of one fish is near the tail of the other, represents the final balance resulting from complete destruction of the polarity which is the cause of all manifestation.

In the diagram for Pisces, two semi-circles joined together by a horizontal line in the middle ♓ , the way the two semi-circles are placed suggests the involutionary and evolutionary impulses. Joined together they form a full circle which stands for the wholeness of manifestation. Disjoined they indicate that evolution is no more the direction of manifestation. They are no longer impelled by the cycle of necessity to proceed further. In this sense the diagram symbolizes cosmic stability, the sea about which we have spoken.

However, the delinking of the two tendencies, evolution and involution, does not imply their complete cessation. They still repose in Mother Nature. The horizontal line linking the two semi-circles represents Nature, the feminine aspect of life eternal. The two semi-circles are placed in such a way as not to form a circle. The existence of the two tendencies but not reacting to the external stimuli can occur only in a state of perfect understanding of the law of nature. The formation of the circular arcs assumes the presence of real wisdom. The emblem in its wholeness represents complete annihilation of any further movement. This is the stage when matter cannot sprout and give birth to any further manifestative impulse. It expresses, in this sense, a balance. The seed for future growth, however, is not destroyed. Everything remains in nature, well poised.

Whether we consider the emblem or the symbols connected with Pisces, they represent the primary impulse of quiescence, which is a mystical state of being. The nature of psychological transformation that precedes this situation is not spelled out clearly. As one goes deeper into the symbology of these signs and symbols, one perceives that Pisces is full of storm and stress, inwardly as well as outwardly. To expect that nature will be quiet when all forms of manifestation ceases is unrealistic. Hiranyagarbha, Mother Nature, or the feminine aspect of creative energy, is a situation of intense subjective activity sustaining an equilibrium, so that it cannot be taken as simply inert. Pisces represents the influences that confront the manifesting soul with the enormity of cosmic existence, whose understanding through the dawn of wisdom annihilates all the material dross in it and peace returns to the soul.

Blavatsky *(IU Vol. II, p. 465)* equates Pisces with Noah, and states that "Noah (Pisces), who appears in the generations as the twelfth patriarch counting Cain and Abel, is Adam again under another name, for he is the forefather of a new race of mankind, and with his three sons, one bad, one good, and one partaking of both qualities*, is the terrestrial reflection of the super-terrestrial Adam and his three sons." The idea of regeneration is highlighted by the fish symbol, as well as by the presence of two semi-circles which stand for the seeds for the future birth. This is the essential nature of the twelfth zodiacal impulse. Pisces represents the quietude and repose before the beginning of the whirlwind of the next cycle of manifestation.

---

* They seem to refer to the immovable, moveable and dual signs of the zodiac and to their classification according to Tamas, Sattwa and Rajas — the primary attributes within which all the zodiacal signs are been categorized.

IV

THE NAKSHATRAS

SYMBOLS OF THE
ZODIAC AND NAKSHATRAS

THE NAKSHATRAS
THE TWENTY-SEVEN ASTERISMS

Nakshatra means "that which never decays." It is the name given to the asterisms or mansions of the Moon, as the Moon resides in each of these constellations for one day. The system of the asterisms is very ancient. Even during the earliest Vedic period, it was important. The *Atharva* and *Yajur Vedas* give complete lists of them and associate them with the oldest Vedic gods. The asterisms are twenty-seven in number. Mythologically they are the daughters of Daksha Prajapati, a great cosmic progenitor, specially charged by the celestial creator Brahma, to assist him in the cosmic evolutionary process. Out of the numerous offspring born to Daksha, his twenty-seven daughters who married the Moon became the repository of astrological influences.

These lunar mansions appear in Chinese and Arabic astrology but have not received much attention in Western or European astrology. Each of the twenty-seven asterisms consists of 13° 20' of the zodiac and is divided into four quarters of 3° 20' extent. The asterisms are classified in various ways, as according to basic attribute, primary motivation, sex, caste, species and so on. They are particularly revealed by their presiding deities, ruling planets and their symbolic form.

Each of the twelve signs of the zodiac consists of two and a quarter asterisms. The asterisms and the signs of the zodiac both begin from the same point. The beginning of the first Nakshatra or asterism of Ashwini is the same as that of the first sign Aries. Each sign contains the combined influence of the asterisms falling within it. Compared to the signs, the asterisms or Nakshatras possess a deeper effect. The signs are merely "a heap, mass, or collection" of influences as their Sanskrit name Rashi suggests.

The planets are the cosmic creative powers. Each planet radiates certain specialized forces. The planets make their impact on the zodiacal field. This specialized circle divided by the signs and asterisms is the negative or passive field of influence, while the planets are the positive or active forces. The signs and asterisms create the necessary milieu, the environment, while the planets are the precipitating factors.

Prakriti, the female creative impulse, is the force that sustains the general background of the zodiac. Prakriti produces the basic conditions on which the seeds sprinkled by Purusha, the male consciousness factor, fructify and grow. The asterisms and signs of the zodiac, are the passive creative potency whereas the planets are the active or generating forces. The planets are active causes whereas the signs and asterism are the material substratum of the action. The asterisms and signs constitute the horizontal arm, while the planets represent the vertical arm in the cross of cosmic creation.

See the Appendix for information on the sex, class, specie, temperament, Animal type, directions, primary, secondary and tertiary qualities, rulers of the sign, rulers of the individual Nakshatras and rulers of the quarters of the Nakshatras as well as a summary of the symbols, presiding deities, primary and movitating impulses, and characteristics of the Nakshatras.

NAKSHATRA	DEGREES	RULER
1. Ashwini	000°00′ — 013°20′	Ketu
2. Bharani	013°20′ — 026°40′	Venus
3. Krittika	026°40′ — 040°00′	Sun
4. Rohini	040°00′ — 053°20′	Moon
5. Mrigrashira	053°20′ — 066°40′	Mars
6. Ardra	066°40′ — 080°00′	Rahu
7. Punarvasu	080°00′ — 093°20′	Jupiter
8. Pushya	093°20′ — 106°40′	Saturn
9. Ashlesha	106°40′ — 120°00′	Mercury
10. Magha	120°00′ — 133°20′	Ketu
11. Purva Phalguni	133°20′ — 146°40′	Venus
12. Uttara Phalguni	146°40′ — 160°00′	Sun
13. Hasta	160°00′ — 173°20′	Moon
14. Chitra	173°20′ — 186°40′	Mars
15. Swati	186°40′ — 200°00′	Rahu
16. Vishakha	200°00′ — 213°20′	Jupiter
17. Anuradha	213°20′ — 226°40′	Saturn
18. Jyestha	226°40′ — 240°00′	Mercury
19. Mula	240°00′ — 253°20′	Ketu
20. Purvashada	253°20′ — 266°40′	Venus
21. Uttarashada	266°40′ — 280°00′	Sun
22. Shravana	280°00′ — 293°20′	Moon
23. Dhanishtha	293°20′ — 306°40′	Mars
24. Shatabhishak	306°40′ — 320°00′	Rahu
25. Purva Bhadra	320°00′ — 333°20′	Jupiter
26. Uttara Bhadra	333°20′ — 346°40′	Saturn
27. Revati	346°40′ — 360°00′	Mercury

1
ASHWINI

Ashwini, the first asterism or lunar mansion starts at the beginning of the sign Aries and extends from 00° 00' to 13° 20' of the zodiac. It consists of three stars in the form a horse. The Vedas represent the asterism by two horses. Classical texts link it with a celestial nymph who in later times was considered the mother of the Vedic gods, the Ashwins. Ketu, the south node of the Moon which relates to the abstract intellect, is the planetary ruler of Ashwini. Mars, which aids in the expansion of the internal to the external in order to carry forward the evolutionary process, owns the sign Aries which contains it. The asterism has the basic attribute of Rajas, activity, which occurs on all levels. Its primary motivation is dharma, principle or honor. The Sun is exalted here.

Ashwini is related to the activation of the primeval energy from its state of latency. In Hindu mythology no one is able to withstand the radiance of the Sun-god (Surya). The Sun-god was therefore left alone without anyone to share his life. To enable him to have a wife, the first task was to reduce his effulgence.

The resplendence of the Sun was so unbearable that his mother, Aditi, approached her husband, the sage Kashyapa, for help in reducing it. Kashyapa divided the fetus into twelve parts, and made each a Sun in its own realm.

The Sun belonging to our universe was married to the daughter of Tvashtar (also called Vishwakarma), the celestial architect, but the girl found it difficult to discharge her marital responsibilities with such a dazzling spouse. In order to discover her own dharma (responsibility), she went to perform penance. As she left to do so, she instructed her handmaid, Chhaya (meaning shadow), to look after her husband.

This allegory describes the beginning of solar evolution and provides a hint to the mysterious process of activating the primeval energy. The word Surya, which means Sun, is derived from the root 'Su' which means "to produce, bring forth, a parent" and is also related to courage, valor and so on. Tvashtar means a carpenter, a builder, a workman. Tvashtri as his daughter has these capacities as well. Aditi, the mother of the Sun, means the earth and is also the mother of the gods. It stands for that which is the beginning and the end, the alpha and omega. Aditya, meaning the son of

Aditi, stands for the Sun. Sanjna, another name of Tvashtri the wife of the Sun, means consciousness, understanding and intellect, as well as a sin. Chhaya ordinarily means shadow, but it also means a reflected image, the blending of colors, protection and darkness.

Returning to the story, while the Sun was taken care of by Chhaya, who always remained with him, he mistook her for his real wife and became infatuated with her. When his real wife returned, she was upset and felt hurt. In remorse, she left the Sun. She did not wish to return to her father, so she began to wander in the form of a mare. When the Sun realized the deception, he began to seek his real wife. He found Tvashtri in the form of a mare, so he assumed the form of a horse. He pursued her and became united to her. From this union was born the twin Ashwins, the two horsemen, and they were placed in the sky as the first asterism, Ashwini*.

The Ashwins possess great healing and rejuvenating powers. Their powers are described in the story of an old sage, Chyavan by name, who married some young princesses who were thereby eager for a full marital relationship with him. In pursuance of their request, the Ashwins made the sage young again so that his consorts could enjoy him. This same power was displayed on other occasions. When Parikshit, the last of the Dwapara Yuga kings, was condemned to die by the bite of Takshat — the principle serpent of the underworld — the Ashwins were about to restore his life. However, Takshat insisted that they should consider whether it was right to do so. After thinking it over, they left king Parikshit to die according to the course of his own destiny.

The asterism Ashwini also represents rejuvenating power capable of restoring youth to the old and decrepit and of life to the dead — even when death is by the bite of the most venomous serpent. But this healing power needs the guidance of spiritual teachers (Takshat was a Naga, a wise teacher) to judge whether or not it should be used.

Ashwa, the horse, the symbol of this asterism, is associated with the number seven, the most sacred of all the numbers. Everything important and auspicious is connected with seven. The creative energy which emanates from the Absolute, moves in seven channels. These are the seven flames of the eternal fire. The horse is also a symbol of vitality and

---

*   After the birth of the Ashwinis, the Sun took his wife *Tvashtri* home where her father, *Tavishtra* the celestial architect, to remedy their plight, put the Sun on his lathe and reduced his effulgence to one-eighth of its original power, cutting from every part of him but his feet.

contains within itself the seven flames which energize all the forms of the manifestation. The seven horses that draw the chariot of the Sun refer to this same life-force. As such, the first lunar mansion stands for the energy through which the Sun, the central deity of this region of the universe, arouses the different forces of creation. The concept of perfection, the sense of wholeness, is contained in Ashwini. It is the storehouse of all forms of power. It is the producer of all creative possibilities, though they are present in it only in their latency.

The horse represents physical power and stamina. If a rider is able to break and subdue a wild horse, he can use it to travel far. The asterism can also enable the individual who can master its power to attain great heights in both the material and spiritual realms. The Absolute, represented by the Sun, is the storehouse of all energy and is able to control and direct the universe under its attractive power. Ashwini, as an offspring of the Absolute, stands for that power under which the imperishable subjective effulgence begins its movement towards materiality — the shadowy world.

The rulers of the quarters of the asterism — Mars, Venus, Mercury and the Moon — are important in developing and assisting the growth of material proclivities, while Ketu, the overall ruler of the asterism, represents the subjective qualities of the Supreme. These impulses link the asterism with fierce activity, tenacity, dynamism, the activation of inert matter into electrifying energy and lightning activity. The resulting impulse can rejuvenate inert matter into divine energy. It can bring radical transformation to the human being. Under the influence of Ashwini, an individual can experience an overpowering thirst for life, a desire for leadership and a dauntless spirit for exploring new lands and establishing new kingdoms. Aggression, lust, indiscretion, and impulsiveness are negative qualities of its impact. Quietude is not a characteristic of this asterism. Great dissatisfaction mixed with an urge to avoid unpleasant responsibilities often mark it.

2
BHARANI

Bharani extends from 13° 20' to 26° 40' of the zodiac, thereby also falling within the sign of Aries ruled by Mars. The asterism itself is ruled by Venus. Bharani has the basic attribute of Rajas or activity on primary and secondary levels, with Tamas on a tertiary level. Its primary motivation is Artha, directed activity. Three important keys to reveal its inner meaning are found. First is its symbol, the yoni or female reproductive organ. Second, is its basic principle (tattwa) Shakti, the cosmic passive principle, and third, is its presiding deity is Yama, the god of death.

Ashwini, the first asterism, represents the cosmic energy in its latent state, differentiated from the void or nothingness, yet not in its kinetic potential. The second asterism symbolized by the yoni or female reproductive organ establishes this potential as the channel for creation.

The Sanskrit name for the female generative organ, bhaga, has several meanings. In Hindu rituals and observances the feminine creative energy has great importance. It relates symbolically to the arghya, the chalice used for pouring water on statues of deities, signifying thereby a means or channel for expressing one's devotion to the supreme. The cosmic feminine force is often compared with a boat which transports people and goods from one place to another. Water symbolizes the movement of the life-force. The second asterism also has the connotation of transporting souls from one realm of existence to another, or from the realm of subjective to objective manifestation.

The word bhaga also means that which is auspicious, and is derived from the root 'Bhaj' which is connected with nourishment. It shows Bharani's function as a conduit through which the divine energy flows to nourish the manifestation.

The Arghya with which water is poured to express one's devotion also symbolizes a bridge between the human and the Divine. Noah's ark, which resembles arghya, is also a conduit, a channel through which the divine seed or energy is transported to a safer time and space for its flowering. It also is a symbol of the feminine creative power.

In Vedantic philosophy, the two primary powers of manifestation are said to be Shiva tattwa and Shakti tattwa, the active and the passive principles, the centrifugal and the centripetal forces in nature on whose polarization and interaction depends all subsequent manifestation. Ashwini is of the nature of Shiva whereas Bharani represents Shakti. As a powerful attractive center drawing to itself the kinetic potential, it directs the energy on its course. Even passive energy can be highly electrifying, which is the basic nature of Aries within whose field both these asterisms function.

Yama, the god of death ruling this asterism, can be interpreted in two ways. One meaning of the word is the deity itself, the other is a yogic term. Yama refers to various yogic practices, disciplines and observances (Yamas and Niyamas) through which our inner nature is harnessed and energized. In both senses, Yama refers to the means which enable new life-forces to permeate the physical form. As the god of death, Yama directs the life-force towards a new birth for the soul. When the old form becomes decrepit and unable to manifest the soul further, the god of death Yama enables us to detach from the old form to assume a new one. In this sense, Yama is the deity providing suitable channels for a more efficient flow of life-energy.

The central purpose of yogic practices like breath control or observances of truthfulness and non-violence, is to cleanse the physical form of the being so that the spiritual forces can flow freely into it. These yogic practices are similar to the rejuvenating process occurring at the time of death. The difference is that in Yoga the process is assumed voluntarily while at death it occurs involuntarily.

Bharani thereby indicates the passive potentiality capable of providing the essential environment where the different kinds of life-forces can fructify. The female sex organ is not so much a channel for the satisfaction of personal sex craving as a means for providing nourishment for the future expression of the life-force. It is a center of energy where evolutionary and generative processes can fructify and prosper.

Bharani is the productive zone of Aries where originality and impulsiveness are much in action. Bharani provides impetus for new forms of manifestation to concretize, or for the actualization of any concept. Psychologically, the attraction which the female sex represents to the male has an element of the unknown within it, a kind of darkness: this unknown realm of darkness is ruled by Yama, the god of death. It is this unknown aspect behind all creative energy, which springs from the deepest layer of being, that is the passive or Shakti principle. This element is the real fountain of all inspiration which transcends all known laws of logic. In ordinary human beings, the sudden downpour of universal energy is often expressed as human love, which is generally blind. Bharani is not so much rationality as emotion, or action under cosmic forces.

In predictive astrology, Bharani makes the person very sensitive. The individual registers the slightest expression of kindness and helpfulness. He keeps in his heart any distasteful treatment given to him. He is often restless, impatient and uncharitable with those individuals and activities that do not conform to his highest ideals. He himself lives in the realm of ideas, trying to create heaven on earth. His weakness is carrying everything to the extreme. If he undertakes the practice of Yoga, he disciplines himself to the breaking point, but if he indulges in sex, to which he is greatly prone, he can carry this also to the furthest degree.

3
KRITTIKA

Krittika extends from 26° 40′ to 40° 00′ of the zodiac. Its first quarter, upto 30° 00′ of the zodiac, falls within Aries ruled by Mars, while the latter three quarters of the sign, are in Taurus ruled by Venus. The asterism as a whole is owned by the Sun. Its presiding deity is Agni, the god of fire. Its symbol is a razor. Its attribute is Rajas, or activity, on both primary and secondary levels, with Sattwa at a tertiary level. Its primary motivation is Kama or desire.

Krittika consists of six visible stars with a seventh invisible one added to them. These are the stars of the constellation of the Pleiades. These seven stars, also called the seven sisters, are said be the wives of the seven great rishis or seers, who are figured astronomically as the seven stars of Ursa Major, the Big Dipper. Imagined as a razor, this asterism is a destructive one. Being connected with the ancient sages responsible for the evolution of our planet, it channels their guiding force. The relationship between the seven sisters and the seven rishis, between the Pleiades and the Big Dipper is very profound and much of its meaning has been veiled.

Krittika's presiding deity Agni, the Vedic fire god, is the central figure in ancient Vedic literature. Fire in its subtlest form is the initial manifestation of the Absolute, the Imperishable. Fire is the essence of the Life-force inhering in every form of existence. On the cessation of this inner fire the cohesion between all forms of existence disintegrates. There are seven flames enabling the seven planes of existence to manifest.

On the physical plane, this septenary principle operates through both the macrocosm and microcosm. In the microcosm, there are the seven sheaths of the human being and the seven principles vivifying them (see *SAO, pp. 220–239*). The highest of these principles is the Atmic or Self principle and the corresponding sheath through which it operates is known as the Atmic sheath, which is difficult to comprehend or to describe. The god of fire connected with the third asterism is this deepest flame of the Atmic principle, which sustains the wholeness of the being. The aspiration for radical changes in life comes under Krittika.

The seventh or invisible star of this asterism, the seventh sister, is said to be married to Dhruva, the pole star or the rishi who governs it. As the entire globe rotates around the pole, Krittika is the seat of this guiding impulse and its sevenfold manifestation through which life on Earth proceeds. The relationship of Krittikas with the pole star emphasizes the importance of a central and invisible principle from which the laws of life derive.

An important characteristic of Krittika is its feminine or passive quality, the Shakti tattwa, which is abundantly represented by Bharani, the second asterism. Under the third lunar mansion, differentiation of the feminine principle begins. This aspect is emphasized by the myths connected with it. Karttikeya, the son of Lord Shiva, is linked with Krittika, from which his name derives. Shiva is the most powerful of the Hindu gods. His power is rarely used for cosmic creation. His procreative seed is employed only when the other gods prove ineffective.

In Hindu mythology, it is said that there was a time when the demons were destroying the world and creating tremendous problems for all creatures, even the gods. To defeat them, the gods obtained the seed of the Lord Shiva, which refers to his virility, energy or power. When the gods got Shiva's seed, it required special arrangements to preserve it. It had such a fiery quality that an ordinary receptacle or womb could not hold it. The seed was thus cast in fire and protected by water. The Krittikas were requested to nourish it in their womb. Karttikeya was thereby born and on the seventh day after his birth killed the mighty demon Taraka, and thereby delivered the gods from the demons who had defeated them.

Those of spiritual knowledge are aware of the importance of the divine seed, the essence of fire or solar positive creative energy. They also recognize the importance of the principle of water, the lunar passive preservative quality. Essentially, man is a son of God, a fragment of the Absolute, the nature of which resembles fire. For his development the fluid, the bythos, is necessary. It provides the ever changing conditions under which the primeval essence is enabled to manifest at different levels while preserving its essential nature. For the growth and nurturing of the individual soul, the fiery seed fragmented from the Absolute, the motherly influence and care bestowed by the third lunar mansion Krittika is necessary.

The influence of Krittika builds the divine qualities in man. The materiality of existence, the demonic forces, expressed in many forms such as false humility and self-centered docility, is incongruous with the radiation of Krittika. The Pleiades are the collective womb of the passive septenary principle. They enable the divine downpour that cleanses all the sheaths of the soul and enables them to operate on spiritual planes. When such vibrations occur, the life of the individual changes radically. He becomes a pillar of light and center of spiritual forces. These are the higher qualities that hold the universe together.

Krittika provides the appropriate milieu for these centralizing spiritual forces and the destruction of all dissipating energy. It has a constructive and destructive potential. In its constructive aspects, it heightens the creative urges in the individual. This can be felt as the sexual urge that creates children, or it can increase sensitivity for artistic and intellectual productions. On the destructive side, Krittika destroys those tendencies which impede evolutionary forces. It can affect the individual as well as society. Anything that is contrary to the Divine plan is importantly affected by this asterism.

These characteristics of Krittika are represented by a razor or a curved knife, which is not an instrument of war but a tool in the hands of a surgeon. Doctors use a knife to remove foreign bodies lodged in human tissue so that the natural functions of the organism are restored. The asterism is destructive in this sense. Any impediment in the natural course of human or social development, especially from the soul's standpoint, is removed under its impact. Krittika links Aries and Taurus, subjective activity and the beginning of creative impulse. Like every precursor of new exploration, the divine creative impulse also encounters difficulties and to succeed in its mission has to surmount them. Such confrontations are presented by this asterism.

The nature of confrontation is indicated by the planets which are located in the asterism or aspect it. They represent the surgeon who uses the razor. If the north node of the Moon, Rahu, is in Krittika, there can be explosions in social and worldly relationships so that the annihilation of worldly attachments can sow the seed of spiritual consciousness. The Sun in this position can activate the thinking principle and give incisive intelligence leading to a sense of dissatisfaction with one's physical involvements and relationships. Depending upon the nature of the planet connected with the asterism, the change occurs but the asterism by itself is neutral in creating the impact. It merely shows the influence. It is the instrument which causes an operation, but the actual performance of the operation depends upon the doctor represented by the planets involved.

Krittika, as a mother of Karttikeya, was effective in discharging the difficult responsibility of his birth only after Karttikeya was given to her as an embryo. Karttikeya was nurtured by her but she did not produce the seed from which he arose. In life the basic potential, represented by Krittika, remains quiescent until a planet begins to operate its influence. The influence of the asterism is passive, requiring other forces to take advantage of it. The asterism becomes highly charged when an active influence comes within its field of energy.

4
ROHINI

From ancient times the asterism Rohini has been clothed in many mysterious myths and stories. The advent of the Divine Force is preceded by preparations which remain hidden and obscure. Only when the appropriate time comes are these supporting angels brought to light. Such preparation requires many behind-the-scene activities. Rohini represents this kind of cosmic preparation. For this purpose it is assigned the symbol of a chariot, as well as other characteristics.

Rohini is a constellation of five stars, some of the most beautiful in the sky, including the bright red giant Aldebaran, alpha Taurus. The asterism extends from 40° 00′ to 53° 20′ of the zodiac. It covers a major portion of the sign Taurus, ruled by Venus, which represents creative potential of the cosmic being. The asterism itself is owned by the Moon. Its primary motivation is Moksha, liberation. Its basic attribute is Rajas, with Tamas at a secondary and Rajas at a tertiary level. The deity of the asterism is Brahma or Prajapati, the creator of the universe, who unfolds the cosmic plan given to him by the higher gods.

The *Atharva Veda* refers to Rohini as the consort of Rohit, the ruddy Sun. The *Puranas* mention Rohini as one of the main daughters of Daksha Prajapati who, along with her other sisters, was married to the Moon. In connection with the birth of Lord Krishna, Rohini is described as a foster mother of Balarama, Krishna's elder brother. These indicate the same preservative principle in the cosmos which requires careful preparation before any important evolutionary influx takes place.

The relationship between Rohini and Rohit is mentioned in poetic terms. Rohit, with whom Rohini consorts, is eulogized as the producer of heaven and earth. He is such a powerful deity that he makes the heaven and the earth firm. By him the heavenly light is established, and by him the firmament is sustained. By him space and the atmosphere are measured, and through him the gods attain immortality. He is red in color and associated with the Sun. Thus he represents the very life-force which gives form to the entire manifestation, which concretizes it, making it measurable. Being red in color, he stands for the circulation of blood through which vitality is maintained.

Associated with this mighty creative power, Rohini shows the quality of great creativity. Rohini, being the mistress of the universal life-force, represents the inherent condition which enables creative forces to fructify. She is the feminine center of attraction towards which the active male is drawn for reproduction. It is through this asterism that the fruits of one's actions are realized. This is suggested by the hymn which states that through her all wealth can be conquered and all victories won. Very appropriately, the Vedic seers considered Rohini as a channel for connecting with the cosmic energy. If it is mobilized suitably, it can satisfy all human aspirations. Rohini operates at the supramental level of consciousness, beyond all rationality of the logical mind. Through Rohini flows the transcendental consciousness to the world manifestation.

The reference of Rohini to the birth of Krishna is full of implications relating the arousal of cosmic awareness represented by Krishna. Balarama, whom Krittika fosters, stands for the power of Great Delight. His mother is Devaki, which means the daughter of God, and his father is Vasudeva, the lord of celestial light. Balarama is their seventh child, as Krishna is the eighth. Before birth, Balarama was transferred to the womb of Rohini to save him from the wrath of Kamsa, the demon king who tried to slay all the children of Vasudeva. Balarama received motherly affection from Rohini until his true identity was finally revealed along with Krishna at the house of Yashoda and Nanda, Krishna's foster parents. Balarama carried a plough as his weapon of war. He was fond of pleasure and very haughty in temperament. He was born to assist Krishna in his mission. As a foster mother to such a mysterious person, Rohini enjoyed a special status without whose tact and sacrifice, the advent of the Divine Consciousness on earth would not have been possible. Rohini as foster mother of Balarama functions similarly as the consort of Rohit. Both of them channel the Divine energy for the benefit of the world.

The story of the infatuation of the Moon with Rohini gives greater detail to this linkage. This Puranic story describes the stage in cosmogenesis at which the Kumaras, the youthful yogi-ascetics, refused to enter into the creation for which purpose they were manifest. Thereupon Brahma, the creator, produced the ten Prajapatis, the cosmic progenitors, for this purpose, of which Daksha was one. He fathered sixty daughters of which twenty-seven became the asterisms married to the Moon.

The Moon is the nourisher of the earth and is primarily concerned with the mind-principle in man. Rohini was very attractive and the Moon became infatuated with her. This aroused jealousy among her sisters. They complained to Brahma and in return he cursed the Moon, who thereby became sick. On realizing what they had done to their husband, they felt sorry for him and once again pleaded with the Creator to forgive him. But such a curse, once pronounced, could not be taken back. It was, however, softened by making the Moon gradually lose his splendor, after which he could gradually regain it.

Spiritual illumination requires close association with the mind-principle in order to operate on earth. The conditions under which this relationship can be established are given in this myth. Such illumination is a Divine gift, the child of the Cosmic Patriarch so to say. It must be united with the Moon, representing the mind-principle, for the furtherance of the Divine Will. But in this operation, if the individual becomes possessive and begins pursuing the objects of the senses to the detriment of his other faculties, he is caught in tidal waves of growth and decay. This is the status of the Moon after being cursed by Brahma for his infatuation with Rohini.

The mind principle in man can discharge its obligations correctly and escape the swing of pleasure and pain only with the utmost equilibrium. Personal indulgence, which is likely to be accentuated in association with Rohini because of its supreme brilliance, may lead the individual to shed his Divine glory and become entangled in the fluctuations of time, the cycle of karma and repeated birth and death. Rohini is that attraction which compels the Divinity in man to lose its pristine memory and become immersed in worldly gratification. In this process it aids the creative impulse in manifestation. Rohini is a powerful procreative force. It attracts the Divine Energy towards the world of manifestation, as suggested by the allegory of Balarama and Krishna. Balarama was protected and nourished by Rohini until Krishna revealed himself. Rohini paves the way for the birth and growth of the Divine potential. It is by activating the Divine Energy and directing it towards matter (one is reminded of Balarama's plough, a tool for tilling land) that Rohini involves the individual in sensory pleasures and inevitably causes suffering as its consequence.

Astrologically, the symbol assigned to Rohini is a chariot. It is a means of transportation for royalty, especially on the battlefield. Swift and dignified movement is its special feature. It is led by horses which stand for virility and Divine kinetic energy. Rohini functions to transport the universal life-force, which is essentially regal and dignified in nature, protecting it at its initial stages until it reaches the time when it is strong enough to meet its adversaries. These are the various allurements of the outer existence.

Rohini leads the soul into the mundane world with all its pleasures, attachments and drunkenness (as in the case with Balarama). It is an asterism which directs the individual towards the physical world of illusion, with all its comforts and luxuries. Under Rohini the mind principle in man, represented by the Moon, is in its state of exaltation and is able to experience the newness of its ventures. It immerses the individual in worldly involvements but like Balarama, even while indulging in intoxicating situations and bending the world to his whims and fancies, he finally helps his younger brother, Lord Krishna, to unfold his Divine mission.

In Sanskrit, Rohini also means a girl having her first menstruation. It is only after attaining this stage that she is able to bear children. Rohini, in fact, represents that cosmic stage which enables the human soul to become ready for creative manifestation. It is the acme of creative potential. It is the asterism which leads to symbiotic relationship with those who are complementary with oneself and in union with whom there is the possibility of receiving some greater experience. Acting on the lower levels, Rohini brings about a deeper involvement in sexual relationships often going beyond traditional social mores, induced by strong impulses and in a state of intoxication. Whatever Rohini does it imparts a sense of mission and there is the feeling that one's action will have important repercussions.

5
MRIGASHIRA

Mrigashira stands for an auspicious beginning and the newness of experience. Its characteristics have been figured in various ways, suggesting dissatisfaction with existence or confusion and disorientation created by cataclysmic events. Following the turmoil, a new relationship is established which imparts a different momentum to life.

Mrigashira consists of the three stars of the head of Orion, extending from 53° 20' to 66° 40' of the zodiac. It first half is in Taurus ruled by Venus, while its second is in Gemini ruled by Mercury. The asterism itself is ruled by Mars. Its primary motivation is Moksha, liberation, while its basic attribute is Rajas, activity, with Tamas or inertia at secondary and tertiary levels.

The presiding deity of Mrigashira is the Vedic god Soma, the God of the mystic nectar that imparts great sensitivity and gives enlightenment. Soma is identified with the Moon, and the story is told how he eloped with Brihaspati's (Jupiter's) wife, from which union Mercury was born. This seduction of Jupiter's wife by the Moon caused a great war in heaven, about which we have spoken elsewhere. The symbol assigned to this asterism is the head of a deer, which in Hindu mythology also relates to the Moon.

Many auspicious events are associated with this asterism. In *the Bhagavad Gita* Lord Krishna identifies himself with the month ruled by it (Margashira). The *Shiva Purana* states that the birth of Shiva's consort, Uma, took place under Mrigashira and they were also married under the same asterism. Kali Yuga, the dark or Iron Age, the present era of human history, also began with the vernal equinox in Mrigashira. In some occult literature mention is made of the shift of the earth's poles from North to South and vice versa. The last shift of the poles, which caused important geological changes as well as the influx of new evolutionary impulses, was said to have occurred under this asterism. All these phenomenon relate to the revival of life on a global scale.

The beginning of a new life-giving impulse is described in the story of the Moon and Jupiter's wife. In this connection, one should note that the word Tara, the name of Jupiter's wife in the story, means a star in general, and the asterisms in particular. Soma, the Moon, found himself attracted to Tara and under the pretext of getting Jupiter to begin his religious rituals earlier than the scheduled time, got Jupiter to leave his house. Then Soma went to Jupiter's house, eloped with Tara, and seduced her. Not finding Tara at home on his return, Jupiter went out and searched for her. When he found her with Soma, he demanded her return. Soma refused to give her back and Tara was also reluctant to return. When the gods intervened, the Moon was persuaded to return Tara to her rightful husband. But Tara, pregnant from her relationship with the Moon, would not disclose the identity of the father. However, even when the Moon became known as the real father of the child, Mercury or Budha, the child was so charming that Jupiter agreed to be a father to him.

A similar story exists about Tara, who was a wife of Sugriva, the younger brother of the powerful monkey king Bali. Bali was so powerful that he kept Ravana under his armpit. Ravana was the demon king who abducted Sita, Rama's wife, and was finally slain by Rama in a great war. This powerful monkey-king once went to subdue another adversary of his and did not return for some time. Believing him to be dead his younger brother Sugriva took his throne. On his return, Bali, thinking his brother had stolen the throne, drove Sugriva away into the forest and captured his wife, Tara. On befriending Rama, when he was on his way to fight Ravana, Sugriva made Rama kill Bali to enable him to recover his wife Tara.

In both these myths, Tara, the wife of the main character, is stolen from her rightful husband. This gives rise to a feud, after which she is returned to him. In Hinduism, the status of a wife is equal to that of the husband. The wife complements her husband and enables him to discharge his religious duties, especially by having children. The common feature in both these allegories is the abduction of the wife by someone less noble, and the intermingling of magnetic influences between her and this more materialistic personage, followed by her final restoration to her rightful husband.

What is important to note is the nature of the impulses which bring about the change. The wife undergoes an inner change from contact with a lower kind of person that creates a situation for the more religious husband to live in a better manner. The spirit in man, which in its original purity cannot effectively mix with the materialization process, is to some extent defiled under Mrigashira so that the further evolutionary process can be carried out. The dawn of Buddhi, intelligence personified by Mercury, is an important stage in the spiritual evolution of man. This asterism stands for all that a curious, sensitive and outward directed intelligence is capable of.

The word Mrigashira consists of two words: 'Mriga', meaning an antelope, and 'Shira', meaning a head. The word Mriga also means to seek, search for, strive for, as well as to seek or investigate inwardly. Shira means the head, the top point of anything, the tip of any material creation. The compound word Mriga-Shira represents the beginning of a search, either outwardly or within oneself. The fifth asterism is associated with the beginning of the creative impulse resulting in concrete manifestation. When the Lord Krishna associated himself with this lunar mansion, it referred to the initial point of manifestation, the spring which energizes all seeds and causes herbs to sprout. The marriage of Lord Shiva also indicates the great cosmic fusion of the Shiva-Shakti tattwas enabling the process of manifestation to begin in the realm of objectivity. The birth of Uma or Shakti, the consort of the Lord Shiva, is thereby the beginning of the world of manifestation. Unless the matrix or cosmic womb, Hiranyagarbha, is created, there can be no manifestation.

Mrigashira stands for a search, either inward or outward, under which the spirit penetrates the outer crust of materiality with a view to ultimately reveal its own reality and the illusory nature of matter. This is the idea of chase, seeking, investigation. In the life of the individual, the impulse radiating from this asterism causes one to be surrounded by material affluence in order to realize ultimately the wider significance of life. One can obtain many good things of life under the influence of Mrigashira, which is why it is considered auspicious.

The antelope is a special, elusive animal. Represented as the golden deer, symbolizing a mirage, it stands for illusion captivating human beings in different forms of worldliness. The antelope seen in the Moon suggests the same idea, an appearance fabricated by imagination. Seeking comfort and pleasure in life is a sort of chase after the golden deer. Such an individual seeks something that is really non-existent, which can only be held momentarily.

A deer is an object of love and admiration. It has much attraction to women, particularly young girls in love. An antelope arouses the desire for romance. The idea of marriage contained in the stories mentioned earlier shows the romantic urge intensified under Mrigashira. Sexual activity when the Moon is in this asterism is astrologically said to be very effective for producing children. Sensitivity, grace, agility, and loveliness of appearance are some of the features of a deer which one experiences under this asterism. The quick prancing movement of a deer resembles the radical change and the quickness with which it occurs under Mrigashira. It is at this stage of cosmic evolution that subjectivity takes a sudden leap, a kind of prancing, to objectivity. It is not a mere accident that Mrigashira is half in Taurus and half in Gemini. Taurus is the zone of subjectivity looking outward, while under Gemini the cosmic impulse gets differentiated and duality of mind arises.

The eyes and ears of a deer are prominent. They are the main organs of perception and receptivity. The deer is quick to register sound. It is quick in its observation and unexpectedly fast in its responses. These features characterize the asterism.

The gradual change of influence of the asterism from the formless spiritual, to mental, perceptual and physical levels of operation is suggested by the rulership of its four quarters assigned to the Sun, Mercury, Venus and Mars, while Mars rules the asterism as a whole. These planets contribute their energy, agility, and the quality of inquisitiveness to probe into every activity. As the basic nature of Mars is perennial dissatisfaction and the search for something higher and formless, even though under Mrigashira there is inertia leading to materialization, there is also an urge toward Liberation. This gives a constant element of contradiction in the effect of the asterism.

6
ARDRA

Ardra consists of one star, the bright star Betelgeuse or beta Orion. It extends from 66° 40' to 80° 00' of the zodiac within the sign of Gemini ruled by Mercury. Its symbol is a human head and it is often said to resemble a precious stone or jewel. Its presiding deity is Rudra, the god of destruction and its planetary ruler is Rahu, the north node of the Moon. The primary motivation of the asterism is Kama, desire or passion, while its basic attribute is Rajas, activity, with Tamas at a secondary and Sattwa at a tertiary level.

Ardra means green, fresh, soft, moist, not dry. It is also a name of the demon Taraka, referred to relative to the asterism Krittika. An understanding of the spiritual implications of Ardra are made easier by a closer study of the story of this demon.

The main point to consider in this regard is the devotion of Taraka to Brahma, the creator of the universe, for whom he practiced severe austerities to get his desired boon of undefeatable power. He did not desire immortality but great prowess. He asked for such strength that only a seven day old child could slay him, which he thought impossible. Having received this boon, he began to oppress the gods.

The meaning of Ardra is also indicated by the softness and freshness of new growth attributed to it. The effusiveness of activity, enthusiasm and the urge for expansion are inherent qualities of Ardra.

Ardra represents the mind or thinking capacity, the essential characteristic of human beings, symbolized by the human head. The nature of the mind is the ability to comprehend. This asterism refers to the power to comprehend generally and not with knowledge of anything in particular. The possibility of recognizing oneself, seeing the working of one's mind, and thereby acquiring self-knowledge, also occurs through the mind. Such a comprehension, that is, the direct perception of a reality, whether within oneself or outside, is always new. It does not assume any previous knowledge.

Having become aware of one's existence under Mrigashira, under Ardra the individual looks, perceives, searches within as well as without, and through this mental activity arrives at the perception of things. The understanding of the relationships in which one exists is the outcome of the mind. It is the mind which imposes itself on the things we perceive and establishes connection with them. This faculty is generally described as intelligence. The ethereal nature of intelligence is comparable to the tenderness or freshness of any pure experience like that of first love or affection. Ardra means freshness, wetness and newness. Intelligence has the same qualities which arise as a result of direct perception, which occurs through the inquiring mind signified by the previous asterism, Mrigashira.

The reference to the demon Taraka, who was highly devoted to the creator of the universe but also engaged in tormenting the gods, becomes apt when we consider mind or intelligence as a double-edged sword. While acting without self-identification with the objects perceived, it can reveal the mysteries of the world, and lead to release from material bondage. This is the goal of all sadhana or spiritual practice. This is what Taraka did in penance and attained the supreme boon from it. The other side of intelligence, making the individual self-conscious, induces him to lust after material attainments. This aspect of the asterism is suggested by Taraka oppressing the gods.

The relating of the God Rudra to this asterism also points to the great potential inherent in it. The Rudras are mighty powers, the different aspects of Lord Shiva himself who have fallen into generation. The lust for immortality characterizes the middle part of this asterism under the rule of Saturn, while the Jupiterian influence associated with its first and last quarters shows the positive side of intelligence.

The human head assigned to Ardra has additional meanings. The head is the seat of the brain and the other glands related to the mind, the jewel in man. The brain is formed according to our past karma, and on the basis of the present prompting of the mind our future course of action is dependent. The possibilities of the human mind acting for constructive as well as for destructive goals are almost unlimited.

No particular name is given for the jewel associated with Ardra. Gems have the capacity to absorb influences from the central storehouse of energy, the Sun. Each gem concentrates certain forces and directs them to us. These effects can act either for good or ill depending upon how they are used. Each individual also has a uniqueness like a gem. This depends on the special divine energy inherent in him. It is reflected through the activities of the mind, which is a like gem through which the light of consciousness is reflected.

The various factors relating to this asterism point to the same thing, the Mind Principle which is dual in nature. It wreaks havoc in the life of ordinary people who seek fulfillment in the material world, while higher on the evolutionary scale, it induces one to seek spiritual knowledge and live in the reality of consciousness. The emanation from this asterism relates to the cosmic principle of Mind, Mahat, which in Yogic philosophy is the main element for the manifestation of the universe.

PUNARVASU

Punarvasu extends from 80° 00' to 93° 20' of the zodiac. It consists of five stars, including both Castor and Pollux, the two main stars, alpha and beta, of the constellation Gemini. It is given the symbol of a house as well as a bow. The asterism is ruled by Jupiter. Its first three quarters lie within Gemini, ruled by Mercury, while the last quarter is in Cancer, ruled by the Moon. The asterism is presided over by the Goddess Aditi and has the strong quality of Rajas or activity at both primary and tertiary levels, with Sattwa at a secondary level. Its primary motivation comes from Artha, or directed activity.

The name of the asterism is a compound consisting of two words, 'punah' and 'vasu', the former meaning "again" and the latter, "a ray of light, a gem, or a jewel." The Vasus are a special class of Vedic deities, eight in number, and this asterism is indirectly related to them. The emphasis of meaning for the asterism falls on the first part of its name, punah meaning "repetition." It is a condition of return or restoration, becoming once again a jewel, a gem, or a ray of light. The asterism represents the universal life, which is like a ray of light or a jewel that has appeared again. It stands for the revival of certain aspects of the original life-essence as it manifests through the evolutionary process.

The Vasus are deities that appear at various levels. At the stage of cosmic evolution represented by this asterism, the same impulse as in Krittika and Rohini is repeated in one form or another. The Goddess Aditi, like Krittika and Rohini, nourished Kartikeya and Balarama. Punarvasu is concerned with the reappearance of the different Vasus who personify cosmic phenomena and energize them.

The eight Vasus are named Apas, Dhruva, Soma, Dhara, Anila, Anala, Pratyusha and Prabhas. They have the same status as the Solar Logos, but with subtle differences in their functions. Apas, which means water as well as sin, provides the foundation for manifestation. What Christianity calls Original Sin, or what elementally is Water is necessary to sustain and nourish living beings. Under Ardra, the Divine warmth is condensed to give wetness. With Punarvasu the radiation of the Sun changes this wetness into water vapor or physical life-particles. The exile of the human soul from its celestial abode of tranquility is due to certain compulsions, which are often called Sin. Apas on the macrocosmic level suggests the emergence of water as the life giving energy, whereas on the microcosmic level it is the sin which deprives the soul of its celestial poise.

Dhruva, another Vasu, is related to the pole star around which the zodiac rotates. It indicates the gravitational attraction that gives cohesion to all forms of manifestation. At the psychological level Dhruva gives determination, the unswerving will essential for every human action. Soma is the sap which nourishes all plants and the psyche which provides the framework within which the human being lives and acts. Dhara is the supportive principle in manifestation and sustains the intrinsic law in things. Bhava is the power to persevere and the quality to contain. It also means shaking and trembling and refers to a man, a master, a rogue or a thief. In fact, Bhava refers to those impulses whether in the external world or inside man, which give perseverance, endurance and determination amid catastrophic upheavals. Anila is the god of the wind, another name for Vayu, whereas Anala is the god of fire, another name for Agni. Pratyusha is the morning Sun while Prabhas is splendor, beauty, luster. The eight Vasus thereby represent the manifold sustaining power necessary for the terrestrial and human manifestation on all levels. These qualities are channeled by Punarvasu so that they can nourish and assist the evolutionary process.

Aditi, the deity of asterism, being a female principle, shows that the qualities of the asterism cannot fructify by themselves. In order to bear fruit, they must come in contact with an external, positive, or masculine force. The asterism provides the suitable soil on which healthy seeds can effectively sprout.

The bow as a symbol is the launching pad from which arrows are shot. The will of the person directs the arrow. The bow establishes the link between the archer and the target. An arrow also establishes a link. This contact is perceived when the object is hit. The impelling force to activate the contact comes from without, while the necessary background preparation for achieving the goal is made by Punarvasu. When the operative force is energized, then only this asterism can show its result.

The intellectual impulse aroused under its influence is protective as indicated by its Jupiterian ownership. The quarters of this asterism that fall under Mercury's sign, Gemini, emphasize the predominance of the Mind principle, finally culminating in Cancer where its last quarter spreads. This indicates that the subjective life-sustaining energy under the last phase of Punarvasu ends in the materialization of thought. For the fructification of these creative energies, the role of Mercury, Jupiter and the Moon are important. These three planets are intimately related to Punarvasu. They intensify the qualities, whether good or bad, contained in it. Punarvasu, in this way, acts like a spring-board for the expression and development of latent virtues as the bow symbol suggests.

The same idea is expressed by the symbol of a house. The house provides a resting place for recuperation of creative energies. The householder works elsewhere but stays at home to rest. A house is a place to leave and go to work from and to return to after the work is over. In this way, it is like a launching pad. It is a station where one can stay for a while before commencing one's journey.

The Vasus are the Divine Agents evolving and nourishing the Divine plan. Punarvasu manifests the powers which materialize ideas at a higher plane and transfer them to lower ones. The asterism provides the impulse under which abstract ideas are concretized. At this stage, the creative agents are imparted fresh impetus for the performance of their arduous work primarily on a mental level. This asterism provides a resting place for the downward flow of Divine energy with a view to enabling it to function with increased energy. Punarvasu is not so much concerned with results as with providing the essential conditions for the onward journey of the soul.

Whether the arrow is aimed at destroying the Gods as was done by the demons, or aimed at protecting the Divine seed from perishing depends upon the person discharging it. The agent who receives the impulse generated under Punarvasu determines the nature of the decision. As far as the asterism itself is concerned, it is merely the preparedness for greater action towards the concretization of the will.

8
PUSHYA

Pushya extends from 93° 20' to 106° 40' of the zodiac within Cancer, the sign owned by the Moon. The Vedic God Brihaspati, who is identified with the planet Jupiter is its presiding deity, but Saturn, which is specially associated with tamasic proclivities, rules it. Jupiter is exalted here. The relationship of the asterism with these two opposing forces has given it a special status. Its primary motivation is Dharma, honor or principle. Its basic attribute is Rajas, activity, with Sattwa at a secondary and Tamas at a tertiary level.

Jupiter aids expansion, it protects and nourishes its beneficiary, while Saturn concretizes, condenses and crystallizes nebulous matter. The combined effect of these two planets helps stabilize materializing energy, and then enables it to fructify in an entirely new form. At this stage, the subjective aspect of cosmic evolution becomes objective as an archetype. This asterism links the subjective idea with the objective archetype. This impulse is symbolized by a flower, an image present for the first time among the asterisms, showing a complete picture in its fullness. Other symbols for the asterism are a circle and an arrow. These three symbols point succinctly to the essential features of Pushya.

It is noteworthy that the symbol for Pushya is a flower in general, not a lotus, or any specific flower by name. A flower represents the blossoming of latent faculties, the possibility of attaining the archetype. The lotus, on the other hand, is the symbol of spiritual perfection. It contains within itself the image of its progenitor. The lotus is said to be the most spiritual plant, and is called "the child of the universe bearing the likeness of its mother in its bosom." A flower is not considered to contain the likeness of its mother in its bosom, it is actually an alchemical crucible in which the base metal lead is turned into the precious metal gold. The flower is considered a symbol of the process of making the subjective or the latent faculties, inner symmetry and perfection, into an objective reality and a thing of beauty. In a different way, this symbol represents the 'bythos', the great deep in which all the potentialities lie ready to be made manifest. It is a popular way of representing Hiranyagarbha, the radiant or golden egg or ethereal stuff from which the Universe was formed.

At this stage, the formative phase of cosmic ideation is over. The idea has been concretized, the archetype formed, and this ideal, which must be actualized, is deposited in the Mother Deep. Pushya, symbolized by a flower, represents the specific limited destiny assigned to the individual which, during the course of his evolution, he must aspire to and achieve. The flower symbol does not indicate that the acme of achievement has been attained. It represents the beauty and symmetry destined to be gained. The act of blossoming is more emphasized here than the attainment of perfection.

These ideas are differently expressed by the circle and the arrow. Both these symbols refer to the cosmic wholeness, a portion of which is energized. They show the possibility of attaining wholeness. The circle relates particularly to the cosmic matrix which energizes one of its seeds to fructify during the specified duration. Some of the qualities of the soul must mature during its incarnation. The complete blossoming may require thousands of incarnations and a considerable uphill journey but the Divine mission for the soul is inevitable. The circle as a symbol of Pushya does not represent finality; the position where the individual has nothing further to learn. It does not show that the soul has blossomed to its maximum. The circle here merely shows that the final dimensions up to which the soul must manifest have been demarcated and the necessary forces required for its fulfillment have been apportioned. The plan for the individual is now complete.

The arrow takes the idea further. As the support for carrying out the mission has been bestowed, the arrow symbolizes the aspiration necessary for attaining the goal. It indicates the psychological preparedness prerequisite for externalizing latent faculties. The arrow is a missile to hit a target. For this purpose, the various faculties given to the soul will be used. The previous asterism, Punarvasu, has the symbol of a bow, suggesting that under it the individual is equipped for the mission. Under Pushya he gets his marching orders. Now he has the arrow, the instrument to set his forces in motion towards their goal. Pushya endows the individual with strength and power in fullness for the mission assigned to the soul.

The symbols that represent Pushya — flower, circle and arrow — have a common quality of vibrant tranquility, absence of undue agitation, a faith in oneself and the fullness of life. Such a psychological structure can exist only when the individual has attained a stage of growth where there is full faith in the Divine plan and an unflinching confidence in oneself. At this stage of development the individual integrates the unfathomable cosmic height and his deepest inner self. The purification of the psyche and an intuitive perception of the Divine plan are the unique characteristics of Pushya.

9
ASHLESHA

Ashlesha extends from 106° 40′ to 120° 00′ of the zodiac and concludes the first third of the asterisms that are primarily rajasic, that is active, initiative or energetic in character. The asterism itself is ruled by Mercury while it lies in Cancer, ruled by the Moon. Its motivating force is Dharma, honor or principle and its attribute at both secondary and tertiary levels is Sattwa.

The presiding deity of Ashlesha is Naga, the serpent king, and the symbol representing it is also a serpent. The serpent symbol has enjoyed a special status in all the religions of the world. A poisonous reptile capable of ending the life of a person by its fatal bite has not been the primary feature of its symbology. The serpent is generally considered the embodiment of wisdom arising from spiritual enlightenment. The Serpent Fire, or Kundalini, is the mysterious power located at the base of the spinal cord coiled like a serpent which properly aroused bestows spiritual enlightenment and occult powers. The knowledge of this highly danger-ous power was known to the ancient yogis and seers. The special role of the Kundalini in cosmic evolution has been described in many teachings in a highly concealed manner.

The reference to the serpent inducing Eve to partake of the apple in the garden of Eden shows directly the function of the serpent in starting the drama of human creation. In several Hindu myths this revelation is more indirect. According to one, the world is balanced on the head of Shesha-Naga, the celestial serpent. He is the cosmic float for Vishnu, the preservative principle, when in the form of Narayana, Vishnu moved on the ocean of primordial matter, known as Kshira-Sagara, the ocean of milk. When the churning of the ocean by the gods and the demons took place at the time of cosmic creation, Shesha-Naga functioned as the churning rope.

These allegories are very profound but one aspect of them is very clear. Whenever the serpent symbol is used in spiritual allegories, it represents the mystic power which assists the successive stages of cosmic evolution. For this very reason, there is a wide tradition of snake worship. Serpents have been considered protectors of many communities and races. Despite the fact that they contain poisonous venom, which often can be fatal, they are also considered the embodiment of wisdom and enlighten-ment. The assignment of the serpent to Ashlesha indicates the deeply mystical power radiating from the asterism which rightly absorbed can produce great electrifying energy, but in case of misuse can be fatally dangerous.

A unique characteristic of the serpent is its bipolarity, its forked tongue. The serpent represents immense good. It is for this reason that almost every god and goddess of Hindu mythology has serpents in their ornamentation. Lord Krishna is fabled as subjugating the serpent lying at the bottom of the Yamuna river when his ball, with which he was playing, fell into its waters. In the churning of the ocean, the serpent was instru-mental in extracting both nectar and poison from its depths. Indian teachings consider the serpent as capable of both good and bad. Classical Indian texts have made the serpent a symbol of wisdom, procreation, wealth and prosperity, as well as of sex, trouble, danger and unexpected attack. The asterism Ashlesha is associated with these contradictory qualities. The effect of Ashlesha is thereby difficult to predict.

The serpent symbol reveals the complex and often misunderstood psychology of Ashlesha. People under the influence of this asterism are deeply philosophical, thoughtful, austere, self-reliant and reclusive, but they can on occasion behave in the most ordinary and crude manner - harsh, selfish and venomous. They cannot tolerate any personal humilia-tion. These characteristics are well represented by the serpent. The venom in a serpent is not a part of its general constitution. It is found under its fangs and is not absorbed into its own system. It is used only when it is induced to bite something. At times the serpent is found sucking milk from the udder of a cow or a buffalo without injecting any poison into the animal. Ashlesha people can be good or bad depending upon circum-stances and the psychological situation. The serpent remains in isolation, generally in a hole, a cavity, a bush or in a crack in the rocks. The serpent does not make its own home. Such places are also associated with yogis — ascetics — engaged in arduous penance. Every Ashlesha influence leads to this kind of psychological segregation which unabsorbed by the person makes his life unhappy. Otherwise he may become austere or ascetic.

Sloughing of the skin is a special feature of the serpent by which it continually renews itself. Under Ashlesha also, there is transformation, especially when the individual has outgrown his experiences and is capable of absorbing new vitality for new endeavors. These changes are very unexpected and Ashlesha does not yield to any well established course of events. This characteristic is revealed by the fact that the serpent appears suddenly and at unexpected moments without the slightest prior however, it makes a straight movement. The glistening eyes of a serpent are hypnotizing and attractive, suggesting the tremendous magnetism latent in Ashlesha people.

The importance of Ashlesha arises from the fact that the Moon, related to the human psyche and changes within it, and Mercury, concerned with intelligence, rule this asterism and the sign in which it is located, and thereby endow it with great potential for mental development. This characteristic is well expressed by the Nagas presiding over it. The Nagas are spiritual teachers concerned with the propagation of wisdom. Ashlesha is the asterism which imparts intellectual and mental development, enabling its beneficiaries to change their perception of life. These changes occur in the most unexpected ways. After the transformation, the individual is catapulted into a radically different condition of existence.

10
MAGHA

Magha extends from 120° 00′ to 133° 20′ of the sign of Leo, governed by the Sun. Its main star is Regulus, the bright first magnitude star of alpha Leo. The deities presiding over it are the Pitris, the Fathers, the great ancestors of humanity. The planet Ketu rules it and its primary motivation is Artha, the seeking of specific goals or objects. Its basic attribute is Tamas or inertia, but it has Rajas, activity at secondary and tertiary levels. Two symbols, a palanquin and a house are assigned to it.

The Fathers are Vedic deities who have the special responsibility of guiding the evolutionary course of the families and races entrusted to their care. They intervene in their progeny's lives and relationships only when serious digression or major diversion from the right course occurs. As long as progress is according to the desired pattern, they merely watch and nourish by their influence. They function like guardian angels giving protection in the event of major calamities. Otherwise they are mere overseers, trying to unfold their descendant's faculties and growth in the exuberance of Divine blessing. Their influence is also directed towards maintaining the tradition and cultural purity of those they look over.

Up to this point in the zodiac, the various asterisms are concerned with formulating the matrix of growth. With Magha begins concretization. At this stage, the soul in its individualized form begins to manifest outwardly its archetype. The contraction of idea into form induces the spirit to long for the freedom lost in the process of encasement. This craving for its lost original nature is expressed as ambition, family pride, racial superiority, class status and the urge to jump from the actual to the ideal. Restlessness arising from the feeling of restriction, and through restlessness, the arousal of the urge to reacquire the lost paradise, characterize this asterism.

Magha marks the beginning of Tamasic proclivities. It is expressed as sloth and the desire to stay put instead of the moving forward which comes through the Rajasic tendency of the first third of the asterisms. Rajas impels the incarnating soul to immerse itself in materiality which attains its deepest point under Ashlesha. At this stage, the Nagas impart ultimate wisdom and bid the soul to proceed further according to the intelligence thus acquired to complete the evolutionary impulse. The archetype is thereby impressed on the finer atoms of the being and the soul acquires the power to actualize it. This situation produces a contradictory tendency. The earlier impulse induced the soul to proceed further, while the new influences of a Tamasic nature, beginning with Magha, exert a decelerating motion. Under Magha, therefore, one experiences conflict. This is emphasized by the secondary and tertiary rajasic or active qualities of the asterism. One part of the being urges the soul to swift action while the other puts on a brake to bring movement to a halt. Magha leads to substantial psychological tension and frustration.

The symbol of the palanquin associated with Magha reveals its inner drive. At this stage, the soul in its fullness as a representative of the Supreme, embarks upon its material journey. Ashlesha bestows the wisdom of the Nagas enabling the soul to hold within itself all the Divine attributes necessary for completing its mundane journey. Under Magha, the soul begins the outer journey ordained for it. The palanquin symbolizes the soul's preparedness for the journey. On a chariot the king goes to the battlefield but on a palanquin he undertakes his usual visitations.

The palanquin and chariot are both modes of transportation but quite different from each other. This distinguishes the basic nature of the two asterisms with which they are associated. The chariot is related to Rohini, while the palanquin refers to Magha. A chariot is generally associated with the army, while the palanquin is for the nobles and the elite. A chariot is pulled by horses, an inferior level of creation, while the palanquin is carried by human beings. This shows that the individual in the palanquin enjoys special status among people. A chariot is pulled on wheels but the palanquin is built around the central, generally undulated, pole.

The wheel represents Divine perfection and the nature's inherent creative impulse. This impulse leads to gradual involution of the spirit into matter. Such is the influence of the fourth asterism, Rohini. But the undulated pole, usually made of bamboo, has several knots in it, which symbolically relate to the spinal cord within which is concealed the serpent fire or Kundalini. The servants who carry the palanquin represent the five organs of action and five sense organs which carry the soul where it wants to go. At Magha, the human individual is bestowed with Divine capabilities. The soul is informed of its Divine mission and is stationed at the place wherefrom it can make its onward journey. This also shows the significance of the house, the other symbol of this asterism. At this stage of evolution, the individual has to make up his mind, take decisions and direct his faculties towards the destined goal. The human soul has reached a situation where the natural impulses guiding his progress cease and he is required to take a stock of his resources and regulate his own actions.

The house emphasizes the human body as a vehicle of the Supreme, while the palanquin refers to an external means of transportation. The comparison between the human body and a house is often found in spiritual literature. The great Vedantic philosopher Shankara explains this comparison in great detail in *Vivekachudamani* (verse 92). The physical sheath sustains and nourishes the individual as well as provide the necessary means of action for it. Even in the *Bible*, there is mention of the tabernacle, as the seat of the Supreme. The tabernacle was made so that "I may dwell among them." The purpose of this tabernacle is to transport the experiencing soul from one stage of development in another. At Magha, the Divine radiance produces the human being complete in his material sheaths so that he can fulfill his Divine mission.

This characteristic of the asterism is accentuated by the fact that it starts the fifth sign of the zodiac ruled by the Sun. Leo is full of life-giving energy. Under Magha, the soul is pushed out into the world with abundant energy and courage. This is the stage of reproduction. Regeneration and reproduction are necessary to continue the process of manifestation. Ketu which rules this asterism is a karmic planet under whom the past is worked out. The soul, imbibing the influence of Magha, is induced to carry forth its earthly pilgrimage under the karmic impulse. Its personal tendencies are subordinated to the Divine mission. But in this involvement, the individual, though not specifically attached to material ease and comfort, often experiences them. The four quadrants of the asterism gradually lead the soul towards materialization. Mars, Venus, Mercury and the Moon, which rule them, progressively increase this process of densification. Under favorable influences, Magha bestows much affluence and physical comforts, sexual happiness and the luxuries of life. But the individual concerned is not psychologically so much involved with these. He wants to follow the ideal and carry out his inner purpose in life. Generally speaking, Magha makes the person an idealist amidst material affluence. This makes people suspect his integrity and honesty of purpose, which often makes the individual feel sad. But this is what all true idealists must suffer.

11
PURVA PHALGUNI

Purva Phalguni, the eleventh asterism, extends from 133° 20′ to 140° 40′ of the zodiac occupying the central area of Leo, owned by the Sun. The asterism itself is ruled by Venus. Its primary motivation is Kama, desire, while is basic attribute is Tamas, inertia, with Rajas at a secondary and Tamas at a tertiary level.

The two asterisms Purva and Uttara Phalguni together form one constellation consisting of four stars represented as the four legs of a cot. The two asterisms, however, have subtle differences reflected by their presiding deities. Purva Phalguni is ruled by Bhaga, the Vedic God of bliss. The symbols assigned to it are a couch, platform, and fireplace. The deity for Uttara Phalguni is Aryaman, who possesses a more active character. Both Vedic deities, Bhaga and Aryaman, are very auspicious. They bestow riches, affluence and material prosperity. The Vedas referred to them as "whom they protect are victorious over their adversaries."

During the course of one's hectic life, a time comes when rest is necessary before taking up the next period of labor. The couch provides such a rest. The fireplace has a similar significance. In ancient Indian society, the teachers assembled their students around a fireplace and discussed matters of spiritual knowledge. This is how the *Upanishads,* the great wisdom teachings of ancient India, originated. A platform is also a resting place for launching such activities. All these symbols thus have a common characteristic. Purva Phalguni consolidates the Divine impulse for its materializing activities. It expresses that phase of cosmic evolution under which the descending soul receives its marching orders.

Under this asterism, one may think that the king has arrived, the war has begun, great religious observances have commenced but the next phase of development has not yet been disclosed. This is suggested in the *Shiva Purana* by stating that Lord Shiva started on his marriage procession under this star. His marriage, with all its deep significance, represents the Divine energy beginning to penetrate deeply into matter in order to spiritualize it.

Purva Phalguni provides the avenue for the expression of dynamic energy. It enables the soul to work in the external realm in order to discharge the Divine responsibilities entrusted to it. The basic feature of this asterism is its readiness to plunge into activity. Other characteristics arise during the operation of this asterism which support this basic impulse. The impelling force of Kama, passion, makes an individual enthusiastic about all that he undertakes, so that he pours forth his inner strength and vitality into every act. But he is purposive, acquisitive, and calculative of the advantages and disadvantages of the outcome. There is often a streak of selfishness in his approach to life and relationship. The amount of vitality pouring forth from him makes him generally successful in his endeavors. It draws to him the attention of those in power. He receives recognition and royal favor. The same thing makes him attractive to the opposite sex. For the man, his virility is strong and women are drawn to him. His material proclivities also make him pleasure seeking and prone to self-aggrandizement.

Bhaga as well as Aryaman bring many material gifts to men of the world. They bestow material affluence, prosperity, worldly comforts and renown. The feeling of uniqueness, being specially gifted and better qualified than the majority are some of the psychological traits of the asterism which often impart the feeling of being original. People who are strongly influenced by this asterism often suffer from feelings of superiority. Their natural tendencies are self-centered and they have an insatiable thirst for personal glorification. This is expressed as sexual conquest, establishment of new empires or eagerness to undertake competitive enterprises. But when planetary influences arouse spiritual urges in the soul, the individual cannot remain content unless final liberation is achieved and all selfish impediments are overcome. Essentially, the asterism is the launching pad for spiritual as well as material conquests.

Bhaga, the deity assigned to this asterism, has other significance. The Sanskrit word Bhaga also means the female reproductive organ. It has a special power because through it all human beings are born and the family and society are formed and perpetuated. The ancients saw it as a symbol of Divine creativity and the power of nature. In this regard, Purva Phalguni is the crucial radiation which is the cornerstone of the future edifice of soul development and its expansion into the supreme. Bhaga is also one of the names of the Sun, the ruler of the sign in which this asterism is located. Purva Phalguni is additionally related to the Sun. This asterism nourishes the individual in many ways, and provides energy for growth and expansion.

Such growth is necessarily the result of Trishna, the thirst for experience. The soul at this stage is let loose to wander forth and gain knowledge of the world. The diverse avenues in which one can unveil one's inner qualities are now open. The individual has to conquer them according to his growing capabilities. This arouses insatiable thirst, which in the early stages of development is expressed as lust. But Venus, the ruler of this asterism, bestows much sensitivity, sociability, and flight of intuition.

With the recognition of the expanding horizons of human experience, Purva Phalguni makes the person ambitious. If spiritual energy is mobilized for the achievement of purer delights of awareness, the individual can devote himself to arduous penance, but generally he does not do so. He usually gets mixed-up with his dreams and existing mundane opportunities. He often rationalizes the necessity of involving himself in the world of matter. Success in life due to special planetary influences make him over ambitious even in spiritual matters. Unless they are on guard, such persons may end up practicing black magic or left-handed Tantra. They may like drinking and gambling. These features of Venus may completely upset the balance of life unless one is very careful. Yet in such situations, the individual is more excited about the novelty of experience than the act itself. This experience is indeed the beginning of a new way of life. It opens the gate to a new dimension of existence. Purva Phalguni is the planetary radiation which opens the floodgate of inner potential for involvement in material existence.

12
UTTARA PHALGUNI

Uttara Phalguni, the latter part of the Phalguni, extends from 146° 40′ to 160° 00′ of the zodiac. The first quarter of the asterism is in Leo ruled by the Sun, while its remaining three quarters fall within Virgo ruled by Mercury. Leo is a sign of immense activity, whereas Virgo has the ability to develop the latent potentialities in man including various yogic powers.

The asterism itself is also ruled by the Sun. Its primary motivation is Moksha, liberation, while its basic attribute is Tamas, inertia, with Rajas at a secondary and Sattwa at a tertiary level. Aryaman, a Vedic deity renowned for his leadership, presides over it. As a continuation of the previous asterism, Purva Phalguni, it has similar features. Both asterisms are assigned the symbol of the four legs of a cot, which emphasizes their unity.

Phalguni as a unity represents the creative energy bestowed on the individual soul. The four legs of the cot represent the lower quaternity of the human being consisting of his physical sheath, the etheric double which provides the channel for the flow of vital energy, the astral sheath which radiates and responds to emotional vibrations, and the mental sheath which enables the individual to think. This quaternity is also represented by the four heads of Brahma, the four dimensions of space, and the four Vedas. These aspects of cosmic evolution provide the arena in which the individual acts and the vehicle through which the soul can express itself. The Phalgunis represent the unity existing between the various capabilities of the human individual, which during the course of his evolution are brought into function.

Uttara Phalguni provides the basic power, the inner urge, the restless energy which can concretize under favorable circumstances. In order to attain this state, there must be many disturbances. Uttara Phalguni presided over by Aryaman, renowned for his fights and leadership, shows the courage and endurance that descend on seasoned fighters who are confident of their strength, the righteousness of their mission and the final victorious outcome of their efforts. Uttara Phalguni is the asterism which enables the individual soul to appear with all its capabilities developed as a result of fighting his way through the realm of matter. It is an asterism of ambition, difficulties and righteous struggle.

The four legs of a bed, the symbol of the asterism, emphasizes the number four and the need for rest. The four directions of space are indicated here. Within this parameter the entire universe is enclosed and the four natural forces operate. Uttara Phalguni in its basic energy is a passive magnetic field wherein the individual soul has the scope in which to operate. The first quarter of the asterism within Leo is ruled by Jupiter. The solar influence which enables the Divine spark to consolidate receives favorable conditions for protection and expansion by Jupiter. The four directions, or the entire universe, is provided to the soul for its activities. Depending upon planetary dispositions, the person under the first quarter of Uttara Phalguni does not encounter restrictions. There is perfect security and immense opportunity for growth and expansion.

The last three quarters of the asterism, which fall within Virgo, are ruled by Saturn (the second and third quarters) and Jupiter (the fourth). They indicate the possibility of the individual delving deep into nature's mysteries. The hidden powers of nature, which are directly related to Virgo, find under this asterism the best conditions for their unfoldment. The possibilities of spiritual growth and mental expansion under Uttara Phalguni are immense. The central impulse covered by its second and third quarters under Saturn concentrates on the consolidation of faculties acquired, while those unfolded under Jupiter get impetus for expansion.

The vastness of space causes great bewilderment for the individual who is not interested in playing an active role in the universal unfoldment. The great loneliness which often arises when the Moon is in this asterism is mainly due to the exposure of the human individual with all his limitations to the vastness of the universe and its manifold inner depths. Such persons like to stand alone and live in isolation, but once they have decided to engage themselves in action, the deity associated with the asterism, Aryaman, assures them victory and laurels in the fight. Uttara Phalguni is the star wherein the safety and peace of the individual can be assured only if he is actively engaged in externalization of his inner qualities.

Such activities, however, should not be merely impulsive reactions. The Martian approach to life is alien to this asterism. What is required here is well directed effort, as if one is engaged on a battlefield and required to have a clear idea of the goal and a good strategy for its achievement.

Uttara Phalguni has the quality of making a person ambitious, especially when he begins to achieve and feel secure. The vastness of the realm of operation creates dangers in the absence of ethical preparations and spiritual discipline. The danger of meddling with black magic may arise under this impulse. If the individual is turned outward, his ambition and certainty of himself may take him to great heights but he needs well directed efforts.

13
HASTA

Hasta extends from 160° 00′ to 173° 20′ of the zodiac. It lies entirely within the sign of Virgo, ruled by Mercury. The asterism itself is ruled by the Moon, the receptacle of cosmic energy, whereas Mercury establishes the link between the human and the divine. Mercury is exalted here. Its primary motivation is Moksha, liberation, while its basic attribute is Tamas, inertia at both primary and secondary levels, with Rajas, activity at a tertiary level. The deity presiding over Hasta is Savitar, the Sun god, particularly as the reservoir of all generative energy in the universe. The word Hasta itself means the hand. The human hand, or more specifically the palm of the hand, through which the entire individuality of the person can be read, is the symbol of the asterism.

Hasta gives self-reliance and control over the outgoing cosmic energy that is always ready to proceed further. Various impediments arise in this enterprise as natural reactions to it. Whenever any kind of kinetic energy moves over static matter, there is resistance to it. Such an individualistic approach to life as is natural under this asterism must bear this kind of confrontation. The inner faculties can develop only through such an exercise.

The hand stands for prowess or the capacity which enables the individual to withstand confrontation. The hand also refers to full confidence in the soul's capabilities to march ahead. This self-reliance springs from the fact that the individual is aware of his own faculties through an understanding of his real nature and the laws of the universe. This is the basic and most important characteristic of Hasta.

Hasta contains within it an immense regenerative power. Savitar, its ruling deity, is the form of the Sun god that imparts creative and transforming energy. This energy enables life to grow and assume innumerable shapes. The cycle of birth, growth, decay and death shows the transformation of the energy content of the incarnate soul. This asterism impels the individual under its impact to change, take new shapes and grow. This process of growth results from the inner urge to march ahead, while external conditions exert resistance. Thus conflict and different levels of crises are the natural features of this lunar mansion. The impediments, difficulties and obstructions which are experienced occur due to the opposing forces impinging on the individual. The ruler of this asterism, the Moon, and the rulers of its four quarters, the quick moving planets Mercury, Venus, Mars and the Moon, are all connected with regeneration and readjustment of the outer sheaths of the soul and aid in its concretization and individualization in the material world.

On a spiritual level, Hasta is the seat of the interplay of nature's finer forces. The two basic impulses in nature are attraction and repulsion, the expression of positive and negative energy impulses. This duality is the primary cause of all movement and growth in the universe. The universe itself is circumscribed by the twelve radiations of the cosmic creative force, which astrologically is reflected through the twelve signs of the zodiac. This basic differentiation results from the four primary motivating causes in the universe namely Kama, desire; Artha, purposeful activity; Dharma, sustaining principles; and Moksha, liberation. These four impetuses motivate the incarnating soul. They are affected by the three primary attributes of all activity, Sattwa, harmony, purity or goodness; Rajas or self-seeking activity; and Tamas or inertia. The hand succinctly represents these forces.

The symbolic hand can refer to the actual organ and its operation, by which the individuality of the person is expressed. It also suggests a spatial dimension because the most fundamental units of measurement are based on the hand. A cubit consists of two spans of three times the four finger width of the hand. The two hands represent the positive and the negative energy currents, the centripetal and centrifugal forces, attraction and repulsion, Purusha and Prakriti, the male and female aspects of all existence.

The four fingers stand for the four primary motivating forces of Kama, Artha, Dharma and Moksha mentioned above. They also refer to the four divisions of the cosmos which in Sanskrit are Annamaya Kosha, Pranamaya Kosha, Manomaya Kosha, and Vijnanmaya Kosha, the sheaths or layers respectively of matter, life, mind and intelligence. These four kinds of impulses or four levels of existence, can be of Sattvic, Rajasic or Tamasic in nature. Together they stand for all the latent forces in the human individual as well as the cosmos. The twelve signs of the zodiac as the twelve digits of the fingers of the hand, are all contained in this asterism in which their cosmic impulses become fully differentiated.

This asterism therefore operates on the entire universe. It functions both on subjective and objective planes of existence. Wherever the soul can have any existence, there Hasta as an asterism has its affect. This makes it a very deep acting influence. Consequently, Hasta is said to represent *Duration,* Time itself. All activities can fructify only in the time-space continuum. In consciousness, there is no real difference between space and time, nor between the subjective and the objective. There is either the complete negation of all manifestation, or everything is pure reality.

On an ordinary level, there is a field in which action occurs. Hasta refers to the field of action. This action can be performed only in field of Duration, which combines within it the functions of both Time and Space. The urge to create aroused under Phalguni meets its reaction. That reaction can follow only when this urge meets the space-time matrix of cosmic ideation. The combination of the two, or the confrontation of action with its field or matrix results in many kinds of difficulties. The emergence of this reaction can be tackled only when there is the quality of individuality. Hasta represents the situation when the individual is ready to meet the universe with all its physical and non-physical potentials. The various perfections that can be attained through this interaction are outside the domain of the asterism. In objective as well as subjective realms, the preparedness of the soul to embark and act is what Hasta represents.

In predictive astrology, the effects of Hasta can be observed in two directions. If the individual is unmindful of any higher purpose, he will engage in many types of voluntary and social work. If he is cognizant of the true goal of life, he will practice yoga or other practical techniques of inner development. Under Hasta, when the soul is not yet developed and is still engrossed in the material world, life will deprive him of many things. Such a person will engage in activities perennially without success. There will be hardships, impediments, difficulties, ill health, poverty and all kinds of resistance to his efforts to arouse a yet greater power of application in him.

14
CHITRA

Chitra extends from 173° 20′ to 186° 40′ of the zodiac. Its first half is in Virgo ruled by Mercury and its second half in Libra ruled by Venus. Mars is the ruler of the asterism itself. Its primary motivation is Kama or desire. Tamas or inertia is its attribute on all levels, while the celestial architect, Tvashtar, is its presiding deity. Chitra represented by a single star, Spica, the bright white first magnitude star of the sign Virgo. This single star shines like a pearl, which is the symbol of the asterism.

Chitra itself means bright or transparent and also refers to a fairy as well as a serpent. Superficially, the pearl, the asterism's symbol, conveys a pleasant and an alluring appearance but this should not beguile the student. It has the potential of a serpent. It contains wisdom and danger simultaneously. In fact, Chitra is one of the most mystical asterisms.

The Sanskrit word Mukta, meaning a pearl, is derived from the same root as the words Mukti and Moksha, both meaning liberation. No one has ever suggested that the liberation process for the human soul is a pleasant experience. Yogis resort to difficult practices and severe austerities before they hope to get any intimation of the final realization. During the process of unfoldment of one's real nature and the dawn of the vision of Truth, the aspirant must discipline himself and forego the comforts of life. Even those who do not undertake this task voluntarily but find themselves on the path of spirituality have to pass through severe ordeals. The process of releasing the soul from the thraldom of matter is a hard one. On this path, the individual's wings are clipped and his activities fettered. He feels tremendously frustrated. He must be completely broken before he can become free. His feet have to be washed in the blood of his heart before he can really move forward.

In this regard, we should note that Virgo represents the Sixth house of the cosmic man, the house of disease and opposition. This house represents the ordeals of the seeker prior to his being ordained in the silken dress of 'Initiation' or direct insight into truth. It is the stage of trial and tribulation which must precede the activation of the soul's faculties. When the inner life-force begins to break the outer material crust, there is trouble and pain. The individual feels like he is being torn apart. But this act of the churning of the ocean is the inevitable prelude to the discovery of inner reality. The real image hidden in the uncut stone must be carved out by the sculptor. When the stone chips are cut, they must cause sorrow. The celestial architect has to ultimately produce the archetype destined for the individual and for each entity of the universe. Tvashtar must cut off the unwanted pieces of the stone which are not essential for the true image to come forth. The word Chitra also means an image or reflection. Under the impulse of this asterism, the archetype, latent within, forces the outer, the external, to dissolve so that the real image can be perceived.

The story of the origin of the pearl, whether true or false, is similar to the process of unfoldment of inner consciousness. It is said that rain drops, under the influence of the asterism Swati, fall on oyster shells to form pearls within them. To get the pearls, the hard outer shells of the oysters have to be broken. In life, impulses from above, from the supramental level or the Divine itself flash on the consciousness of the individual and begin the churning operation. They arouse the urge to realize the true Self. The momentary flash becomes the guiding star to drive the aspirant to traverse the difficult path. The asterism Chitra represents the sudden flash of inspiration, the urge to realize one's true image. For it, the individual undergoes different kinds of suffering. Before the pearl is obtained and polished, the oyster, the outer physical sheath, has to be dissolved and the shell discarded. All these sufferings are for a cause, the realization of the inner self, the real man which resembles the pure shining pearl lying hidden within the reeking hard shell of the body and ego.

The celestial architect, Tvashtar, is the father of Sanjna, the wife of the Sun. The celestial architect had to clip the wings of the Sun and reduce his radiance to allow Sanjna to withstand his light. In life, the individual has to adapt himself to actual external conditions. Selfish feelings must be discarded before one can realize the truth about oneself and one's relationship with the world. Chitra represents this realization of the true self through the ordeals of life and complete subjugation or destruction of one's material nature and self-centeredness.

Mars as ruler of Chitra reveals the basic urge towards externalization. Mars does not accept any defeat. Any confrontation provides it added incentive to fight and attain its goal. When the soul reaches the stage of Chitra it has already discovered the goal of its mission which must be achieved at any cost. The attempt made at this level is primarily on intellectual and inspirational planes. This is why one finds the asterism extending from Virgo, ruled by intellectual Mercury, to Libra, owned by inspirational Venus. The Venusian inspiration lightens the burden of the struggling soul. The first two quarters of the asterism in Virgo, as governed by the Sun and Mercury, represent the nature of the struggle taking place on the intellectual plane. The confusion which may arise at this stage is due to lack of clarity or confidence in the ideals held by the individual. In the last two quarters of this asterism in Libra, conflicts and adjustments in the realm of social relationships become prominent.

Chitra brings a great upsurge to build and to reach to new levels of achievement. For this reason, one can find wonder workers, efficient leaders, people desiring intellectual attainment and extremely honest personages born under this star. But those who are not able to imbibe the full radiation of this asterism may become smug, self-content, stagnant, self-indulgent types. Whatever the level of spiritual development, the individual under this asterism must glimpse the vision of perfection, struggle in some way to attain the ideal and concretize the vision, and come a little closer to the final goal of his destiny. Depending upon his capacity to imbibe the energy of the asterism and the disposition of other planets, the outcome of the struggle begun under this star can be foreseen.

15
SWATI

Swati lies in the middle of Libra from 186° 40' to 200° 00' of the zodiac. It is marked by Arcturus, the bright star alpha Bootes. Libra ruled by Venus represents the stage where materialistic and spiritual tendencies are finely balanced. Swati resembles this influence though with some differences. These are highlighted by Rahu's rulership of the asterism. Its primary motivation is Artha, directed activity, while its basic attribute is Tamas, with Sattwa at a tertiary level. Swati is presided over by the Vedic deity Vayu, the God of the wind or life-breath. This makes the asterism more concerned with the spirit flowing through it than the vessel that contains it. The difference between the sign and the asterism is further clarified by the difference between the symbol of the balance for the sign and that of coral for the asterism.

This stage of spiritual evolution, described by coral, has several unique characteristics. Coral is the hard calcareous skeleton secreted by certain marine animals. It produces its own offspring from within itself. This represents the stage of evolution when the spirit is encased in its outer physical sheaths while its further evolution depends upon the unfoldment of its inner potential. When the pearl-like spirit begins to move in the realm of matter, it has all the potential contained of its Divine creator which it expresses, creates and multiplies. Coral is a living entity though it outwardly looks like stone. The outer physical fringe of the human being also appears like a solid mass, though in our essential nature we are spirits or consciousness. At this stage of manifestation, the two primary impulses, the centrifugal and centripetal forces or attraction and repulsion come into prominence. The subjective spirit has the natural inclination to expand, while the material sheaths restrict it. The equilibrium attained by these opposing tendencies enables the formation of a human individual and sustains him.

Coral is a sea product but it is not essentially a marine creature. The marine condition gives it a solid foundation, but coral has a strong psychic impact on those who come in contact with it. Coral is affected by its marine environment, but it has its own unique contribution to make on its environment which it reshapes. The same is true of human beings who are affected by the surrounding environment but also change it in a dramatic way.

Swati is the primeval stage of human evolution when human beings produced offspring from themselves in a non-sexual manner. There are many stories in Hindu mythology in which the ancient sages produce offspring from their speech, sweat, ears, or in other non-sexual ways. Human reproduction through sexual union came later in evolution according to the occult view of it. The sexual stage is also included under Libra, particularly relative to the next asterism of Vishakha. Under Swati, reproductive activities exist but in an asexual way. At this stage, the outer environment and physical conditions do agitate and affect the soul. This leaves the inner nature practically isolated. Some contradictions in the life of various saints have been depicted which occurred as a consequence of this stage of spiritual development. Their outer stoniness is not the mirror of their inner spirituality, sensitivity and vitality.

Along with Agni (fire), and Surya (the Sun), the presiding deity of the asterism, Vayu (air) forms the trinity of gods who rule the formation of the material world. Though all three are present together in all the worlds, Agni has as his seat the earth. Vayu, who is considered to be an aspect of Indra, resides in the atmosphere surrounding the earth. Surya, the vibrant spirit ensouling every living being, resides in heaven as the Sun. In the microcosm, these three cosmic principles correspond to Kama, desire or vital passion; Kama-manas, desire-mind or feeling based on thought; and Manas or intellect. Vayu is related to desire-mind, the main impulse inducing and motivating creatures to mundane involvements and activities. Under Swati, one is aroused to act according to the primary objective of personal gain.

Coral as a symbol for Swati shows the crystallization of the spirit in the physical sheath and inducing it to act for self-gain. This results in its projection and reflection of itself into the world around it. This feature is also indicated by another astrological condition; the Sun, representing the highest spiritual force, is debilitated in this asterism, that is, the spiritual force is at its lowest level here. The human being under this asterism has the predominant motivation of self-gratification which is often the root of all his actions. Saturn in exaltation in this sign indicates the increasing hold of materialism. The pure spirit is now a stone-like entity engaged in outward activities. Here also, he functions in a self-centered manner: the socialization influence of the sexual process is absent at this stage. Such a person who has Swati as an important influence in his life is however very dynamic in several ways. Though he is susceptible to outer influences, yet he has much capabilities by which he impacts the surrounding world.

In predictive astrology, Swati produces self-centeredness. Under every impulse the individual is motivated by the goal of personal gain. Even when the individual is undergoing pain and deprivation, the feeling that these conditions will lead to some kind of spiritual or material reward is always present. There is intense passion in every act. The complete personality is engrossed in every action pursued. Such an intensity of involvement is not necessarily due to the work in progress but because of the feeling that the individual engaged in it that he is important. Generally, it is the pleasure principle in life which is important for the person, but to say that the person is pleasure seeking is not entirely correct. What is most characteristic is the desire to have a long lasting condition of achievement. Often the emphasis on personality is so deep and hidden that it has to be inferred from action, the way of performing it, or the experience gained from it.

Swati is an asterism that transforms the psychological orientation of the person concerned but after bestowing upon him a condition of affluence. In order to lead to this transformation, psychological dissatisfaction occurs. The person feels that he deserved more success, more happiness, greater recognition and so on. If he manages to get these things, he feels that they do not give him the necessary satisfaction that he should derive from them. There remains a kind of airiness in life, expressed as a vague discontentment; not knowing what one wants, feeling unfulfilled with everything one gets.

16
VISHAKHA

Vishakha extends from 200° 00' to 213° 20' of the zodiac. Three quarters of it lie in Libra, ruled by Venus, while the last quarter falls in Scorpio under the sway of Mars. The asterism itself is governed by Jupiter. Its primary motivation is Dharma, honor or principle. Tamas or inertia is the primary attribute flowing through it, while its secondary attribute is Sattwa or harmony and its tertiary attribute Rajas or activity. A unique feature of this asterism is the dual rulership of it; the two Vedic deities associated with it are Indra, the lord of the gods, and Agni, the God of fire. The symbol assigned to it is that of a potter's wheel, but sometimes in ancient texts it is indicated by an archway. Saturn is exalted here.

Vishakha stands for transformation. The manifesting soul has already been individualized and under Swati's radiation has achieved a self-perpetuating metabolism. The Vishakha phase makes the individual look forward to discover what lies within him. It arouses the urge to change in order to achieve something which is not entirely known. The beginning of spirituality and the urge to move towards the source of existence or Divine origin of things occurs under this asterism. A kind of spiritual discontent or dissatisfaction with the existing conditions of life, restlessness in the personal life, and a great psychological turmoil are some of the main characteristics of Vishakha.

Such an impulse often leads to infidelity in marriage, non-fulfillment of promises in personal relationships, and it minimizes the contribution of others to the person. There is great non-attraction, which is not necessarily repulsion, to existing conditions. The infidelity does not arise due to any fault of the partner, and letting down friends does not arise due to their lack of warmth for the person. These reactions are caused by a feeling of dryness at the central core of one's being, which is outwardly expressed as restlessness. Dissatisfaction at the surface, the urge to look within, the discovery of an impersonal existence, and the need to revolt lead the individual to a great turmoil in his personal life.

This kind of turmoil is represented by the potter's wheel. Vishakha has inertia as its guiding impulse and harmony is the foundation on which this impulse acts. As a result of these attributes, intense activity occurs on a physical level. Such complex forces act on the person because Tamas is the primary attribute of the asterism, Sattwa the secondary and Rajas the tertiary attribute. In a potter's wheel the central axis around which the wheel rotates is almost stationary. There is no apparent movement at that point. The greater the proximity to the center, the less movement. Tamas is that attribute which desires no change in the existing condition which is what the center of the wheel represents. Remain wherever you are, whatever else happens, exert no will of your own. This is where the clay to be shaped is put. Harmony prevails by conforming to the will of God or by surrendering to the impulse generated by nature. The clay does not resist. The shape visualized in the potter's mind is gradually imprinted on the clay by the wheel, which works according to the potter's fingers.

Under Vishakha, the Divine Will arouses the urge to explore one's inner self, one's real nature, which, however, arouses dissatisfaction with its existing state and urges the person to act in order to transform oneself.

The potter's wheel as a symbol is commonly found in Vedantic literature. The cosmos itself is compared to it. Within this field the crystallized coral that contains within itself the vibrating divine life is shaped into different forms and sizes according to the archetype in the potter's mind. Every impetus, whether external or internal, is a part of the cosmos which operates according to the Divine design in the Creator's mind, the Mahat of Vedantic philosophy. Under the impulse of this asterism, individual genius finds expression, its main impelling force being the externalization of that which is within. It leads to a radical transformation. This transformation, however, is according to a plan, a design. The individual performs his assigned duty or responsibility in the cosmic drama. But this takes place at a tremendous sacrifice of personal pleasure and convenience.

One may remember that this asterism is owned by two deities: Indra, the god of luxury and sensuous enjoyment, and Agni, the god of penance, under whose influence the dross is burnt out completely. With a new beginning, the process of transformation occurs in numerous ways; the shape of the clay is also fashioned in many forms depending on the potter's objective. The potter's mind and the role of the presiding deity, Agni, are identical in many ways. The potter's mind can be better understood by examining the nature of Agni as given in classical literature. There are many kinds of fire, but seven are identified as the main ones. These seven are the seven flames which are the seven human temperaments, or the seven channels on whose current the seeds of manifestation are carried through the different planes of existence. The One Supreme Principle becomes actively energized under this impulse.

The dual ownership of the asterism by Indra and Agni implies that the course of evolution can be either on the path of materialization, on which one gets all the luxuries in life, or on the path of spiritualization where all kinds of deprivations have to be met. The two function within one primary force — that of Tapas or asceticism, the process of destroying the non-essential.

The archway, another symbol given to Vishakha, marks the transit from one place to another. In this allusion, the focus is not on the material, the clay which is fashioned on the wheel, but on the living entity, the man on pilgrimage. Passing through an archway indicates the entrance to a sacred or important place. When Vishakha affects any aspect of one's life, it must move it towards its inherent goal, the shrine of one's true nature. The onward movement under such an impulse entails important changes. Generally it is observed that the person affected by Vishakha becomes austere, hard-boiled, detached and such changes which result from the burning away of lower passions, as happens in the case of yogis performing tapas. In everyday life one notices its influence as a feeling of uneasiness, not the usual unhappiness that occurs during periods of psychological stress, but a feeling of vague disillusionment with the superficial experiences of the pleasures and happiness in life.

The basic nature of Vishakha is revealed by its very name. The word derives from the word which means "readiness," like the attentive preparedness for shooting an arrow. It is readiness when the archer keeps his feet apart, holds the bow and stretches the cord holding the arrow, aiming at the target but not yet deciding to shoot. This asterism itself covers primarily the sign of Libra but towards its later part extends to Scorpio which provides the preparatory impulse to enable the soul to receive the radical transformation under Sagittarius which has the shooting centaur as its symbol. Basically, Vishakha is the asterism where the necessary attention of the archer is turned towards the butt of the arrow. This asterism prepares the individual for the forthcoming change which takes place under Sagittarius. For this purpose Vishakha induces a change in attitude; the clay under the potter's wheel only changes form while it still remains clay and retains its inherent material nature. Only under Sagittarius radical transformation of the whole being occurs: it is only then that the horse becomes a human being, that the person motivated by physical propensities and emotional passion becomes a conscious individual. This emphasizes the role of Vishakha as a preparatory stage; under it, the psychological orientation needed for spiritual change in life begins to take place.

17
ANURADHA

Anuradha extends from 213° 20′ to 226° 40′ of the zodiac. The asterism itself is ruled by Saturn, but it lies in Scorpio ruled by Mars. There is great turmoil raging in Anuradha as Mars and Saturn are inimical planets, one being fiery and the other being cold. The same churning process is indicated by its primary and tertiary attributes as Tamas, density and inertia, while its secondary one is Sattwa, lightness and harmony. Tamas and Sattwa do not vibrate at the same wave length, rather the friction between the two is pronounced. The astrological symbol assigned to Anuradha is a lotus flower and the Vedic deity Mitra presides over it. Mitra is addressed in the *Rig Veda* as the power that brings people together. He is the deity of friendliness and cooperation among men. Mitra, as the light of the day, is worshipped along with Varuna, the light of the night. The power which brings to light what is attained during the night is found under Anuradha. All the efforts of men done in order to cultivate their natural powers, or to wrest them from the hidden recesses of Mother-Earth are watched over by Mitra. It is through the benevolent influence of Mitra that our efforts succeed and the secret powers begin to open and come out. Mitra as the light of the day heralds the dawn, the beginning of new possibilities. At the dawn of a new life the fruits of past labor yield their result.

The *Atharva Veda* is more explicit in stating Mitra as 'uncovering' in the morning what Varuna conceals during the night. Up to Anuradha the individual soul has been collecting matter, immersing itself in deeper layers of the outer world of manifestation, to become unconscious of its divine heritage and original nature. Anuradha strives to rend the veil of ignorance and uncover our central core to show what is hidden within us. Mitra uncovering in the morning (the intimations of our divine heritage) what is concealed by Varuna in the night (the ignorance under the influence of Maya) indicates the impulse to arouse us to the ultimate truth. With this awareness grows understanding, empathy, friendliness and union with the universal energy. This realization is not a smooth process but full of turmoil and conflict. As an aftermath of these conflicts of the dematerialization process, the individual is able to identify himself with the universal, the macrocosm.

Scorpio, the Eighth house of the Cosmic Man, the sign in which Anuradha is found, is regarded (see Scorpio) as a secret cavity. During the period of night or mental obscurity and ignorance, the individual loses his sense of oneness with the universe. This darkness Mitra dispels under his watchful care. The manner in which the "un-covering" takes place depends upon individual circumstances. In some cases, it may give pleasant experiences that enable the individual to recover his primeval memory, while in other instances it may give heart-rending pain leading to the same goal. Either way it is a process of dematerialization.

Anuradha, the name of the asterism, means the "smaller Radha," or "the follower of Radha." Radha is, in one sense, a small lightning flash or spark. In this way, Anuradha implies a small sparkle or fragmented lightning representing the microcosm. The perception of our fragmentation from wholeness arouses the urge to unite with it, to be the whole once again. In another meaning, Radha is the beloved of Lord Krishna. Radha, deeply attached to Krishna, stands for the same relationship of the microcosm with the macrocosm. She was separate physically from Krishna, Divinity, but psychologically and in essence was with him every moment. This made her a great devotee of the Lord, though on this account she had to suffer much pain and anguish. Under Anuradha the deep psychological urge to unite with the original source is aroused, and the individual is made to feel as a fragmented unit of divinity.

The astrological symbol for Anuradha is a lotus flower, whose Sanskrit name is Padma. It also refers to sexual intercourse and can refer to the evacuation of excrement. The lotus stands for Lakshmi, the consort of Vishnu, who appears in the form of Radha for Lord Krishna. From the naval of Vishnu arises the macrocosmic lotus on which is seated Brahma, the creator of the universe. The lotus flower contains within itself the entire creative process. It mystically reflects the various stages of cosmic evolution.

Padma stands for manifestation occurring from the ever-concealed seed. The lotus grows from the mud, symbol of the deepest level of materiality equivalent to the unpleasant smelling oyster (see Chitra) from which the pure pearl is taken out. There is, however, a significant difference. The pearl can be taken out of the oyster by suddenly breaking it, while in the case of the lotus, the development occurs gradually, step by step, mirroring the stages of manifestation. In the case of the lotus, the seed takes root in the mud, which represents the original ignorance or primeval matter. It pushes itself up in water which stands for the emotional life of the person. From it, attracted by the Sun's rays, sprouts the stalk. It comes to the surface, representing the soul's growth through various lives, which by the experience of divine attraction struggles to emerge from the lower earthly realm. Having emerged from the realm of emotion, the soul opens in mental activities, symbolized by air, but the long journey of the lotus does not stop at this stage. Its aspiration for the Sun continues, and it finally flowers to greet the Sun. It then withers away, but its seed falls back into the mud to repeat the process again. The lotus symbol in this way emphasizes the soul's thirst for union with the source. Though it may fall again under the sway of the cycle of birth and death, a radical psychological change has occurred.

Under Anuradha, the latent powers in man begin to manifest. The ignorance gained during the period of night, resulting in attachment to worldly existence, must be purged. The dirt of the mud of materiality has to be cleansed in water. Emotional purity must be attained prior to regaining one's original nature. At this stage of emotional purification, the aspirant must seek union with the Master. The individual must strive to unify himself with the Ultimate. This is not easy and there are many pitfalls and hardships to be endured. All these stages are represented by the lotus, either in its physical form or as implied in its Sanskrit name. The lotus of the soul has to pass through various stages of unfoldment, for each phase of which are required corresponding efforts of the aspirant.

The impediments and struggles experienced by the aspirant are indicated by the planetary rulership of the asterism. Saturn is essentially a planet of spiritual trials. As the aspirant can succeed only with courage and perseverence, Mars the lord of Scorpio, has its place in the process. The difficulties on the path of the soul's evolutionary journey and the misery experienced at important stages of its unfoldment are expressed by Saturn.

The impulses flowing from Mars provide for the appropriate courage and competence for "uncovering" our latent powers leading to the attainment of the light of the dawn, the understanding of our original nature. Courageous endurance for the sake of Divine Love is the keynote of this asterism.

18
JYESHTA

Jyeshta extends from 226° 40′ to 240° 00′ of the zodiac marking the end of Scorpio ruled by Mars. The asterism itself is ruled by Mercury. With it ends the second third of the asterisms under the primary flow of Tamas, the attribute of inertia. Its secondary and tertiary levels give the influx of Sattwa. Jyeshta's primary motivation is Artha or directed activity. The Vedic deity presiding over Jyeshta is Indra, the king of the Gods. The three stars constituting the asterism resemble an umbrella or an earring, which are the symbols assigned to it. The main star is the bright red giant at the heart of the Scorpion, Antares.

Jyeshta means the eldest sister, the middle finger, or the holy river Ganges. A sense of reverence is connected with it. The association of the eldest sister, who is regarded with almost as much respect as the mother in Hindu society, and the river Ganges, which is also regarded as the holy mother, suggest that this asterism functions like a female guardian angel protecting and guiding the development of its earthly children. In Pranayama, yogic breath control exercises, the middle finger is used for stopping the left nostril so as to direct the breath to flow through the right. The primary function of Jyeshta is to guide the individual to his spiritual evolution. There has to occur radical transformation at this stage of the soul's pilgrimage.

Indra, the king of the Gods in Hindu mythology, controls all the pleasures of life. He has achieved this august status after arduous preparation and severe discipline. The name Indra is derived from the root word meaning "a drop." It is the individual who has attained the supreme heavenly position as a result of great austerity. The sudarshana chakra, the invincible disc with which anything can be annihilated in an instant, remains balanced on his forefinger. It is the reward he has won for his great sacrifices. It is a kind of thunderbolt, a circular disc, ever active and auspicious, a great and mysterious weapon. The circularity of the disc has an important similarity with the symbols, the umbrella and earring assigned to Jyeshta.

Indra uses this disc to protect the universe and the kingdom of the gods against the deadly onslaughts of the demons or Asuras, the anti-gods. The Sudarshana chakra can be used for attacking the most dangerous enemy. This weapon used for protection is not bestowed by another but is earned by one's own severe penance and austerities, by control over one's senses and nature's subtle forces.

These symbols — the disc of Indra, the earrings on the earlobes of Divine kings and the protection given by umbrellas for the elite — yogically stand for the Serpent fire, which is said to resemble them. This Kundalini Shakti, the secret (female or negative) energy coiled like a serpent at the base of the spine, when rightly energized gives control over the subtle forces of nature. In order to unfold it in the right way, the individual is required to master his lower nature and to go beyond attachment to the outer world. Upon the successful completion of this discipline, the soul becomes the ruler of all the world. Angels and fairies dance at his will and he gains miraculous powers. These potentials are contained in Jyeshta, which enables the human individual to communicate freely with spiritual powers. This relationship is suggested by Mercury ruling over this asterism.

Jyeshta bestows much status. The earring and umbrella are status symbols. In ancient India, as in other ancient civilizations, kings who attained spiritual and occult powers wore special earrings to signify their mastery over the serpent fire. Nobles and aristocrats who attained a high social status because of their wisdom and erudition were offered the royal umbrella. The energizing of special latent faculties in the individual opens himself up to the macrocosmic force occurs under Jyeshta. At this stage, the soul qualifies itself to embark upon a new direction. The soul's personal evolution reaches its end. Even if the soul is still under the spell of materialism and has to go yet deeper into the outer world, it meets a severe reaction as it is now open to the energies of other realms of existence. A new life-wave springs from the inner Self to provide the experience of a new kind of existence.

It requires considerable psychological growth to be able to absorb the cosmic impulse so that the individual can be spiritually transformed. This psychological impact is indicated by the rulership of the various quarters of Jyeshta. The first quarter is governed by Jupiter, the planet of religion. Under its impact the materiality of the individual is gradually spiritualized. This is expressed by attraction to outer religious practices. Attraction to earthly things remains important but inside the individual, a voice intimates their ultimate futility. Such people are often misunderstood. The contradiction in their behavior is glaringly visible to their friends. Outwardly the individual does religious practices while psychologically, he is still entrenched in materialistic pursuits. These contradictions force his friends to consider him a hypocrite, but both aspects of his behavior are reflections of sincere beliefs. The contradiction arises due to the beginning of the differentiation between the outer and the inner self.

In the second quarter, ruled by Saturn, Saturn gives the effect of its rulership of Capricorn, while in the third, the effect of its rulership of Aquarius becomes evident. The individual is thoroughly broken under the second quarter. His personality is disintegrated. Saturn grinds very slowly and very finely, always keeping the ultimate goal clear. Mastery of nature's finer forces cannot be gained by any person who has the slightest speck of selfishness or materiality, or who seeks personal status. For Saturn to produce the kind of complete detachment required, he must use the only method known to him: the complete shattering of the personality. This change occurs during the second quarter of Jyeshta. The third quarter follows the transformation achieved during the second. The new impulse enables the individual to operate for the good of all. At this stage the energy contained within the individual is put forth for universal welfare without any personal calculation of gain or loss. For an individual who is completely detached from himself, such opportunities are very fulfilling but from an earthly standpoint it can be very trying to work for the expression of this impulse. The individual has no remorse if he suffers poverty or is afflicted with personal sorrow as long as these do not obstruct his compassionate activities.

The fourth quarter is again under the domain of Jupiter and inner contentment becomes pronounced. The characteristics of Jupiter in Pisces are prominent at this stage. Under this impulse there is no confusion. The individual knows that fulfillment of the Divine mission in life is all that really matters. The hardships of physical life become insignificant compared to the higher goal.

Jyeshta prepares the individual for the new kind of influx he will have to endure. In this preparation he must be linked with his inner life. This process of psychological exploration is accompanied by material deprivation. The outer expression of the asterism depends upon the level of soul development of the individual concerned. If the soul is functioning at a material level, the power bestowed by it gives arrogance, on a spiritual level it gives the expression of Divine Benediction.

MULA

Mula extends from 240° 00′ to 253° 20′ of the zodiac and marks the beginning of Sagittarius ruled by Jupiter. This sign transforms animal man into a spiritual being aspiring toward the Supreme. The asterism is assigned to the shadowy planet Ketu, which also produces spirituality. Mula also marks the point where the galactic center intersects the zodiac, which further emphasizes its spiritual influence. The spiritual implications of this lunar mansion are further indicated by the symbols of an elephant's goad or prod, and a lion's tail assigned to it.

The presiding deity of Mula is Niritti, the Goddess of destruction or negation. Mula itself means "the root." It marks the end of materialism and the beginning of the spiritualization process in man. Its basic attribute is Sattwa, harmony, while it has Rajas, activity at secondary and tertiary levels. Its primary motivation is Kama or desire.

Niritti is a demon, a personification of death. The word Mula refers to Ravana and Kamsa, the two mighty demon kings of the Indian Epics, the *Ramayana* and *Mahabharata*. The dreadful impact of this asterism can be comprehended by examining the terror perpetrated by these demons to force men and women to change their nature. Ravana was a pious and mighty king born in the highest class. He performed the most arduous penance, pleased Lord Shiva and thereby received the most precious gifts from him. But his prowess and rich materialistic attainments made him so drunk with power that his egotism reached the culminating point. He abducted the wife of Rama, Vishnu's incarnation on earth. Rama destroyed him but death from the arrows of Rama, a great avatar, carried Ravana to the highest celestial realm.

Ravana's story is similar to the story of king Kamsa who was killed by another incarnation of Vishnu, Lord Krishna. Kamsa's story refers to human hostility towards the Divine. Kamsa had a sister, Devaki, who married Vasudeva. As the newly married couple proceeded to their nuptial abode, angels announced that their eighth child would destroy his uncle, king Kamsa. On hearing the angelic voice, Kamsa imprisoned the couple and killed their offspring as soon as they were born. When the eighth child, Lord Krishna, was born, he was transferred by divine assistance to safety and grew up unknown to Kamsa. Eventually Kamsa found out that the child was alive and a conflict began between them. Krishna destroyed the cruel king and finally the reign of terror came to an end.

Thus, whether Mula stands for Kamsa, Ravana, or the king of death, the asterism stands for foundation, it points to a change, a radical transformation in the nature and life expression. It has a special position in the evolutionary scheme of the soul. With the termination of the Scorpio impulse in Jyeshta, the soul reaches its acme of material attainments. Whatever lies within its material sheaths is realized. For this reason, at the beginning of this asterism Mula, the arrogance or the egoism in man knows no bounds. This Tamasic proclivity has to be completely wiped out in order to enable the spiritual forces to flow. Releasing such destructive impulses, Mula justifies its role as the goddess of death. But this death is inflicted with the purpose of arousing the dormant spiritual energy in the soul. In this sense, the asterism fulfills its role as the foundation of a new beginning. It initiates spiritual unfoldment. The deaths of Ravana and Kamsa brought about the destruction of their egotism as well as their personal salvation, their spiritual awakening. Mula marks the advent of spiritual awakening, a new spiritual era and the downpour of Sattvic forces.

In this context, the two symbols, the elephant's goad or prod and the lion's tail are very suggestive. The huge elephant, like the physical body of man, is subjugated under the Mula impulse. The goad is used to control and guide the elephant to move in the desired direction. The force exerted by the goad is painful. This pain reminds the elephant of the elephant driver and his will. Mula inflicts pain but the pain is intended to set the course of action along the right track and to remind us that the outer nature has become negligent to the real purpose of the soul. The elephant is an auspicious animal capable of much service to its owner. In the same way, the human body has a noble purpose and can be immensely helpful to its inner immortal ruler.

The lion has a similar significance. The lion is a symbol of the indomitable spirit within man. When this spirit is aroused, it is capable of expressing itself in powerful ways. When it appears as anger, it can be extremely dangerous. The tail of the lion is very sensitive, and if disturbed at that point, the lion becomes alert and attacks the cause of the disturbance in order to destroy it. The stories relating to this asterism point out this characteristic. Ravana became angry when the lust and arrogance behind his abduction of Sita were pointed out as unethical. When Kamsa was reminded of his brutalities he become more cruel; the beast in him was further aroused. Mula directs the soul by inflicting pain, it "goads" the soul towards the path of spiritual unfoldment.

Mula is motivated by Kama, the desire for sensate pleasures. As a result of the soul's involvement with matter and the physical forms of existence, its cravings have become intensified. Any resistance to these greatly upsets it. One feels extremely disturbed if impediments are created against the satisfaction of one's desire. But this is exactly what happens under Mula. It makes the individual violent and cruel. His mental balance is deranged. The need to control his passions, which, of course, is an arduous task, directs the latent energy towards spiritual unfoldment.

Mula is male by sex and butcher by caste. Its masculinity expresses its active quality. The individual is not very receptive, he wants to act and is eager to move forward and achieve supremacy. The cruelty of the butcher is typical of the Mula ego once its vehemence is aroused. It can be ruthless in perpetrating its demonic excesses. But as it has been classified as human as its animal type, it affords adequate spiritual possibilities to transform our animality into divinity. The possibility of transmuting the animality of the ego into spirituality is Mula's most important characteristic.

The different planets associated with the quadrants of the asterism reveal its subtler influences. Its four quarters are ruled by quick moving Mars, Venus, Mercury and the Moon which are intimately connected with the astral and mental sheaths. The various planetary forces impinging upon the individual are thereby primarily emotional and mental in nature. Such an individual can be quickly impressed but their impressions can also easily be wiped out. Ketu as governing the asterism, makes a person thoughtful. The enduring impact of Ketu is to spiritualize the individual. Mula being located in Sagittarius, a Jupiterian sign, works to lead a person to seek Divine help. But if the person is still on the lower rungs of evolutionary growth, his possessive instinct will be intensified and he will become cruel — almost like a butcher or a demon.

20
PURVASHADHA

Purvashadha extends from 253° 20′ to 266° 40′ of the sign of Sagittarius ruled by Jupiter. The asterism itself is ruled by Venus, the planet of sensitivity. The Vedic deity presiding over it is Apas, the water goddess. The primary quality of the asterism is Sattwa but it is affected by Rajas or activity at a secondary level and Tamas or inertia at a tertiary level. Its primary motivation is for Moksha. The symbol assigned to it is the elephant's tusk.

The basic characteristic of Purvashadha is the general spiritual environment in which the soul dwells. Like an elephant unconcerned with the surrounding commotion and activity, the soul is attuned to the harmonious interrelationship of all things in creation. On a superficial level, inertia prevails, but under appropriate conditions, the elephant can be aroused to courageous deeds. The tusk is more valuable than any other part of the elephant's body. It is a sort of externalization of the inner possibilities of the animal. When the tusk is severed it has the power to grow back again. Under Purvashadha many unknown and unsuspected possibilities of the person come to light. Under its impulse, the individual may receive flashes of intuition and valuable insight into the working of Divine Law. One gets much wisdom under it.

The quality of wisdom that grows under the influence of Purvashadha is of great practical importance. Like water, it sustains life as well as cleanse its impurities. The Vedic sages worshipped the water goddess as one who destroys all poisons, wards off jealousy and disease, and bestows eternal creative energy. These are the vitalizing impulses flowing through this asterism. The Sun and Moon provide the polarized energy impulses, which in turn protect water to support and nourish every kind of manifestation. What Purvashadha produces for an individual goes a long way in sustaining, nourishing and making him creative. Much sensitivity is developed at this stage.

Great significance is attached to water and water deities in every religion. The great Vedantic philosopher Shankara equates water with Sattwa itself, the spiritual quality in life. He mentions Sattwa as water, which in conjunction with Rajas (activity) and Tamas (inertia) creates the conditions responsible for the rebirth of the soul. According to him, the reality of the Self (Atman) is reflected in Sattwa, like the Sun in water. Purvashadha, by cleansing the impurities of ignorance collected during previous incarnations, opens out the soul to the universalization of consciousness and thereby to universal sympathy. This energy of water or Sattwa is a reflection of Divine Unity, its activation brings forth the inmost and Divine quality latent in man, symbolized by the elephant's tusk.

When the individual becomes aware of his inherent qualities, the uniqueness with which he is born, there is often a sense of pride. Such a psychological weakness arises if the unity between the individual and the Universal Life-force is overlooked. This situation may arise due to the influence of Venus, the lord of the asterism. With the change in the basic nature of man, he becomes more spiritual and much power begins to pour through him. His creativity is augmented to a great extent. Venus gives sensitivity and an inclination towards personal pleasures. This influence accentuates the ego of the individual. He begins to think that the creativity resulting from the Divine energy is his, and does not come from another source. This ignorance veils the Supreme force energizing him. The psychological transformation possible at this stage is indicated by the forces of Sagittarius as beauty, harmony and noble aspiration. Persons born under Purvashadha are amiable in disposition, have many friends but are also very proud. Their friendship, however, is dependable and sincere. As a married partner, the individual can be very trying, always changing his nature, primarily because of the constant unfoldment of his inner being. This change is often misunderstood and considered as hypocrisy or contradictory behavior. The allegation of deception can be levied against him. Yet if life conditions provide opportunities for rendering social service in a spirit of dedication to humanity, he takes to this course of action and finds much happiness in it.

The nature of the purification and transformation under this asterism is indicated by the planets ruling its quarters. The first quarter is ruled by the Sun under whose impact the individual begins to experience the omnipresence and omnipotence of the universal life. This experience draws one nearer to the center as a result of which psychological transformation begins to take place. The second quarter is ruled by Mercury whose main function is to energize the mentation process. Under the overall radiation of spirituality resulting from Sagittarius and the primary flow of the Sattvic attribute, Mercury enables one to perceive unity in diversity. Such an understanding of the universality of nature around oneself makes an individual yet more religious oriented.

The Venusian energy of the third quarter is related to sign Libra, implying thereby the satiety of material affluence and the growth of spirituality. At this stage, the individual is not argumentative; he intuitively perceives the universal spirit prevailing everywhere. As the asterism itself is ruled by Venus, this feeling is very pronounced. The inborn attraction of the soul towards the religious life is accentuated under Purvashadha. In the fourth quarter under Mars, a mild form of fanaticism may be noticed. Whatever the quarter, the psychological change is pronounced. This directs the individual towards universalization of his spirit. In such activities, there is much of sacrament, the outward expression of religious activity, and a strong urge for dedication to the Supreme. Devotion to a personal form of God is more attractive at this stage than the philosophy of one universal being existing and manifesting everywhere.

The classification of this asterism by sex, class, species, and animal type show that its impulse is active in inducing the soul to take initiative in changing its nature. The species being that of the monkey, there can be much experimentation. Such a person finds it difficult to adhere to any one way of life. He may change the deities he worships quickly or frequently. His philosophy of life will also be shifting. But, in all his expressions, the individual is guided by two main objectives. First he will endeavor to be religious, whatever it may mean to him. Second, he will like to be serviceable to others. The underlying consideration for these pursuits is to purify one's life so that merging in the Divine becomes possible.

Purvashadha induces the divinity of the person to externalize to aid in the purification of the ego. Wrong actions from past incarnations produce trying situations in life to rectify the karmic account.' These experiences are at times extremely unpleasant. Jupiter, the planet of Divine grace, purges such past karmic effects to transform them into a spiritual force. If the individual born under this asterism is careful to note, instances of Divine help, sometimes appearing like miraculous assistance, can be discerned in one's life. Such Divine aid makes the person Godfearing, religious and helpful to others.

However, there are other instances, particularly if the soul is on an early rung of spiritual growth, where the ego becomes inflated. The individual becomes unduly proud. This shortcoming must be eradicated whatever the pain to allow for the onward journey of the soul. For this reason one often finds in predictive astrology that Jupiter, the best benefic, does not always provide the material affluence usually associated with it. The clue to this contradiction is given by the disposition of Purvashadha within Jupiter's sign of Sagittarius.

21
UTTARASHADHA

Uttarashadha extends from 266° 00′ to 280° 00′ of the zodiac. Its first quarter occurs at the end of Sagittarius ruled by Jupiter, while its following three quarters are in Capricorn ruled by Saturn. The asterism itself is governed by the Sun. The Vedic deity ascribed to it is the Vishwedevas, the Universal Gods. Its primary and tertiary attributes are Sattwa, harmony, while the secondary attribute is Rajas, activity. Moksha or liberation is the primary motivational impulse radiating from the asterism. Its symbol is the rods or planks of a bed.

Uttarashadha is a baffling constellation. It is an extension of Purvashadha, but in nature it has great differences from it. The impulses generated at this level primarily affect the psychological makeup of the individual. The earlier asterism shows the inner reality of the being concealed within the outer physical garb trying to purify and spiritualize it. The realization of inner spirituality has to be absorbed and assimilated in one's psychic nature. This is the inevitable consequence of every true understanding. With the realization of the Real, the universal laws of nature begin to manifest to the individual. One begins to perceive life in a different light. With such an understanding, the individual begins to weave a pattern of life in which the universal rather than the individual, social or the personal are more important. This is the role of the Vishwedevas, the Universal Gods who personify universality.

The rods of a bed, or the bed itself, as a symbol of the asterism do not merely represent a place of rest and relaxation. The rods serve to hold the bed up. The symbol therefore indicates the provision of the necessary means for securing rest and peace. The asterism in this way provides the necessary psychological condition for the universalization process that affords peace. The psychological orientation received under its impulse allows the wider unfoldment of the individual. The asterism arouses in the individual those faculties and powers which later provide the foundation for ultimate rest, Moksha or final liberation of the soul.

Under Uttarashadha, there is constant activity. The experiences gained as a result of incessant change lead to psychological readjustments which necessarily produce much pain. Our personal defenses in life break down and material supports are destroyed. The process of sacrificing the individual on the cross of universal consciousness is always painful. This process is intensified at Uttarashadha.

The Sun, as the lord of the asterism, cannot leave the individual isolated, while Saturn has the supreme quality of restricting and destroying all materialistic foundations. The influence of Vishwedevas can be felt on intellectual development and the urge towards socialization. The foundation of harmony is empathy, and the rod of the bed also represents human relationship, which depends upon empathy for its endurance. Only on such harmonious relationships can the individual experience lasting repose. Before one attains the universalization of consciousness, there has to occur empathy, which is born out of humility. It can be truly experienced only when the individual has passed through the devastating fire of life's struggle and turmoil. The rod of the bed represents the asterism in this sense. There is nothing lower than the rod of the bed; this part of the bed is treated without much care.

In understanding the significance of this asterism, it is necessary to examine the attributes that flow from it. The harmonious impulses coming from the primary and tertiary Sattvic attribute emphasize the urge to merge in the universal nature, the aspiration to delve deep into nature's mysteries in order to utilize them for the good of all. Such ideals and aspirations will not remain merely academic. There is a strong tendency to translate them into action. Thus the influence of Uttarashadha enables the individual to be earthly in action according to a stimulus from some kind of spiritual goal. Each earthly activity is explained in terms of the higher objectives in life.

The planetary ownership of the different quadrants of the asterism indicates the nature of the reaction that follows the involvement of the individual in different types of relationships. Under the influence of Jupiter, ruler of the first and fourth quarters, one finds many ritualistic activities. There may be frequent worship of gods and regular attendance of temples, churches or other religious places. Such individuals can be found practicing prayers or mantra. They may be engaged in rituals or austerities to obtain material benefits or may perform them for the sake of society, or do them simply out of a sense of duty. Such persons are generally blessed with affluence in life but inwardly there has to be a quest for the spiritual unknown for their true fulfillment.

Saturn's rulership of the middle quarters leads to different results. Saturn produces restrictions. Its impact is very intense and the annihilation of personality is very deep. The entire life may seem barren and without any core. Everything may be taken away and the individual may be left with nothing substantial. This can happen as a consequence of deep or philosophical thinking. It may arise due to scientific knowledge of the essentially empty nature of matter as a mere fabrication of minute energy particles. All energy operates because it contains within itself the potential of growth and a pattern for its own unfoldment. The know-how potential of the energy particle is a reflection of the Intelligence of the Divine Mind. In each of these approaches, the individual comes to an understanding of the nothingness of his own self, and the enduring nature of the Supreme.

The characteristics of the asterism show the central nature of its influence. Its masculine nature indicates its active or positive approach. It is dynamic, kinetic and takes initiative in order to carry out the Divine purpose. Its warrior caste represents the same motivated force. People born under the influence of Uttarashadha often become the leaders of social organizations they serve. Having the characteristics of a mongoose, they display a dogged persistence in their pursuits, and as a deadly foe of serpents, they have great hostility to deceit and duplicity. Possessing the quality of the human being, they have the potential to rise up to the Divine level. Only matured human beings have the potential for spiritual upliftment. Animals grow and develop slowly under the inertial impact of natural forces, while the gods have already attained their status and have no further development to achieve. Men still have the stupendous heights of spirituality to scale.

Uttarashadha leads to the universalization of the individual. The individual is imprinted with the goal of cosmic unity. Under the influence of this asterism an individual may become very humble, or self-centered, but in both cases the objective is the spiritualization of the nature. To achieve this goal, however, he may suffer immensely.

22
SHRAVANA

Shravana extends from 280° 00' to 293° 20' of the zodiac in the sign of Capricorn ruled by Saturn. Its main star is Altair, alpha Delphinus. The asterism itself is ruled by the Moon. Its presiding deity is Vishnu or Hari, the preserver of the universe. The symbols of an ear and an arrow are assigned to it. The basic attribute of the asterism is Sattwa, the secondary is Tamas and the tertiary is Rajas, while the primary motivational impulse is Artha, directed activity. The basic orientation of Shravana is towards the Great Silence on which background subsists the entire scheme of manifestation. The asterism leads one to meditation. If the individual is still on the materialistic side of evolution, under this asterism he develops the qualities of obedience or service.

These characteristics of Shravana emphasize the profound nature of the impulse flowing through it. The primary Sattvic attribute enveloping it indicates that every impact under it must arouse a deep perception of the harmony that prevails around oneself. This is possible when the personal dissatisfactions an individual feels when confronted with life's problems are set aside. This requires an attitude of complete negation of one's conditioning, complete freedom from the past, the non-expectation of any preconceived results. Such a state of complete attention to what exists in the present moment is the main spiritual impulse of Shravana.

Shravana provides the main impulse that attunes the human personality with its spiritual goal. Mars, whose main function is to externalize the inner aspects of life, is exalted here providing tremendous courage and endurance. Mercury and Venus governing two of its quarters impart harmonizing influences. But the Moon and Jupiter do not vibrate harmoniously under Shravana and their impact on it is not good. They are related to intelligence, receptivity, and to the channeling of the solar radiation of universal energy. Clarity of vision and direct perception of cosmic laws depend upon these influences. Perception and alertness are essential for attuning oneself to the spiritual goal of life. The role of Shravana is significant in achieving these qualities.

The name Shravana means listening. In every spiritual teaching, the act of listening is given much importance. In the *Mundaka Upanishad,* the teacher and students pray for the capacity of listening together. "Oh

Gods! May we hear together with our ears what is auspicious." *The Voice of Silence* also states, "Before thou has't thy feet upon the ladder's upper rung, the ladder of the mystic sounds, thou has't to hear the voice of thy inner God." J. Krishnamurti gives much importance to the action of right listening. He states that "it is very important to know how to listen. If you know how to listen, you will get to the root of the matter immediately. If you know how to listen to what is being said, there is immediate understanding. Listening is complete focusing of attention." The Lord Buddha put succinctly the importance of listening, when he emphasized Right Attention and Right Meditation as two steps of the Noble Eightfold Path. Shravana is the stage of cosmic evolution where the individual receives universal impressions. At this stage one comes immediately in contact with the beauty of life. One receives immediate understanding, as one listens to the voice of the Divine within. But such an exalted prize is not obtained easily, for it one has to suffer materially.

Shravana and Nada are two aspects of cosmic intelligence which are intimately linked. Nada is the cosmic sound regarded as the primeval silence from which all the forces of creation have arisen. This sound of the Silence can only be perceived by self-discipline in the practice of Yoga. The perception of the voice of the Silence resulting from the annihilation of personality is a result of Shravana, of listening in the true sense of the term. The physical basis of this listening is the ear, the symbol assigned to the asterism. Whatever preparation is needed for this perceptive faculty is the result of Shravana.

One pointedness is an essential requirement for Right Attention as required in the Noble Eightfold Path. It is represented by an arrow, the other symbol of Shravana (see Sagittarius). The arrow is an ancient sign suggesting the substantial amount of preparation by the individual necessary for attaining his spiritual goal. The sign Sagittarius is symbolized by a centaur who shoots an arrow representing higher aspirations. The Upanishadic literature uses the arrow in a similar sense. In the *Mundaka Upanishad* the soul, aspiring towards God, is compared to an arrow while the great mantra Om represents the discipline essential for attaining the goal. Under this impulse all peripheral activities are trimmed, though the reduction may be full of painful sacrifices. Such a preparation is made so that the inherent reality of the individual and of the manifestation around him is revealed.

Vishnu or Hari as the presiding deity relates this asterism to the cosmic preservative principle whose primary function is to harmonize and eradicate all impediments to the growth of the soul. In this role Vishnu floats on the sea of primeval matter reclining on the coils of Shesha-Naga, the cosmic serpent. He balances all the divergent forces and harmonizes the rough sea of worldly existence. He works to help the evolving soul out of the turmoil and encouragingly guides it along the evolutionary path. In order to guide the soul on its perilous journey, Vishnu creates situations in which the aspirant relinquishes Asat, the false, and embraces Sat, the true.

This radical transformation requires clear perception of one's true nature beyond the veil of ignorance. Under Shravana, one begins to perceive the truth of the manifestation concealed in the illusory appearances. This unveiling results in the tearing of the old and transcending of the hard crust of primeval ignorance. It is always a trying experience. The lordship of Saturn over Capricorn which contains this asterism, contributes to the hardship. Shravana is not an asterism of comfort and enjoyment, but one of difficulty and disillusionment. The trying experiences it gives can only be borne with endurance and patience. Yogic teachings give instructions for the necessary psycho-physical preparations. On such a path of listening to the pure sound of the cosmos — Nada — it is essential to have a sound intellect bestowed by Mercury and good intuitive insight granted by Venus. These allow the individual to seriously set foot on the path and move toward the attainment of his enduring goal.

The endurance of personal pain and suffering in order to listen to the cosmic voice without any distortion is possible only with the benediction of a strong Mars. Before the voice of the cosmic Great Silence is heard, there must be the persistence of a mongoose, and the eager intellect of a monkey. But these make the individual isolated from his friends, turn him away from society and make him live in a world of his own. This is the life of an outcast. Yet having gone through these ordeals of Shravana, the individual is ready to function as a man of knowledge.

23
DHANISHTA

Dhanishta extends from 203° 20′ to 306° 00′ of the zodiac. It is half in Capricorn and half in Aquarius, both ruled by Saturn. The asterism itself is ruled by Mars. It is primarily influenced by Sattwa or harmony, but the secondary and tertiary qualities relate to Tamas, inertia. The asterism is presided over by the eight Vasus, the personifications of the cosmic energy. The symbol assigned to Dhanishta is a drum called mridanga. Its primary motivational impulse is Dharma.

The word Dhanishta a bamboo-cane flute as well as a drum. Both these musical instruments are hollow inside. They resound and reverberate the tune played by the musician. Depending upon the touch on the drum or the blowing of the flute music comes forth. The instruments are merely links between the music and the musician. Similarly, under Dhanishta, the basic impulse is to purge the soul from whatever it considers its own so that the Divine plan for it can be unfolded smoothly. The individual must come to function like a reed through which the Divine music is played uninterruptedly and without distortion.

Lord Shiva's miniature drum, shaped like a time-jar, represents the bipolarity of personality. On both sides of it the hollowness is covered by stretched leather, and tiny knots tied to two threads attached at the center strike the stretched leather alternately and rhythmically. The drum of Shiva represents the spiritual view of man, as does Krishna's flute. When Krishna plays the flute, his devotees, the Gopis are attracted to the tune and renounce all self-consciousness. The representation of Dhanishta by these instruments shows that it prepares the soul for its ultimate unity with the cosmic plan. Such changes can be astrologically deciphered by examining the relationships between the various sheaths of the human personality and the planets vibrating them. The individual passes through tremendous strain in order to be lifted from mundane existence to spiritual reality.

Between Shravana and Dhanishta, which are complementary in many respects, the soul first comprehends and then reverberates the Divine Music. In order to intelligently cooperate with Nature, it is necessary to completely eschew self-consciousness and even so-called prudential considerations. That is what the Gopis attracted to Krishna's flute had to achieve before the consummation of Divine Love. It requires complete renunciation of personal and social considerations. The soul has to become hollow like a reed or flute before it merges in the Supreme and the spark becomes one with the Flame.

Having listened to the message of the Universal Spirit under the influence of Dhanishta and giving up the personal point of view, the individual begins radiating the Divine message and power. With the emptying of selfish, personal, and Tamasic Impulses, the hollowness of the individual is filled with universal sympathy and compassion. When the Aquarian pitcher begins to pour the water of life, it gains enormous vitality to nourish the world around it. Yet a person under Dhanishta can magnify and exaggerate his own deeds and beat his drum loudly. This happens if one is on the lower rungs of evolution, otherwise one is a Divine messenger of hope, courage and enlightenment to his fellow beings.

Dhanishta as the drum links the individual soul to the very root of manifestation which it begins to reverberate. The Maha Shunya or Cosmic Void radiates sound waves which concretize cosmic ideas. Sound allows perception of the void on whose substratum all sounds arise. Beneath the noise and agitation of the outer world, there is the great silence which resounds the real nature of things. This is the medium which enables the soundless sound to be perceived, towards which all meditation practices aim. Under all forms of manifestation, there is the Void which reveals their Divine purpose. Perception of this original cause affords the individual different intensities of spiritual experience. One experiences the Divine energy circulating everywhere.

This perception depends upon the purification of the psyche which necessitates purging of personal emotions and self-centered ideas. At this stage, the individual may experience great sorrow and suffering, bleeding of the heart, but this is the only way to enlightenment. Divine strength, power and light can only be poured into the individual after his crucifixion. Within the hollowness of the drum there is the capacity to resound the tune played by the cosmic dancer, Lord Shiva. The trial of the neophyte is a necessary stage for experiencing universal harmony. The drum in the hands of Shiva, the supreme God, and the flute on the lips of Krishna, the great avatar, are intended to evoke spirituality in man, to make the soundless manifest in sound. Dhanishta among the lunar mansions prepares the individual to realize the Divine.

The presiding deities, the eight Vasus, are assigned to Dhanishta especially in their role of energy sources. Each of one of them is a sun, each has a special domain on the different realms of existence. None of them can exist along with materialism: they are the very antithesis of matter. Dhanishta therefore completely, though gradually, eliminates material attachments from the individual and enables the soul to express itself directly.

Mars, governing the asterism, provides courage, strength and devotion. Saturn, ruling the signs in which the asterism falls, gives it the patience and protection which sustains the person through his trials. Having endured the ordeal of purification the individual's consciousness is attuned to the universal harmony; spiritual knowledge is opened to the mind. Behind the interplay of light and shadow in the outer world, beneath the fleeting images of the senses, one deciphers the inner reality. Within the increasing perception of Ultimate Reality, the mind resounds the celestial harmony. Great yogis are born under such stars. For mundane results, the Moon in Dhanishta makes the person liberal in giving, and bestows wealth and courage. Poorly placed it makes one greedy, conservative and stingy.

An important point to remember is the difference between the first half of the asterism under the influence of Capricorn and the second half under Aquarius. The impulses under Capricorn cause more trial. The person under its influence has to purify and universalize himself. Under Aquarius one becomes a servant of the Divine, uncovering the unifying principle in life and attuning his own will to it. If this does not occur, a devil or a Mephistopheles is born to plague the world. Such a person will be ruthless, inconsiderate, and heartless, striving to acquire everything for his own selfish aggrandizement. No depth of degradation will be too low for him. But in the end, he will suffer and cry. Retribution takes place so that ultimately he turns his gaze to the inner light.

24
SHATABHISHAK

Shatabhishak, which extends from 306° 40' to 320° 00' of the zodiac, has the quality of producing ultimate harmony in spite of the trials and tribulations it creates achieving this result. It lies entirely in Aquarius, ruled by Saturn, while the asterism itself is governed by Rahu, the shadowy planet which brings karmic rectification. The mystical character of the asterism is further highlighted by assigning to it a thousand petalled flower representing the hundred stars constituting the constellation. The presiding deity of Shatabhishak is Varuna, the bestower of wisdom. Its primary and tertiary attributes are Sattwa or harmony, while the secondary is Tamas or inertia. Its primary motivation is Dharma or principle. It is significant to note that Pracheta, a synonym for the asterism, refers to Manu, Daksha, and Valmiki, the mighty progenitors of the human race.

The flower is a very auspicious symbol standing for fruition of efforts, the attainment of the goal for which a journey is undertaken. In Shatabhishak the flower represents the achievement of the purpose for which the manifestation came into existence. It represents the summit of creation. The thousand petalled flower stands for the ultimate in the multidimensional evolutionary process. In human beings, it relates to the thousand-petalled lotus or crown chakra at the top of the head. Its blossoming indicates the full activation of the Kundalini. At this stage the latent powers in man are fully realized and the individual transcends the cycle of birth and death. One becomes a conscious cooperator with Nature and assists the cosmic evolutionary process.

Manu, Daksha, and Valmiki are beings who guide the evolutionary process. Having achieved Divine knowledge, they devote themselves to the welfare of creation. The Manus are concerned with physical growth, social organization and geological changes. They develop and guide physical processes to enable the soul to express itself effectively through form. The final form of development is imprinted on their consciousness, which they articulate at the physical level. The Dakshas are also engaged in similar activities but they function on lower planes in order to carry out the special tasks assigned to them. They are willing to assume voluntary restrictions and even spiritual deprivations in order to discharge their responsibilities. Valmikis impart spiritual knowledge and influence devotees to purify their daily lives. The last of the Valmikis, we are told, was born in a low caste where he earned his livelihood by attacking and robbing travelers. But ultimately he become a great seer and wrote several great teachings, the most important the epic *Ramayana* in which he showed the destruction of egoism and the victory of truth to sustain the spiritual order of society.

These references indicate that Shatabhishak pours forth mighty influences which can radically transform the life of the human being. Under such an energy, the individual is fired with a missionary zeal. He is willing to undergo heavy sacrifices for the fulfillment of his spiritual mission. Such individuals present future ideals to the world. They are not merely great thinkers. They are engaged in concretizing spiritual ideals in the outer world, which makes them very active in service projects.

Varuna, the deity of Shatabhishak, is one of the earliest Vedic Gods. He is vested with unlimited cosmic knowledge. This knowledge, however, is aimed at producing practical results. It is stated in the *Vedas* that, "He holds together mankind and the earth. He dwells over all the world as its sovereign ruler. He is the god who made the golden Sun to shine in heaven. The wind which resounds through the atmosphere is his breath. He witnesses Truth and Falsehood. He instructs the Rishi Vasishta in mysteries no ordinary man can comprehend." Varuna directs such mysterious powers of wisdom and compassion that the individual under Shatabhishak is radically transformed and a new ray of light shines through him. Such a person is motivated by a new approach to life, its problems have a different significance for him. He is able to perceive the deeper mysteries of life.

Rahu, as the lord of the asterism, and Saturn, ruling the sign in which it is located, refer to the trials and the purification of the soul. Both planets act at a very deep level. Saturn annihilates everything personal, which is what the flowering process requires. On the purification of the outer encasement, the inner spirituality swells, which is the real blossoming of the man. Rahu, however, turns the individual consciousness to materiality and thereby arouses a sense of loneliness and depression. Shatabhishak people are rarely happy within themselves. Life to them is a duty, not an experience of personal satisfaction. A flower is meant for the enjoyment and pleasure of others. It does not enjoy its own beauty, fragrance and freedom. The individual attaining spiritual knowledge may not be happy in his personal life, but having acquired spiritual knowledge, he has a sense of impersonal joy.

The acquisition of higher knowledge and comprehension of universal principles, which Varuna bestows, destroy the hold of the material sheaths and enable a new awakening. Such a process which results in an expansion of consciousness entails abundant austerity and sacrifice on the part of the individual for the good of others. The energy ensouling Shatabhishak turns the individual outward for the good of mankind. If this transformation does not occur, the individual may explode and annihilate himself. Those born under this star are truthful, daring, victorious, but unfortunate from a worldly standpoint.

The difficulties of the asterism arise from its secondary attribute of Tamas occasionally impinging on its generally Sattvic nature. These are the psychological impediments encountered in the fulfillment of one's inner aspirations. Generally, the asterism produces harmony in relationships and leads the individual towards his ultimate goal but the Tamasic proclivities limit this to some extent. This happens because the individual is still susceptible to sloth, lethargy, and psychological stagnation.

Other Shatabhishak classifications help us understand it further. Its feminine nature appears in its passivity or inertia unless it is affected by an active agent. Once the asterism is aroused to action, it can move ruthlessly. Its animal species, the horse, is full of vitality and energy; it is ever willing to serve its master. Shatabhishak is also full of vitality. Once inspiration is received, and psychological lethargy is overcome, it impels the individual to follow his inner direction through all adversity. The demon and the butcher, as its temperament and caste, also signify such traits. Both of them are non-emotional and act in a detached manner. A butcher carries out the operations as ordained to him; the direction comes from an external agency. In the case of a demon, the direction comes from within himself, and he carries it out in an almost unconscious state. In actualizing the dictates of his heart, the demon can brook no interference. Once the Shatabhishak individual has received his marching orders, tremendous force and vitality are put into its execution. In all its efforts, Shatabhishak transforms the basic nature of the person concerned. The basic quality of the human being is the capacity to comprehend the nature of Divinity and ascend to that sublime height. Shatabhishak brings this about.

Before the flowering of the crown chakra, or the fulfillment of one's purpose, the path the individual has to traverse is not very easy. The nature of such trials are revealed by Jupiter and Saturn ruling the quadrants of the asterism. These planets create difficult situations for the individual so that the inner purpose of life can be discovered. When the urge to spiritualize one's life takes place, the first step is toward religion, external forms of religious practice to harness nature's finer forces for one's deeper welfare. This urge is produced by Jupiter ruling over the first quarter of the asterism. Subsequently spiritual practices become more important and the aspirant begins to shed his self-centeredness. Personal trials begin at this stage. When the objects of sense gratification are taken away, life becomes barren and lonely. The individual almost becomes a butcher to himself. With demonic efforts he has to lift himself up in order to universalize his life. This is the function of Saturn ruling the second and third quadrants. Then dawns the phase of expansion, satisfaction and real spiritualization, the flowering of the thousand petalled lotus. This occurs under the fourth quadrant again ruled by Jupiter. Shatabhishak contains within its field of influence all the qualities which enable the individual to pour forth the water of life contained within the Aquarian pitcher to nourish the universe.

Shatabhishak provides the impulse for the blossoming of our inner potential. In order to achieve this objective, there must be the blending of the individual consciousness with the universal. It leads to the experiencing of Infinity, the Illimitable. Such an achievement necessarily entails immense psychological expansion, sacrifice and pain. In order to bear it, the butcher-like quality with demonic vigor is inculcated. Finally, the door of liberation is opened with the full arousal of the Kundalini.

25
PURVA BHADRA

Purva Bhadra extends from 320° 00′ to 333° 20′ of the zodiac and consists of two stars. It is associated with cosmic stability and imparts fearlessness. The first three quarters of the asterism fall within the Saturn ruled sign of Aquarius while the last quarter is in Jupiterian Pisces. The asterism itself is ruled by Jupiter. Sattwa or harmony is its attribute at both primary and secondary levels, while at its tertiary level Rajas, activity, predominates. Its primary motivational impulses is Artha or goal directed activity. Its presiding deity is Aja Ekapada, the one-footed goat. Its astrological symbol is a sword.

An understanding of the nature of Aja Ekapada, the one-footed goat, reveals the deeper implications of the asterism. The Vedic deity Aja Ekapada represents the unborn, transcendent cosmic energy. The goat is a simple, harmless milk producing animal which requires almost nothing for its sustenance. However, in the Vedas this deity has been extolled to great heights: he is considered as infinity, an entity without motion or speech. As Aja, the unborn, he is worshipped as a form of Shiva. He is the vehicle of Agni (fire).

The *Atharva Veda* refers to Aja Ekapada in relation to Rohit, another deity associated with cosmic evolution. Rohit's main function is to produce heaven and earth, where the thread of the sacrifice is extended. In this creation of Rohit, Aja Ekapada establishes himself as the Sun and makes heaven and the earth firm with his strength. Being of the nature of the Sun, which provides life and light, Aja Ekapada is without any objective existence while it sustains the entire creation. It is the un-polarized latent creative energy which produces the different levels of existence. Rohit contains within himself ever-changing impulses without which the various dimensions of manifestation would remain abstract, ethereal and non-existent. The role of Aja Ekapada is to concretize this "essence" of manifestation into the unpolarized positive cell, which subsequently assumes many forms at the different levels of creation. As the vehicle of Agni, the fire which energizes all life-forms, Aja Ekapada takes the abstract image of Rohit, differentiates it, and then provides warmth and nourishment so that it can succeed in completing its journey.

The impulse flowing through Purva Bhadra, over which Aja Ekapada presides, stands at the border of manifestation on one side and the state of latency on the other. It is an energy which can be expressed both in an upward and downward movement. Aja Ekapada refers to the stage of cosmic ideation where on one side is pure undifferentiated energy, Agni or fire, and on the other side are heaven and earth in their existing motion, vibrating with speech and action. Where these two meet, there is unceasing motion at such a tremendous speed that it appears motionless.

Aja Ekapada represents the stage in cosmic evolution where the fire of creation is still in latency, though the area of creation has been well defined. The personification of energy is not fire, but the vehicle of fire. It is infinity. Therein neither motion nor speech exists. Neither subjective nor objective attributes have yet been born. It is only after polarization has taken place that the interplay of different forces can occur giving rise to the multiple forms of manifestation. As far as Aja Ekapada is concerned, it presides over a realm of passivity which actually is not passive. There is unity, undifferentiated latency, but it is turned outward, it is creative. Aja Ekapada is like the Sun which bestows life and light to every form of creation but takes nothing itself. Like Lord Shiva in his cosmic dance, Aja Ekapada arouses the scintillating, outgoing energy which enables eternal motion, but in itself is completely still, with no activity, either subjective or objective at any level.

This enigmatic deity imparts an influence which is very difficult to comprehend. At our level of manifestation it can be observed on the paths of both involution and evolution. It can be seen in all the separatist propensities which must be unified into one essential energy to enable the individual to become attuned to the permanent Ray on which the universal evolutionary impulse has destined him to proceed (*SAO, pp. 240–51*). This emphasis on oneself, arousing the urge to stand completely on our one's without aid or support from any external source can appear as eccentricity, originality, or rebellious tendencies unmindful of the opinions and reactions of the world at large. For the individual already ahead on the path of evolution, it is expressed as an urge to work for a universal principle without any consideration for one's own personal welfare. Those on the materialistic path will become self-centered, maniac, anti-social individuals. Whatever the form of expression of the individual, under the impact of this Vedic deity there will be a great urge to stand on our own feet without any consideration whether it be for our personal advantage or harm.

This complete self-reliance for outer or inner growth is symbolized by a sword. The sword is an instrument for attack as well as defense. The fight can originate from an altruistic cause, or for achieving some nefarious end. Thus the sword signifies the act more so than the motive for it. As a symbol for Purva Bhadra the sword suggests the work for universal unity where courage, vision, and self-involvement irrespective of the consequences excepting the goal are concerned. The asterism leads to universal unity. It urges the individual to fight with a missionary zeal for the universal life. Engaged in such a crusade, one becomes a martyr, dedicating his life for a cause. In such activities, the sword symbolizes courage, martyrdom, and dedication, but the same sword can also lead the person to murder others to obtain some personal advantage. Whatever the expression of action, the important impulse under Purva Bhadra is the urge to become focused upon an ideal. At this stage the individual is motivated by an inner urge, the outer being of little significance. Under the influence of this asterism the life of the individual is radically transformed and becomes much different from what has so far been experienced. The subjective is objectified and the true principles of life begin to hold sway over the person.

Whatever symbology we consider, Purva Bhadra is important as a great centralizing force. The various outlets of one's energy are concentrated and directed towards the goal of harmony and balance. At this stage in the effort to fulfill one's aims, there are serious trials and tribulations. Many critical situations arise on the path. Even life itself may seem meaningless. The determination needed to emerge successful in such conflict and turmoil is also indicated by the sword. The determination is the individual's decision and the urge to fight and die for it are his actions. Whether for good or ill, Purva Bhadra imparts an immensely active impulse. It alters the life of the person in a dramatic way.

UTTARA BHADRA

Uttara Bhadra extends from 333° 20' to 346° 40' of the zodiac in Pisces ruled by Jupiter. The asterism itself is ruled by Saturn. The Vedic deity presiding over it is Ahir Budhnya, the dragon of the deep sea. Purva and Uttara Bhadra taken together consist of four stars, two for each. There is much interchange between their symbols. Together the four stars are said to represent the legs of a cot, but the two stars assigned to Uttara Bhadra are said to symbolize a twin as well as the number two.

The general effect of Jupiter, which owns Pisces, colors the Saturnian impact of the asterism. The primary motivating impulse for Uttara Bhadra is Kama, desire. In regard to attributes, it is under the influence of Sattwa, harmony, at the primary and secondary levels, but at the tertiary level, which is responsible for the immediate reaction to a situation, it is under Tamas, inertia. There are many contradictory forces acting on the asterism. There is the opposition between Jupiter and Saturn, between Sattwa and Tamas, between a warrior and a cow. The symbols assigned to the asterism also refer to its dual character.

Ahir Budhnya, its presiding deity, the dragon of the deep sea, is related to Ahi-Vritra, the dragon of primordial ignorance which lies concealed in primeval darkness. The dual principles of light and darkness, heat and cold, are emphasized by Aja Ekapada and Ahir Budhnya. These two are in eternal conflict. They are the two fundamental principles of cosmic creation. They govern fire and water, heat and cold, and are personified by Agni and Soma. They are the two primary Rudras, a group of gods, eleven in number, which are manifestations of Shiva. Together these two Rudras, representing the unity between Uttara and Purva Bhadra, are the four legs of the cot. The four legs of the cot represent two twins each within itself containing dual or opposing qualities.

Purva Bhadra governed by Jupiter, lies mainly within Aquarius ruled by Saturn, while Uttara Bhadra, governed by Saturn, lies within Pisces ruled by Jupiter. The contradictory or opposite tendencies contained in the asterism of Bhadra as a whole are differentiated between Purva and Uttara. The asterism in its wholeness contains the two basic polarized forces which constitute the universe.

Ahir Budhnya is of the nature of Soma, the Moon, which is associated with water and has the quality of passivity. The passivity of darkness is the mysterious source from which all forms of creation have arisen and this kind of passivity predominates in Uttara Bhadra. This is why it is considered female by sex. Uttara Bhadra becomes powerful only when associated with a planet. Its singular feature is complete passivity, non-action; it is without motion unless another force impinges on it.

Furthermore, Ahi is a serpent, a demon, and darkness personified. In the form of a serpent it is the demon Vritra killed by Indra, the Vedic god who works for the preservation of life on earth. The basic darkness of an individual, from which all forms of ignorance arise that lead to involvement in matter and bondage to rebirth, finally comes to an end with the dawn of enlightenment. Yet when the darkness of ignorance ends, there still remains the darkness of wisdom. The presence of light implies something that it illumines. Only darkness containing nothing, nihil, can be the final negation of existence, good as well as bad. In that darkness there is Ahir Budhnya or the deep sea, suggesting the circularity of the creative process in its cyclic movement. After unity has been established in universality in Purva Bhadra, under Uttara Bhadra the individual soul merges itself in the great deep which is the source of all creative energy. It is from the deep sea that all life proceeds. Under Uttara Bhadra the impulse is of that passivity from which all forms of creation emerge.

The dragon is a symbol of wisdom. All wisdom emanates from this asterism. It enables the individual to comprehend the knowledge concealed in all forms of manifestation. Under the impact of Uttara Bhadra no matter what happens to the individual there is growth and expansion of consciousness. Jupiter bestows wisdom, but under Uttara Bhadra this wisdom results from Saturnian constriction over material attainments. Only when materiality is completely annihilated can Right Understanding — which does not show any Trishna or thirst for material existence — dawn. Only when there is no further involvement in matter can an individual find Nirvana, or liberation.

The four legs of the cot, standing for Purva and Uttara Bhadra together, points to the stage of stability where an individual is poised for the rest which comes during Pralaya, the final dissolution, when the world of manifestation is reabsorbed in the Final Cause. Taken together, the Bhadra asterisms create the situation where an individual is fully prepared for eternal rest, where his detachment from material influences is perfect and his attachments have ended. There is complete disinterestedness, Vairagya, but there is still the urge to work in the manifestation to help the Divine plan. Without this, the attachment to one's individual liberation would remain as a sediment in the psyche and stop the soul from merging in the Infinite. The number two assigned to the asterism represents this situation where the individual has a kind of double personality. He has attained Vairagya, complete detachment from all forms of existence, yet he has the impulse to associate with the Divine plan to make his life action meaningful.

The categorization of Uttara Bhadra among the warrior caste, suggests strong determination to preserve, protect and cooperate in the Divine plan, notwithstanding any hardship one may have to bear. Such an impulse is considered masculine because of its active nature, which arises after attaining complete indifference to worldly matters. The asterism's animal species as a cow is also significant. A cow is almost human except that it does not have any personal life of its own. The cow lives in order to provide nourishment for others. Uttara Bhadra has the inner quality of the cow's surrender for the furtherance of cosmic unfoldment. The primary motivational urge of Kama or desire at this stage represents the Divine passion for being a beneficial influence on the world. It is for these reasons that the asterism leads to the unveiling of Divine wisdom which cannot be distorted by any material attachment or ignorance. Complete disinterestedness flowing from the asterism as its important influence leads an individual towards liberation but if the person is still immersed in matter, it makes him careless, lazy, irresponsible and dull.

27
REVATI

Revati extends from 346° 40' to 360° 00' of the sign of Pisces ruled by Jupiter, where Venus is exalted. The asterism is governed by Mercury. Mythologically, Saturn is born under this asterism. Revati consists of thirty-two stars. The symbol of the fish is assigned to it. The Vedic deity presiding over it is Pushan, a name given to the Sun for measuring the sky. Its basic attribute is Sattvic on all three levels. Its primary motivation is Moksha or liberation.

Revati stands for the great womb in which the Sun dwells in dormancy until the impulse for the next creative cycle arises. Here matter merges in Pure Essence, into the Spirit where God's messenger to the human world, Mercury, dominates. It is the Great Deluge, where the seed for future creation incubates until the next cosmic dawn. The planets associated with different aspects of creation still have an important role to play during this cosmic quietude. The creation becomes possible when the Moon pours Soma, the life sustaining energy. There are many behind-the-scenes activities for souls at their journey's end and many activities to prepare them for the next act of the drama of creation.

Revati is the wife of Balarama, elder brother of Lord Krishna. As the feminine counterpart of Lord Krishna's precursor, Revati, even as the last lunar mansion, has the important task of providing necessary assistance to the forces which operate to herald a new beginning, a fresh Divine Mission.

Balarama was miraculously transferred from the womb of Devaki, where he was conceived, to the womb of Rohini (see chapter). This was done in order to save him from the wrath of the demon king Kamsa. Born from the womb of Rohini, the fourth asterism, he became the helper of Lord Krishna. Revati being the counterpart of this mighty power, who was transferred from one womb to another, can be recognized as the mysterious preservative and protective principle in Nature. It enables the fructification of nature's secret energies. Revati acts in the realm where one cycle of evolution enters into completion and rests until the next beginning of the next. In everyday life this asterism portends the involvement of an individual in earthly things and relationships with possibilities for further evolution and materialization. Under this asterism, the individual is prepared for a new realization of truth and fresh impetus for a meaningful life.

The symbol of the fish is indicative of an auspicious creative influence. The fish gives fertility and allows for rapid growth. It helps the one to become many easily and rapidly. While doing so it also makes an individual turn outward and consider the feelings of others. Having children was considered by ancient people as the fulfillment of one's social obligation. When social obligations are fulfilled, social prestige and contentment afford peace and satisfaction to the person. Under Revati creative faculties enable the expression of outgoing tendencies. A new life begins for an individual under this asterism. Vishnu's avatar form as a fish, Matsyavatara, heralded the advent of a new cycle of evolutionary growth. Similarly, under Revati, an individual begins a more useful existence. Under this asterism there is always a change and an impulse to begin anew, to immerse oneself in the realm of materiality with the intent of beginning at a higher level of existence.

Mythological references relate Revati to the Sun, the source of energy for the sustenance of life. Revati is also linked with Saturn, who was born of the Sun and Chhaya, the shadow of the Sun's wife. Saturn was born on a Saturday at dusk. He is the god of boundless time. Saturn was born when the real wife of the Sun was away, having put in her place an illusory woman called Chhaya, meaning shadow, to take care of her husband. From this illusion under the impact of the Sun's union with it, Saturn was conceived (see Ashwini).

Under Revati, active time represented by the Sun revolving in its cycles as indicated in the allegory of its union with its shadow, becomes passive time experienced as endurance, duration, eternity. The fish symbol emphasizes the merging of Jivatman, the individual soul, in the Universal Soul, Paramatman. At this stage the flame becomes the Fire, the drop joins the Sea and the fish goes back to its home. Mercury, the ruler of the asterism, and Jupiter and Saturn ruling its quadrants, provide the necessary impetus for spiritualizing materialistic experiences and linking them with the world of the gods. Arising out of the desire for spiritual unity caused by Jupiter ruling the first quarter comes the penance and suffering caused by Saturn ruling the second and third quarters, under which material cravings are completely annihilated. By this the individual is reborn in wisdom, signified by Jupiter, ruling the last quarter of the asterism. Under the impact of Mercury, the individual attains pure awareness born out of discrimination and dissatisfaction with external forms of religious observances.

The exaltation of Venus in the last quarter of Revati produces a sense of contentment and tranquility especially if it is placed there with the

Moon which, exalted in Rohini, represents the foster mother of Balarama. Venus, related to sexual relations, encourages and augments procreative activities.

Considered as female, the passivity and receptivity of Revati makes an individual very sensitive to external conditions. The creative faculties both at the physical and psychological levels are considerably energized. Categorized as an outcast, upon whom the social organization depended for support, Revati's influence enables its beneficiaries to do great service for their fellow beings without expecting much in return. A sense of psychological disappointment and feelings of inferiority result under its impact. As a species, Revati is an elephant. It arouses a sense of grandeur, awe, while at the personal level there is little awareness of honor and credit accorded thereby, just as the elephant is unaware of the honor bestowed on it. The psychological transformation which gives rise to such mental attitudes is highlighted by the asterism possessing a godly temperament.

Whether we consider the impact of Revati on the individual or in relation to cosmic evolution, the impulses flowing through it lead to the expansion of awareness. Revati moves us to the cosmic expanse, boundless duration, and preserves the seed of future growth and splendor in the infinite sea of quietude and beatitude. Revati refers to the involvement of the soul in self-preservative activities which extend from Kalpa to Kalpa, from one eternity to another.

V

APPENDICES

GLOSSARY

Aditi	the mother of Adityas; the Earth; Eternal Space or boundless Whole.
Aditya	the Sun, a son of *Aditi.*
Adityas	eight or twelve Suns, or sons of Aditi, taken collectively.
Agni	God of fire, sacrificial fire, one of the Vedic Trinity.
Ahamkara	egoism, selfishness. In Vedanta the same as ignorance, the cause of manifestation. In Sankhya, it is the third of the twenty four tattvas.
Ahi	a Vedic demon of egoism and ignorance, symbolically of drought; also the planet Rahu and Ashlesha asterism.
Ahir Budhnya	the Dragon of the depths of the cosmic sea or wisdom.
Aja	unborn, eternal, Brahma, an epithet of the Almighty. A ram, the sign Aries, a name of the Moon and of *Kamadeva*, the Indian Cupid.
Aja Ekapad	the One-footed Goat.
Akasha	sky, space, ether of the five elements. The primordial substance or spiritual essence which pervades all space.
Amrita	nectar, the ambrosial drink of the Gods which gives immortality.
Angiras	Vedic sage born from Agni.
Anima Mundi	life principle or world soul that pervades all.
Antahkarana	mind in general, including Buddhi, Manas and Citta as main instrument of manifestation for soul or Purusha.
Ardha-Narishwara	The Divine represented as half man, half woman.
Arjuna	companion of the avatar Krishna.

Artha	object, purpose, aim, significance, import; attainment of worldly riches, prosperity, one of the four ends of human life.
Aryaman	Vedic God of friendship, help and assistance.
Ashwins	Vedic twin horseman, Gods of healing and medicine.
Asura	demon, titan or anti-god.
Atman	Divine Self, Soul, Spirit, Essence; the seventh principle in man.
Avatara	incarnation of Vishnu or the Divine.
Balarama	elder brother of the avatar Krishna.
Bhaga	blissful form of the Sun.
Bhakti	devotion or love of God as a spiritual path or way of yoga.
Bhrigu	ancient seer, father of Shukra or Venus.
Bhuta	literally what has been, a ghost, an element: the five elements of earth, water, fire, air and ether.
Brihaspati	Jupiter, the priest or ritualist, also called Brahmanaspati.
Buddha	eighth avatar of Vishnu, the Enlightened one or incarnation of wisdom.
Buddhi	comprehension, intelligence; identified with Mahat, the second of the twenty-four tattvas.
Chakra	circle, potter's wheel or wheel of a carriage; a cycle of Time; Vishnu's disc; the seven force-centers in the subtle bodies activated by the Kundalini Shakti.
Chhaya	shadow, a reflection or image; the astral body. The shadowy body of *Tvastri*, the wife of Sun, made when she left him to visit her father.
Daityas	demons or Asuras.
Daksha	capable, competent, skillful. A Prajapati placed at the head of the creative powers; one of the ten sons of Brahma.
Dakshinamurti	one of the great immortal sages that looks over the earth.
Deva	resplendent deity, the Divine; a celestial being.

Devayani	daughter of Shukra or Venus, wife of King Yayati.
Dharma	principle, law, duty, religion, ethical conduct. Righteous deeds as one of the four goals of human life.
Diti	cutting, splitting, dividing. A daughter of Daksha married to Kashyapa and mother of the Daityas or demons.
Durga	the Goddess as the saviouress or rescuer from all difficulties who rides a lion.
Ganesh	the elephant God, second son of Shiva and Parvati, also called Ganapati.
Garuda	mythical winged eagle, vulture or kite-god, half-bird and half-man, vehicle of Vishnu.
Guna	quality, characteristic or property of substances, three primary as *Sattwa*, *Rajas* and *Tamas*.
Hiranyagarbha	shining, resplendent, the Golden Egg, the nuclear matrix from which Brahma was born; Mother Nature in essence.
Ida/Ila	androgynous daughter of Manu, wife of Budha (Mercury). A channel of Prana on the left side of the spine through which the feminine force flows up.
Indra	supreme Vedic God, the Divine Self, later the King of Heaven.
Indriya/Indriyas	the quality which belongs to Indra, the ten organs of action and sensation. The five *Karmendriyas* (organs of action) are speech, hands, feet, excretory organ, and generative organ; five *Jnanendriyas* (the sense organs) are nose, tongue, eye, skin, and ears.
Jiva	living or existing being; individual soul enshrined in the human body, called *Jivatman* as opposed to *Paramatman*, the Supreme Soul.
Jnana	wisdom or knowledge as a spiritual path or way of yoga.
Jyotish	Vedic astrology or the science of light.
Kala Purusha	spirit or personification of time. In Hindu astrology all personal predictions are made by relating the planetary positions with various impulses generated by the Kala Purusha.

Kacha	son of Brihaspati or Jupiter.
Kalpa	great cycle of time, generally a kalpa represents a 'day' of Brahma and is equal to 4,320,000,000 human years. Each 'day' of Brahma, its period of active manifestation, is followed by a 'night' of Brahma of similar duration.
Kama	sexual urge, the God of love (Kamadeva); the principle of desire, either cosmic or individual; the clinging to existence. Desire as one of the four ends of human life.
Karma	action, duty, fate, consequences of acts done in former lives; the law of cause and effect or ethical causation.
Kashyapa	form of the Sun and a cosmic creator.
Karttikeya	name for Skanda or Mars as born under the asterism Krittika.
Ketu	south node of the Moon, literally a flag or a ray, also a meteor or comet.
Kosha	sheath, covering, body, vehicle of consciousness, of five types subtle and gross.
Krishna	eighth avatar of Vishnu, the God of the flute and Divine Love.
Kumaras	youthful ascetic sages who refused to partake in the process of creation.
Kundalini Shakti	form of the Devi or female cosmic force, the Serpent Fire. It is a seven layered power residing in the base of the spine. In its milder form, it is the nerve force, while its deeper aspects quicken the *chakras* or force-centers. It rises and energizes the seven chakras it unfolds different psychic powers; finally reaching the crown chakra giving Enlightenment.
Lokas	worlds or realms of beings.
Prithvi (the earth) & Naraka (hell).	A fuller classification gives fourteen, seven of which are used by human beings and other evolved deities whereas the other seven are for different levels of demons and degraded beings.
Mahabharata	epic story of Lord Krishna and his era.

Mahat	literally, the great one; the first principle of cosmic mind and intelligence, the second of the twenty-four elements of tattvas.
Manas	mind, intelligence; the thinking principle or synthesizing sense, which organizes and relates the sense organs with the sense objects. When unqualified it means the Higher Self or spiritual soul in contradistinction to its human reflection — *Kama-Manas*.
Manu	Vedic original man or father of the human race, a cosmic progenitor.
Manvantara	time interval between two Manus. Fourteen Manus take charge during the course of a kalpa or 'day' of Brahma.
Maya	illusion, enchantment, unreality; philosophically, matter, wealth and worldly attainments; another name for *Prakriti* (matter).
Mitra	the Divine Friend or lord of compassion.
Moksha	liberation, final emancipation of the soul from cycle of birth and death, *Nirvana*; after death state of rest and bliss. Liberation as the last of the four goals of human life.
Nada	sound, vibration; the primary, all embracing vibration of which all other vibrations in the manifested universe are constituted.
Naga	a serpent; a fabulous serpent-dragon having the face of a man and the tail of a serpent said to inhabit Patala loka; the rishis or seers as serpents, symbol of eternal wisdom and its teachers.
Nakshatras	twenty-seven or twenty-eight lunar asterisms or mansions of the Moon, one of the most important factors in Vedic astrology.
Nataraja	dancing form of Shiva.
Nirvana	liberation from existence; reunification with the Supreme Spirit. In Buddhism, absolute extinction of individual or worldly existence.
Paramatman	Supreme Spirit, Self or Soul.
Parvati	wife or consort of Shiva, mother of Skanda and Ganesh.

Prajapati	Lord of Creation, proprietor, governor; An epithet of Brahma. Brahma created seven and then ten Prajapatis who superintended the creative processes of the universe.
Prakriti	principle of materiality or objective existence, the passive or feminine creative principles, Mother Nature.
Pralaya	destruction of the whole universe at the end of a *Kalpa*; a period of obscuration — planetary, cosmic or universal.
Prana	life-force or vital breath, of which there are five major ones.
Puranas	ancient Hindu mythological and spiritual scriptures from a later period than the Vedas.
Purusha	a male or man, the positive generative force; the Spirit or Supreme Being, Atman. In Sankhya, Purusha is the soul is the inactive witness of Prakriti.
Radha	Krishna's beloved.
Rahu	ascending or north node of the Moon, which causes eclipses, regarded as like Saturn in Vedic astrology.
Rajas	activity, energy, agitation; the second of the three constituent qualities of material substances, predominant in man; gives motivation and ambition.
Rama	seventh avatar of Vishnu, the Divine warrior and savior.
Ramayana	epic story of Lord Rama.
Ravana	demon who stole Sita, Rama's wife and was eventually killed by Rama.
Rishis	Vedic seers.
Rudra	name of Shiva, the roarer or howler, the storm God; the destructive and regenerative force of Shiva.
Rudras	group of gods, inferior manifestations of Shiva, eleven in number.
Samadhi	absorption, equanimity, bliss, spiritual realization; the final stage of yogic practice.
Siddhis	accomplishment, fulfillment, perfection; superhuman faculties gained through yogic practices

Sankhya	enumeration, reasoning; one of the six systems of Indian philosophy, founded by Kapila. It discourses on numerical categories and the meaning of the twenty-four *tattvas* with Purusha. Saraswati.
Sattwa	quality of purity, goodness, harmony and balance.
Shakti	Divine power, Reality as power.
Shani	the one who moves slow, Vedic name for Saturn.
Shiva	auspicious, blissful; the third aspect of the Hindu Trinity associated with destruction of the universe, the personification of the Absolute.
Shukra	planet Venus, the reproductive fluid.
Skanda	God of war who holds all spiritual powers. Shiva's eldest son, also known as Karttikeya or Sub-rahmanya and the presiding deity of the planet Mars.
Sita	wife of Rama, the Earth Goddess.
Soma	great Vedic God of the mystic wine or nectar; the Moon.
Surya	the Sun, or central light.
Swastika	mystic mark denoting good fortune. It stands for cosmic unity; revered in Jainism, Buddhism as well as in the Vedas.
Tamas	darkness, dullness, inertia. An epithet of Rahu, the ascending node of the Moon, one of the three gunas.
Tanmatras	prime qualities of sound, touch, sight, taste and hearing behind the five elements.
Tantra	medieval Hindu teachings. A peculiarity of Tantra is the worship of the *Devi*, the female powers personified as *Shakti*. Some Tantras are connected with sexual rites and the practice of black magic.
Tapas	warmth, penance, austerity. Meditation with self denial.
Tara	star or a planet in general; often used for the lunar asterisms.
Taraka	demon killed by Skanda.

Tattva	cosmic principle. Many classifications of these *tattwas* are made in different metaphysical systems, particularly the twenty-four tattvas of the Sankhya system.
Turiya	fourth, four. The state in which consciousness is raised to the highest or the Nirvanic state of Samadhi, beyond the three lower states of waking, dream and deep sleep.
Tvashtar	one of the cosmic creators; a name for Brahma or Prajapati.
Tvashtri	daughter of Tvashtar and wife of the Sun.
Upanishads	ancient Hindu scriptures and philosophical texts revealing the knowledge of the Self. Their current number is over one hundred and fifty but no more than about twenty are of an early ancient era.
Vach	word or sound, Saraswati, the female creator.
Vaivasvata	the seventh and the present Manu as sprung from the Sun.
Varuna	Vedic God of heaven and the cosmic ocean, the Divine Father.
Vasus	class of Vedic deities eight in number.
Vayu	God of the wind, one of the Vedic Trinity. Vayu is often associated with Indra. In Ayurveda, Vayu or Prana is one of the three humors of the physical system of human body, the others being *kapha* (phlegm) and *pitta* (bile).
Vedanga	branches of the Vedas. Vedangas are six: 1) *Siksha*, the science of pronunciation, 2) *Chandas*, the science of prosody, 3) *Vyakarana*, grammar, 4) *Nirukta*, etymology, 5) *Jyotish*, astrology and 6) *Kalpa*, ritual.
Vedanta	the *Upanishads* which come at the end of the Vedas, the last of the six *darshans* or the schools of Indian philosophy which teaches the ultimate aim and scope of the Vedas, the knowledge of *Brahman* or the Universal Spirit, *Paramatman*.

Vedas	ancient scriptures or books of wisdom of the Hindus. The three Vedas, the *Rig, Yajur* and *Sama* follow the Vedic Trinity of Agni, Vayu, and Surya. The fourth or *Atharva Veda* came later. The Vedas are 'not human in composition' being directly revealed by the Supreme Being. Each Veda has two distinct parts: *Mantra* or *Samhita* and *Brahmana*; the former deals with laws and principles and the latter with rituals and rules of observances. The former is the esoteric aspect of the Vedas, the Jnana Kanda or the division of Divine Wisdom, and the latter exoteric precepts, Karma Kanda, the division of actions and work.
Vidya	knowledge, learning, wisdom. There are two kinds of learning, para and apara, esoteric and exoteric, the former relating to the inner Self, the latter to the outer world.
Vishnu	the Divine as the preserver, the cosmic sustaining power and source of the avatars.
Vishwakarman	architect of Gods and the universe; also known as Tvashtar.
Vritra	demon destroyed by Indra, represents the veiling power of ignorance.
Yama	God of the dead, a form of the Sun God.
Yayati	famous Vedic King.

THE PRIMARY CHARACTERISTICS OF THE NAKSHATRAS

Nakshatra	Sex	Class	Specie	Temperment	Animal Type	Dir.	QUALITIES Primary	Secondary	Tertiary	RULERS Sign	Nak.	1st 1/4	2nd 1/4	3rd 1/4	4th 1/4
1. Ashwini	M	Merchant	Horse	God	Quadruped	South	Rajas	Rajas	Rajas	♂	☋	♂	♀	☿	☽
2. Bharani	M	Outcaste	Elephant	Man	Quadruped	West	Rajas	Rajas	Tamas	♂	♀	☉	☿	♀	♂
3. Krittika	F	Brahman	Goat	Demon	Quadruped	North	Rajas	Rajas	Sattwa	♂ (1/4) ♀ (1/4)	☉	♃	♄	♄	♃
4. Rohini	F	Worker	Serpent	Man	Quadruped	East	Rajas	Tamas	Rajas	♀	☽	♂	♀	☿	☽
5. Mrigrashira	F	Farmer	Serpent	God	Quadruped (2) Human (2)	South	Rajas	Tamas	Tamas	♀ (1/2) ☿ (1/2)	♂	☉	☿	♀	♂
6. Ardra	F	Butcher	Dog	Man	Human	West	Rajas	Tamas	Sattwa	☿	☊	♃	♄	♄	♃
7. Punarvasu	F	Merchant	Cat	God	Human (3) Aquatic (1)	North	Rajas	Sattwa	Rajas	☿ (3/4) ☽ (1/4)	♃	♂	♀	☿	☽
8. Pushya	M	Warrior	Goat	God	Aquatic	East	Rajas	Sattwa	Tamas	☽	♄	☉	☿	♀	♂
9. Ashlesha	M	Outcaste	Cat	Demon	Aquatic	South	Rajas	Sattwa	Sattwa	☽	☿	♃	♄	♄	♃
10. Magha	M	Worker	Rat	Demon	Forest Dweller	West	Tamas	Rajas	Rajas	☉	☋	♂	♀	☿	☽
11. Purva Phalguni	F	Brahman	Rat	Man	Forest Dweller	North	Tamas	Rajas	Tamas	☉	♀	☉	☿	♀	♂
12. Uttara Phalguni	M	Warrior	Cow	Man	Forest Dweller (1) Human (3)	East	Tamas	Rajas	Sattwa	☉ (1/4) ☿ (3/4)	☉	♃	♄	♄	♃
13. Hasta	F	Merchant	Buffalo	God	Human	South	Tamas	Tamas	Rajas	☿	☽	♂	♀	☿	☽

14. Chitra	F	Farmer	Tiger	Demon	Human	West	Tamas	Tamas	Tamas	☿ (1/2) ♀ (1/2)	♂	☉	☿	♀	♂
15. Swati	M	Butcher	Buffalo	God	Human	North	Tamas	Tamas	Sattwa	♀	☊	♃	♄	♄	♃
16. Vishakha	F	Outcaste	Tiger	Demon	Human (3) Insect (1)	East	Tamas	Sattwa	Rajas	♀ (3/4) ♂ (1/4)	Q	♂	♀	☿	☽
17. Anuradha	F	Worker	Deer	God	Insect	South	Tamas	Sattwa	Tamas	♂	♄	☉	☿	♀	♂
18. Jyestha	M	Farmer	Deer	Demon	Insect	West	Tamas	Sattwa	Sattwa	♂	☿	♃	♄	♄	♃
19. Mula	M	Butcher	Dog	Demon	Human	North	Sattwa	Rajas	Rajas	♃	☋	♂	♀	☿	☽
20. Purvashada	M	Brahman	Monkey	Man	Human (1/2) Qudruped (3 1/2)	East	Sattwa	Rajas	Tamas	♃	♀	☉	☿	♀	♂
21. Uttarashada	M	Warrior	Mongoose	Man	Quadruped	South	Sattwa	Rajas	Sattwa	♃ (1/4) ♄ (3/4)	☉	♃	♄	♄	♃
22. Shravana	M	Outcaste	Monkey	Man	Quadruped	North	Sattwa	Tamas	Rajas	♄	☽	♂	♀	☿	☽
23. Dhanishtha	F	Farmer	Lion	Demon	Aquatic	East	Sattwa	Tamas	Tamas	♄	♂	☉	☿	♀	♂
24. Shatabhishak	F	Butcher	Horse	Demon	Human	South	Sattwa	Tamas	Sattwa	♄	☊	♃	♄	♄	♃
25. Purva Bhadra	M	Brahman	Lion	Man	Human (3) Aquatic (1)	West	Sattwa	Sattwa	Rajas	♄ (3/4) ♃ (1/4)	♃	♂	♀	☿	☽
26. Uttara Bhadra	F	Warrior	Cow	Man	Aquatic	North	Sattwa	Sattwa	Tamas	♃	♄	☉	☿	♀	♂
27. Revati	F	Worker	Elephant	God	Aquatic	East	Sattwa	Sattwa	Sattwa	♃	☿	♃	♄	♄	♃

SYMBOLS, DEITIES AND IMPULSES OF THE NAKSHATRAS

Nakshatra	Symbols	Presiding Deities	Primary Impulse	Motivating Impulse	CHARACTERISTICS	
					Evolving Side	Materialistic Side
1. Ashwini	A Head of a horse	*Aswini Kumars:* The Celestial Physicians	Regenerative Potential	Dharma	Leadership	Thirst for Sensations
2. Bharani	*Yoni:* The female sex organ	*Yama:* The God of Death	Preservation of the Germ	Artha	Investigation into Occult Laws	Excessive Indulgence in Sex
3. Krittika	A Razor	*Agni:* The God of Fire	*Primordial Light:* the Latent Active Principle	Kama	Dedicated Divine Service	Quarrelsome and Self-ish Efforts
4. Rohini	A Chariot	*Brahma:* The God of Creation	*Hiranyagarbha,* or the Great Deep: The Incubative Potential	Moksha	Engineering the Divine Power	Social Progress and Love for Wealth
5. Mrigrashira	The Head of a Deer	*Soma:* The Moon	*Tan-Matra:* The Subtil Elements	Moksha	Intelligence	Egotism: I-ness
6. Ardra	Precious Stone, or a Human Head	*Rudra:* The God of Destruction	*Mahat:* The Universal Intelligence	Kama	Study of Esoteric Laws	Conflict
7. Punarvasu	A Bow or a House	*Aditi:* "Visible Infinity"	Union of Sound and Divine Consciousness	Artha	Discipleship	Accentuation of *Kama-Manas,* or of Passional Nature
8. Pushya	A Flower, a Circle or an Arrow	*Brihashpati:* Jupiter	Spiritual Magnetism	Dharma	Tranquil Mind	Emotional Instability
9. Ashlesha	A Serpent	*Nagas:* The Serpent God	Differentiation of Life Energy	Dharma	Initiation in Esoteric Mysteries	Treachery and Immoral-ity
10. Magha	House of a Palanquin	*Pitris:* Manes	Metempsychosis: Trans-migration of the Soul	Artha	Regal Glamor; Prestigious Office	Servitude
11. Purva Phalguni	A Couch; A Platform or Fireplace	*Bhaga:* The God of Fortuen	*Trishna:* Thirst for Experience	Kama	Conquest and Domination	Debauchery, Gambling and Black Magic
12. Uttara Phalguni	A Small Bed	*Aryaman:* The Wooer	*Siddhis:* The Latent Powers in Man	Moksha	Ambition	Black Magic

13. **Hasta**	The Palm	*Savita:* The Sun	Duration; Time	Moksha	Public Service	Earning One's Bread anyway; Penury
14. **Chitra**	One Pearl	*Tvastra:* The Celestial Architect	Space, The Dance of Shiva	Kama	Urge to Build	Pig in the Mud
15. **Swati**	Coral	*Vayue:* The God of Air	*Akasa,* The Sky	Artha	Passion	Pleasure
16. **Vishakha**	A Potter's Wheel	*Indra and Agni:* The Lord of Gods and the God of Fire	Psychism	Dharma	*Tapas:* Purificatory Austerity	Experience of Restrictions
17. **Anuradha**	A Lotus Flower	*Mitra:* A Sun	Spirit-Matter Mix	Dharma	Occult Powers used for Selfish Ends	Depth of Material Whirlpool
18. **Jyestha**	An Ear Ring; Umbrella	*Indra:* The Lord of Gods	*Kundalini:* The Serpent Fire	Artha	Divine Benediction	Arrogance
19. **Mula**	The Tail of a Lion; An Elephant's Goad	*Nritta:* A Demon	*Mumukshutwa:* The Urge for Liberation	Kama	Karmic Nemesis	Cruel; Possessive
20. **Purvashada**	Tusk of an Elephant	*Apas:* The Water	Reflecting the Divine	Moksha	God's Grace	Pride
21. **Uttarashada**	A Small Cot	*Vishwa Deva:* Universe as God	Cosmic Unity	Moksha	Humility	Self-Centeredness
22. **Shravana**	An Ear; An Arrow	*Visnu:* The Preserver	The Great Silence	Artha	Meditational Attention	Obedience
23. **Dhanishtha**	A Musical Drum	*Vasus:* Gods of Light	Radiation of Life Force	Dharma	Occult Attainment	Deprivation of Material Conveniences
24. **Shatabhishak**	Hundred Flowers	*Varuna:* Regent of the Ocean	Maintenance of Law; Nature in Bloom	Dharma	Blending of Consciousness (in Infinity)	Psychological Pain
25. **Purva Bhadra**	A Sword	*Ajaikapada:* One Footed Goat	Cosmic Stability	Artha	Fearlessness	Anguish; Sorrow
26. **Uttara Bhadra**	The Number Two; A Twin	*Ahirbudhanya:* The Serpent of the Deep	Unveiling of Wisdom	Kama	*Kaivalya: Nirvana:* Liberation	Complete Disinterestedness
27. **Revati**	A Fish	*Pushan:* The Nourisher	*Nihil* — The Dissolution	Moksha	Equanimity	Complete Destruction

SELECTED
BIBLIOGRAPHY

BOOKS

Behari, Bepin. *A Study in Astrological Occultism*. Bangalore, India: IBH Prakashan, 1983.

Behari, Bepin. *Solve Your Problems Astrologically*. Bangalore, India: IBH Prakashan, 1988.

Behari, Madhuri and Bepin. *An Introduction to Esoteric Astrology*. New Delhi, India: Sagar Publications, 1986.

Blavatsky, H. P.. *Isis Unveiled, Vols. I & II*. Pasadena, CA: Theosophical University Press, 1976.

Blavatsky, H. P.. *The Secret Doctrine, Vols I–VI*. Madras, India: THP, Adyar, 1971.

Blavatsky, H. P.. *Transactions of the Blavatsky Lodge*. California: The Theosophy Co., 1923.

Dowson, John. *A Classical Dictionary of Hindu Mythology And Religion*. London: Routledge & Kegan Paul.

Frawley, David. *The Astrology of the Seers*. Salt Lake City, UT: Passage Press, 1990.

Frawley, David. *From the River of Heaven, Hindu and Vedic Knowledge For The Modern Age*. Salt Lake City UT: Passage Press, 1990.

Giedion, S. *The Eternal Present: The Beginning of Architect*. New York, NY: Bollingen Foundation.

Hodson, G. H.. *The Hidden Wisdom in the Holy Bible Vol. I.*. Madras, India: TPH, Adyar, 1963.

Jennings, Hargrave. *The Indian Religion or Results of the Mysterious Buddhi*. London: George Redway.

Santhanam., R. *Brihat Parasara Hora Sastra*. New Delhi, India: Ranjan Publications, 1984.

Subba Rao, T. *Esoteric Writings*. Madras, India: TPH, Adyar.

Subrahmanya Sastri, V.. *Varaha Mihira's Brihat Jataka*. Mysore, India.

ASTROLOGICAL JOURNALS

Astrological Magazine. Raman Publications, "Sri Rajeswari," 115/1, New Extension, Seshadripuram, Bangalore-560 020 India.

The Times of Astrology. "Sri Bhavanam," 9/1040, Govindpuri, P.O. Box 4347, Kalkaji (P.O.), New Delhi-110 019 India.

BIODATA

Bepin Behari, primarily an economist, is a noted authority on Vedic astrology, Eastern philosophy and occultism. His penetrating approach to astrology has reclaimed many of its deeper aspects once thought lost. He is the author of many books in both fields and is a regular contributor to *The Astrological Magazine, The Times of Astrology* and other astrological journals. In 1979, his manuscript which became the book, *A Study in Astrological Occultism* won the prestigious international Meyer Foundation Award of Switzerland for philosophy. His forthcoming books from Passage Press include: *A Study in Astrological Occultism; Career, Relationship, Success and Vedic Astrology; The Vedic Astrologer's Handbook Vol. I, Fundamentals;* and *The Vedic Astrologer's Handbook Vol. II, Predictive Techniques.*

Index